NOT IN
KANSAS
ANYMORE

NOT IN KANSAS ANYMORE

A Curious Tale of How Magic Is Transforming America

CHRISTINE WICKER

HarperSanFrancisco

A Division of HarperCollins*Publishers*

HarperCollins books may be purchased for educational, business, or sales promotional
use. For information please write: Special Markets Department, HarperCollins Publishers
10 East 53rd Street, New York, NY 10022.

HarperCollins Web site: http://www.harpercollins.com

HarperCollins®, 📖®, and HarperSanFrancisco™ are trademarks of HarperCollins
Publishers.

FIRST EDITION

Library of Congress Cataloging-in-Publication Data

Wicker, Christine.
    Not in Kansas anymore : a curious tale of how magic is transforming America /
Christine Wicker.
        p.   cm.
    Includes bibliographical references.
    ISBN–10: 0–06–072678–4
    ISBN–13: 978–0–06–072678–2
    1. Magic—United States. 2. Medicine, Magic, mystic, and spagiric—United States.
I. Title.

BF1622.U6W53 2005
133.4'0973—dc22

                                                                    2005046004

05 06 07 08 09 RRD(H) 10 9 8 7 6 5 4 3 2 1

TO MY PARENTS

who encouraged me to think about everything
and never lost their nerve when I did

Let our common experiences be enveloped in an eternal moral order; let our suffering have an immortal significance; let Heaven smile upon the earth, and deities pay their visits; let faith and hope be the atmosphere which man breathes in;—and his days pass by with zest; they stir with prospects, they thrill with remoter values.

—WILLIAM JAMES

CONTENTS

PART THREE: MIRACLES AND WONDERS

Part One

COME TO
THE PARTY

What is important now is to recover our senses. We must learn to *see* more, to *hear* more, to *feel* more.

—SUSAN SONTAG

1.

The Waitress Wears a Pentacle

Two brawny men with tattoos had just allowed me to enter the Vampire and Victims Ball when young Nichole, a divorced mother of two who makes her living as a hairdresser, greeted me with a moan. I'd met the newbie witch some months ago during a gathering of her Salem coven. This night she was looking lovely in a nun's habit. On her forehead, as though branded there, was the blackened image of a crucifix. From her pallor, I gathered that she was supposed to be a dead nun.

Mock-swooning against me, she asked in a whisper, "Is this really me in here?"

A weighty question, particularly when asked by a witch posing as a Bride of Christ. I had hardly an instant to ponder before a red-haired woman in a backless evening gown interrupted.

"Are you beating people?" she asked.

"Yes. I think I am," Nichole answered. Crucifixes were popular that evening. A large wooden one had been set up in the back room so that partyers could be tied to it and lashed.

"Do you know how?" the red-haired woman asked.

Nichole shook her wimpled head.

"Come with me."

The room was dark and the music sounded like African drumming. A witch named Christian Day wandered by to flick his tongue and roll his eyes in what seemed to be a parody of a silent-movie vamp. A totally bald vampire with Spock ears was appropriately stern. A handsome young swain in a frock coat and a high-collared satin shirt looked beautifully sulky. A pasty-faced vamp with a top hat, long white hair, and dark glasses was thin-lipped as he took his blond bride in his arms. On her bosom were two fake puncture marks and a dribble of blood, also fake.

Real vampires, as opposed to those who only dress up as vamps, come in two main types: those who drink blood, called sanguine, and those who feast on other people's energy, called psi, or psychic. For psi vampires, parties raise energy, which makes them good places to feed. For blood vamps, a drop or two was certain to be spilled before the sun rose.

I had come to this costume party looking for magic, not the tricks of conjurers but the real stuff, the kind of magic that bends reality to a wizard's will. I'd been warned that it is dangerous to fool with people who believe they can do magical things—people such as wizards and vampires, Satanists and voodoo priestesses, high magicians and conjurers of the black arts. I had no trouble finding such people. They exist in considerable numbers, and not just in California. They're in Cleveland and Rochester, Milwaukee and Dallas, Orlando and Chapel Hill. They're all over the South. And in New York City, of course. Everything is in New York City. I wasn't warned by magical people themselves, who were often as eager to protest their goodness as fresh-dunked Baptists. It was the mundanes who issued dire predictions. Mundanes are how ordinary people are often described by those in the magical community. Sometimes, borrowing from the Harry Potter books, they're called muggles.

They're power-hungry, the mundanes said of the magical people. They're immoral, people said, and they're scary. Playing with the dark arts could plunge me into evil. I'd be pulled toward depravity, they said. Blasphemy would begin to seem like truth, bad like good, God like Satan. It had happened to people through the centuries, they said. And they were right. All that did happen.

Others greeted my enterprise with derision. You'll be on a journey, they said, but don't expect to arrive at the heart of darkness. The epicenter of silly will be more like it. And they were right too. All the warnings proved true, and yet as Hamlet put it, "There are more things in heaven and earth, Horatio, than are dreamt of in your philosophy." I was soon to find that magic is not only of ancient and illustrious pedigree, not merely an astonishingly alive and widespread way of thinking, but also a valuable, even irreplaceable, part of human experience.

Across the ballroom I saw a dapper gent in shiny white-and-black shoes wearing sharply creased black pants, a sport coat, and a yellow-and-navy tie. His hair was closely cropped and swept back from a pale forehead. He stood stiffly without smiling as though feeling timid.

"Are you a vampire or a victim?" I asked, making small talk. I couldn't have known at such an early moment, almost at the very beginning of my investigation, but I had asked the only question that truly matters. I should have listened more closely as he answered, pressed him further. Instead, I took him for a flake, which he was, of course, and yet also the envoy of truth, as I would find to be the case again and again.

"Do I look like a victim?" he asked, smiling in a way that didn't show his teeth. This was not a good sign.

"Well . . . ," I said, stalling.

"Are *you* a victim?" he asked too calmly.

Still his smile showed no teeth.

"I don't want to say."

"You have to choose."

Tied to the physical, deaf to the eternal, riveted by my own shortcomings, I was thinking only of what a bad choice I'd made when choosing a partner for chat. This guy was faking timidity to lure someone over. If I said victim, he was likely to start gnawing my neck. If I said vampire, he would demand proof. I hadn't fangs enough to back that pretension. Spotting an angel across the room and eager to shift Dapper Gent's attention, I said, "That takes some nerve in this crowd."

"Why do you say that?" he asked. "An angel and a devil are only a breath away."

If I had been wiser, I could have wrapped up my investigation at the Vampire and Victims Ball and gone no further. Everything I needed to understand had been right there before me. That first costume party showed me all of it, the humor and the mystery, the humanness and the divine, the dark and the light. It had been funny, messy, mysterious, absurd, and wonderful, like a great postmodern myth, a little microcosm of life. The Dapper Gent had even put it into words for me three times, a most magical number.

So come, Cinderella, let me take you again to the ball. Perhaps you will see more than I did, or perhaps you will begin to understand how difficult it is to understand. Truth is never easily wrested from the stuff of life, and this stuff was even stranger and sometimes more repellent than the usual fare.

On the night of the Vampire and Victims Ball, our hostess, Mistress Tracy, Queen of the Vampires, wasn't able to make her entrance in a hearse, as she usually did, because the party was on the second floor of a Salem restaurant. Instead, the curtains to a back room parted, and Shawn the Witch emerged resplendent in swirling red velvet. He was happy tonight because he had a new lover, a slight young man who said he was a werewolf and looked appropriately morose, as anyone would if he found himself growing hair in unexpected places. I couldn't see any suspicious tufts. But his skin did look deadly pale against his long black locks and funereal garments, as though he might have received some dreadful shock.

Next came a gleaming mahogany coffin, carried by some of Mistress Tracy's husky minions; the red-haired girl in the backless evening gown was swooning alongside. The Sisters of Eternal Damnation, as the lovely Nichole and another woman dressed as a nun were known, ended the procession. The attendants were holding white candles. As the minions set the coffin down, Shawn and the red-haired girl held their candles over each other so that the hot candle wax dripped on their skin. Nice.

Shawn the Witch lolled over one end of the casket, while the red-haired girl lay across the other end, rubbing herself along it as though she had an itch. Shawn began to declaim. I could tell by his hands that he was in full roar, but I couldn't hear him for the drums beating. He opened the coffin and there, gleaming pale against the satin, was Mistress Tracy. Her hands were folded across her chest, and her eyes were closed. She looked comfy, but she wasn't. Coffins only look padded, she told me later. They don't have any bed in them at all, so her backbone was gouging into the wood, and her bones ached from being jostled about during the grand entrance.

As we all gazed at Tracy, Shawn said loudly, "A victim."

Jeff, Tracy's consort, stepped forward; his shirt was pulled from his shoulders so that it fell down around his waist. He looked hunky and severe. A large tattoo of Mistress Tracy with a sword held before her body was clearly visible on his chest. No doubt whom this victim belonged to.

"Is this blood safe to drink?" Shawn bellowed.

Jeff nodded slowly. Then he lifted his hand. In it was a razor. If the drums hadn't been so loud, you could have heard an *eeech* go through the multitude. A razor? The ceremony's planners had hoped to use a knife, but it was too hard to break the skin with a blade. Hacking his arm in a Monty Pythonish way would not be in keeping with the solemnity of the occasion.

As Jeff cut his forearm, Shawn intoned, "Ashes to ashes, dust to dust."

"They stole that. That's from Ash Wednesday." It was Irene, a woman from New York City who was in Salem for the week with her husband and adult daughter.

Shawn did love churchy phrases. I was relieved that he hadn't cribbed the sentences that introduced Tracy's Internet description of the ball. "I am the Resurrection and the Life. All those who drink of me will never die." That was really stealing.

"Drink deep the blood. For the blood is life," Shawn said.

Jeff moved toward the coffin. "Feed, my mistress," he said, as he held his arm over Tracy's mouth and began to squeeze the wound. Her mouth was open, and blood was dripping into it. The crowd stared, as open-mouthed as Tracy but for a different reason. The bartender grimaced as Tracy's hands came up like claws grabbing Jeff's arm. Pulling it to her lips, she began to suck. I was feeling pretty grossed out, and I noticed that Shawn, still wearing his expression of great solemnity, had shifted his gaze piously upward. The sight of blood makes him faint.

Tracy arose from the coffin and stood swaying, her eyes unfocused and woozy. She did look like a woman who'd had a hit of something good. Not to be upstaged completely, Shawn declaimed, "I present to you the Dark Mistress and her consort, Jeff."

That was a misstep. "Jeffrey" would have been better. The modernity of the nickname was a clunker.

Next Tracy began to go about the circle giving people blessings. They would bow their heads, and she would touch them in a regal way. The music was now a swirling Celtic tune, and the dancers began to flit about, nuns and vampires, angels and victims. Shawn's friend and fellow witch Christian was among them, dressed in a ruffled shirt and black frock coat. As he passed, he gave me a sneer and shouted, "Doth my makeup look all right?" His eyes were rimmed by thick black smudges that looked fine, and his fangs were truly impressive, but they gave him a lisp, which did kind of spoil the effect.

Irene sidled up to me. "There's a witch over there with bigger boobs than I have and it's a man. Now what's that?" she asked, her mouth pursed. "I'm from New York, and nothing shocks me. I see he/shes on the subway all the time. I can't tell for sure with those boobs, but I know a surgeon who does sex change operations all the time, and he told me there's one thing they can't change."

"What is it?" I asked with some trepidation. Irene looked harmless, but she was from New York City, as she'd pointed out, where they've seen everything and for all I know have done everything too. I hoped she wasn't going to suggest that we grope the guy's skirts.

"Their feet," she said. "Their big ol' feet."

"How were the feet?"

"Couldn't see 'em. I'm going to look," she said, disappearing into the crowd.

Wandering into the back room where there were hors d'oeuvres, I saw a wooden crucifix splashed with red paint. Two ropes were used to tie people to the crucifix's outstretched arms, and then they were beaten by the nuns. In line for beatings were two women who had been auctioned off earlier as virgin slaves guaranteed to satisfy their master's most wicked desires. The men were removing their shirts for the flogging, but the women wouldn't. "Flogging, yes," one of them said. "Naked, no."

Shawn invited me to be flogged.

I shook my head. "I'll just watch."

"Oh," he said, arching his brows in a companionable way, "a voyeur. We like those too."

Tracy had promised that the ball would draw real vampires like herself, and I looked for them. I thought the pasty-faced guy with the long white hair and his bleeding bride must be vampires. But the bride said, "Oh, no. We're here celebrating our wedding anniversary." A group beautifully dressed in gauzy Victorian clothes and old-fashioned dark suits seemed like good candidates, but they turned out to be a dance troupe that was going to do an Edward Gorey fashion show. Finally Tracy pointed out the red-haired woman.

Her scene name was Xana, and she was thirty. She had always been into horror, which her parents encouraged. At thirteen, while reading Anne Rice's book *Interview with a Vampire*, she began having intense dreams that led her to begin reading everything she could find about vampires. She started drinking blood at sixteen with her first girlfriend. The Internet helped her find others with similar interests. Lots of Goths are interested in drinking blood, but Xana only drinks from those who've been tested, which means she hasn't had many partners. At seventeen, she had Tracy put a tattoo of a bite and blood drips on her neck. At that time she believed in the reality of vampires and would spend nights roaming graveyards and woods looking for them.

"I completely believed that I would find one and they would make me one of them. That's what I wanted," she said. But it never happened. Sometimes she and her friends felt things, spirits and forces, around them.

"Maybe it was a mass hallucination. It was an intense time, not too intelligent. I don't believe anymore." But she does call herself a vampire.

"It helped shape who I am," she said. She wrote a self-published book called *Limericks for Young Vampires*, which sold five hundred copies.

"I'm still into the cutting thing. I prefer to share. It's a bonding thing. To allow someone to cut you is the most trusting thing you can do. I've never done it with someone I'm not deeply committed to.

"And I do like the pain."

Right.

She and a friend, a big guy with a dozen silver rings hanging off his face, were going to do a public cutting later. They would also give a lecture on safety. "A lot of Goths don't take precautions," she said. As much as I admired her high-mindedness, I wasn't going to stick around. I'm happy people can do what they enjoy, but I'd over-sold myself to Shawn. I didn't want to watch.

We might have talked more, but someone wanted a beating. It was a girl in a wench costume. She must have known Xana would give her a good one, and she did. I could hear the slaps as I left the room.

"Are you a vampire or a victim?" the Dapper Gent had asked, and I thought he meant only which costume did I wear, but the question was much more than that. Will you seize the magical power, step up, and be something awesome—even if it means that you'll look ridiculous and maybe actually be ridiculous—or will you drift along, victim to whatever wind blows you?

"You have to choose," he said.

And then in the last words he spoke to me, one final warning and bit of truth that could have saved me all sorts of disillusionment. "An angel and a devil are only a breath away."

$\mathcal{I}$ am not a vampire, a witch, a fairy, a wizard, an elf, a were-wolf, an angel, or a devil. Two years ago I hardly knew such entities existed outside fiction and religious texts. I am also not a victim, I hope, although that is less certain. I am a journalist, one who is quick to go purse-lipped at anything that seems too airy.

I was in Salem, Massachusetts, chasing magic, specifically good magic. I'd picked Salem to start because this town, whose very name conjures religious intolerance and shame, has been reclaimed by witches and other members of the magical community. Three thousand are said to live here, so many that it calls itself the Witch Capital of the World. The (Good) Witch Capital, of course. Nowadays, all the witches are good, or say they are—a big brag, that one. I'll deal with it later.

As this tale of magic in America begins, I must reassure some of you and dash the hopes of others by confessing that as I began this investigation I believed in nothing except disaster. I had great spiritual faith in my youth, but it went away. Since then I've moved in and out of traditional belief, mostly out, so far out that people who have deep faith in anything generally mystify me. I think, *You're so alien.* Or on my softer days, *Aren't you just the dearest thing? Wouldn't it be lovely if you were right?*

For a good portion of my life I've worked as a reporter of religion. You might think such disbelief would have hurt my work. It hasn't because, first of all, many religious people don't have deep faith either. Poor dears, times are so hard on the faithful that some of them are as bad off as I am. They're merely holding on tighter.

And second, reporters are meant to be observers who do not comment. People with big, strange, life-altering faith fascinate me, no matter how odd a turn that faith takes. I admire them, love them even, for being what I can never be. I am incontrovertibly ordinary, which may be why the more unlike me people of faith are, the more convinced I am that they have something deeply important to tell me. Once I tried to convince my editor to let me follow the travels of a guy dressed like Jesus. He was walking across Texas shouldering a big cross on wheels.

"He's a nut," the editor said.

"He's not. He's not," I said, defensive already. "I've talked to him, and he's perfectly sane. What he's doing makes complete sense if you, uh . . . if you think like he does." The end of that sentence sounded weak even to my ears, so I said it extra loud. But you see, it wasn't weak. I'd uttered exactly the right point and then been ashamed of it, which is often my way. Thinking like someone else thinks *is* the only way to understand people radically different from you, but my editor didn't want a reporter who thought like a guy carrying a cross across Texas.

"Forget him," she said, fearing that I was already halfway toward going native, a term journalists use for reporters who lose themselves too completely among sources. I've done that sometimes.

I didn't intend to do it again, although there would be temptation. I started my investigation into magic for purely intellectual reasons. I planned to write about it as a social trend. I was going to write about "them," which is how journalists best like to work. The old joke about the reporter who shows up to say, "Let's you and him fight," has truth in it.

As a reporter of religion, I knew that a great change was going on in modern faith. I believed looking at magic would open a window into why it was happening and how. Forty years ago, when the current occult revival was beginning to gain strength, the wisest thinkers in the land predicted that faith in the supernatural was shriveling and would soon die back to insignificance. The scientific worldview demanded such a shift. Who could possibly withstand it? Organized religion, mystical meanderings, and magical ideas could not hold up against scientific ideas that were so self-evidently true, or so they reasoned.

But the wise ones were wrong. Instead, such thinking—call it what you will, religious, spiritual, mystical, irrational—has tightened its grip in astonishing ways. This development has been most obvious among the ultraconservative. A portion of their constituency has bullied and preached and agitated and murdered its way into the headlines—always for the love of God, of course. But the drift toward an ancient belief in the—how shall I put it?—more *active* forms of Deity has also penetrated religious groups that don't often make the headlines. Wiccans and Pentecostals are both often cited as the fastest-growing faiths in America. Middle-aged witches are scattered through the hinterlands, and little witches can be found in high schools and colleges all over the country. Healers who use various kinds of energy do a brisk business among middle-class groups.

Some Pentecostal preachers are so familiar with evil spirits that they have names for them and a hierarchy of rankings. Sightings of the Holy Mother Mary are rising all over the world. Some are in visions; so many are images on foodstuffs that there's been a boomlet on e-Bay items, including a Lay's Smokey Bacon potato chip and a grilled-cheese sandwich that appear to represent her.

Millions of Americans are turning to magic, mysticism, and *mythos*—some in ways that radically set them apart, others merely to augment more mainstream beliefs. A Methodist friend who graduated from college with three majors and a Phi Beta Kappa and recently put a voodoo flag on her wall is an example of the latter. She mentioned that she was also fascinated by vampires.

"You don't believe vampires are real, do you?" I asked.

"Of course not," she said. "But maybe. Yes. Sort of."

People with, shall we say, *expanded* kinds of awareness are quietly blending among us, cobbling together spiritual lives that are more freewheeling than anything ever seen before. Quietly, quietly, with a minimum of fuss, they are reenchanting the world—their worlds anyway. The waitress wears a pentacle under her blouse. The computer geek next door is a conjure doc. The mom down the street tells fortunes. Soldiers chant toward gods of war. Nurses send healing power through their hands. You have to know what to look for. You have to search them out, ask the right questions, notice the right signs, but they are there, here, everywhere around us. Deep into the night, with only the blue glow of computer screens lighting their faces, they send streams of energy one to another, small town to inner city, Amsterdam to Houston to San Juan, virtual meets magical and melds.

Reaching back to ancient lore, these otherwise average folk summon wonder and mystery and meaning into their lives. They believe humans can change events with their thoughts. They believe progress is possible, probable in fact. They believe all of life is intricately connected—with the earth, the planets, the stars, and other life. They believe in magic. What does that mean? At its most basic level, it means that there is a stream of power, life, energy, intelligence, spirit, call it what you will, that courses through the universe. Magical practice is the attempt to notice, to understand, to channel, and to control that force. It is a method of connecting with the unseen, or as the anthropologist Tanya M. Luhrmann wrote, "a technology of the sacred." Someone else called it a physical prayer. Or as some Wiccans put it, magic is a form of positive thinking, hypercharged, wonderfully optimistic.

Aren't they just the dearest things? Wouldn't it be lovely if they were right?

For thousands of years most human beings shared such an enchanted worldview. For the past four hundred years it has been steadily abandoned, turned into the occult, which means the hidden—or as one writer says, the rejected—knowledge. But as modern America fills up with astrologers, psychics, magicians, wizards, witches, hoodoo workers, and their many customers, the hidden is coming into light. Ancient occult ideas are radically changing how Americans think about themselves, and most of us don't even know it's happening.

This move toward occult thinking is more amorphous than the faiths that reporters are able to write easily about. It has no doctrine, little organization, few moral codes. It gets no official sanction and is sometimes bizarre beyond comprehension. It marshals no martyrs, wages no wars (at least not the kind most of us know about), and yet it has elements that are more ancient even than the big religions, older than history itself. It offers breathtaking possibilities and soul-shaking dangers.

In twenty years of reporting the actions of human beings, probing their reasons for acting oddly, and watching the effects of their behavior, I've become convinced that when a good number of people start to do something that makes no sense to the society at large, when they cling to it for a long time and increasing numbers of people take it up, they're on to something. Usually it's something that's percolating through the unconscious. The rest of us feel it too, but we suppress it. It's often the outcasts, the iconoclasts, the hyper-religious, the young people, sometimes middle-aged women, those who have the least to lose because they don't have much in the first place, who feel the new currents and ride them farthest. Most of us don't listen to these people because they act strange and look goofy. They often say offensive, dopey things in clichéd ways. I am as put off by such behavior as most comfortably situated, middle-class people are. I believe, nevertheless, that the magical people have something to tell us and I want to hear it.

2.

Eat Only Chicken
the Day of the Game

I don't believe in magic, of course. Hardly anybody does, but we all live by it. It permeates our lives every day, and we wouldn't give it up for all the science on earth. Most of us can't. We can't because we aren't aware of how completely we live within its thrall. Who can break a bond they don't know exists?

My first magical lesson came when I was five. I was playing with the crippled girl who lived down the street. We didn't like each other much, but being the only children in the neighborhood, we made do with each other in a grudging, bickering way. At one point in our play she took two bananas off the kitchen counter and told me to pick the one I wanted. I wanted the bigger one. I knew I shouldn't take the big banana. To take it from a crippled girl would be especially bad. But I wanted it. So I took it.

At this point, in defense of myself, I'd like to mention that I was cross-eyed. I'm not saying that cross-eyed trumps crippled, and to be completely truthful, it wasn't much of a factor in my case—

morally speaking, I mean—because I didn't know I was cross-eyed. No one had mentioned it, and I wasn't an observant child.

I might have forgotten about the bananas by now except that mine had a big brown soft spot in it that ran all the way down the side. About two inches of my banana was edible. Her banana was perfect, and she ate it while I watched. If I had been generous, she would have been eating the rotten banana.

I knew what this meant. Somebody was watching, keeping score. It was God maybe. Who it was didn't matter. What mattered was that I got the message. I never have taken the big banana again. I've never taken the biggest piece of chicken or the last scoop of mashed potatoes or the cookie with the most chocolate chips. I've never pushed anybody aside at the bargain table. I say to myself that I don't care as much about such things. I don't want them as much as other people do, but that's not the truth. The truth is that I am still ruled by the bad magic of the big banana.

I was smart enough not to tell anybody in my family about it. If I had, they would have given me the horselaugh and brayed, "Taught you a lesson, huh?" I didn't call this experience magical even to myself, but it clearly was, just as magical as that bad witch who wasn't invited to the party and got so mad that she cursed poor little Sleeping Beauty.

It was a curse for sure. Luckily the big banana curse was a minor, manageable spell, evoked by my behavior and not by a capricious universe. The behavior it evoked dovetailed well with my Christian upbringing. But the lesson of the banana was deeper even than Christian teachings because it didn't have to be taught. It had been experienced, and it seemed to affirm something basic in the fabric of reality. It didn't, of course. But it seemed to.

Life went on. My eye got fixed, sort of. The doctors call it satisfactory. It turns outward a little instead of inward a lot. It hasn't been much of a handicap, as far as I know, and it has helped me some. I understand outsiders in a way that not everybody does. Or I try to. Not because I'm smarter or more sensitive, but I know how it feels to be among those who can be summed up with one word of physical attribute. There are lots of them—cross-eyed, fat, crippled, bald, weak-chinned, spastic, crazy—and knowing what that feels like makes me listen harder. Or try to. If I wanted to make it a joke, I'd say I look at the world askance. Nobody who knows me would disagree with that.

I grew up. I became a big-city newspaper reporter, which is not a hopeful or fanciful or magical profession. If anybody had asked me two years ago to describe the age we live in, I'd have painted a picture right in line with what the world's wise thinkers expected of me, except that it would be utterly dismal.

I'd have said science is our true God. I'd have said that we live in a world of marvels gone stale, adrift in an empty cosmos. We hear no voices but our own. We believe no omens, listen to no oracles. If otherworldly visions come to us, we close our eyes. And we never, ever think that we might have some great task, noble destiny, or grand calling. Such thoughts are generally believed to indicate a need for medication.

That's how lots of people would describe life, but if an extraterrestrial were to watch these nonbelievers as they go about their lives, it would become quite clear that they do believe in much more than a material, soulless world. I first began to know about these hidden beliefs because I wrote a book on Lily Dale, a western New York community of Spiritualists where people have been talking to the dead for five generations. I wrote the book because I thought people with such extravagant ideas were rare, an oddity, something strange that would excite wonder. What a chucklehead.

Whether the dead talk back is a matter of contention, of course. I was careful about that, not wanting to be branded a crazy. But it didn't matter. In writing the book, I'd been transformed. I'd become a person who could be told things. People all over the country started coming up to me in bookstores, at meetings, during parties to tell me stories they didn't usually share with strangers.

They'd often start by glancing to each side. They would shrug as if they weren't to be held responsible for what was coming. Then they'd say, "I don't know what this means," or, "I'm just going to tell you what happened." One by one they came, butchers and bakers and candlestick makers. Few would have described themselves as believers in magic.

Once, for instance, I was in a Bible Belt state with a group of women who raise charitable funds for children's hospitals. I talked about my book on the town that talks to the dead. When the talk turned to spirituality, heads nodded about the room as several women attested to their strong belief in Jesus Christ as their own personal, living savior and to their complete reliance on the Bible as the direct word of God, suitable for any occasion. I thought, *Oh, boy. I hope they don't go to praying and try to save me.* I hadn't needed to worry. They finished dessert, and then they lined up to tell me *things*.

"My mother read tea leaves all her life. If a relative was about to die, she always knew it," said one. Another told me that her husband had second sight. His whole family had witnessed it.

The eighty-year-old former president of the group reached into her bosom to pull out a silver cross with a little charm next to it.

"Know what this is?" she asked.

"It's the evil eye," I said. According to magical theory, the eye on her charm would stare down the evil eye if it were directed toward her.

"Evil eye. That's right. I'm Greek. All the Greeks wear them. Even the children."

A blond woman of middle years asked, "Have you ever known anyone who had the evil eye put on them?"

"No," I said.

"Well, someone put it on my daughter," she said.

The daughter was about eighteen months old. She and her family were strolling along a New Jersey beachfront boardwalk when a man approached them. He was an actor from a fun house and was dressed in a monk's robe. He had a rope around his waist. From it hung a cross, which he was twirling.

"Oh, what a beautiful child," he said, looking intently at their daughter. Then he began to follow the family, continuing to stare at the little girl.

The man's focus was so strange and his tone so eerie that the father turned the child's stroller around and began pushing it away from the man, faster and faster until the family was practically running to escape. That night the child fell ill. She had a high fever and began throwing up. The next day she was still sick and crying constantly. A child who had always loved men, now she wouldn't go to any of the men in the family. The mother's sister had been on the boardwalk when the actor approached, and she was troubled by his actions. She called their aunt, who was of Polish heritage.

"He's put the evil eye on her," the aunt said. "You'll have to remove it." The mother's sister was to take four straws from a broom and throw them over her shoulder into the corners of the room as she said a litany of Polish words. She was then to take a fifth straw, burn it with a wooden match, and drop it into a glass of water. They were to give the baby a spoonful of water from the glass.

"Make sure you do exactly what I told you," she said, "and don't let anyone who doesn't believe be in the room when you do this."

The mother, who didn't know Polish, was so frightened that she would foul up and kill her daughter that she couldn't do the spell. So her sister did it. The baby fell asleep immediately and slept four hours. When she awoke, the fever was gone and so was her fear of men.

"Are you telling me the truth?" I demanded. But I knew she was. She was as wholesome as Thanksgiving dinner and probably sat in the front pew of the Baptist church every Sunday.

Kids upchucking in the night and then getting better the next day isn't all that unusual, but I didn't say so because she knew that already and my saying it would have missed the point. The point of the story was that evil is alive, and good can defeat it in magical ways. It's a good story, and the last part makes it better. No one told the little girl about that night, and she was too young to remember, but for the rest of her childhood she feared men in monk's robes and would cry whenever she saw them.

As I heard a hundred tales and more, I also began to see magic everywhere, planted deep in the stuff of everyday life and flourishing. Britney Spears appeared on the cover of *Entertainment Weekly* wearing a red Kabbalah cord on her wrist. Paris Hilton had one, and so did Madonna, who adopted the name Esther to go along with her new faith in Jewish mysticism. The cords, which deflect the evil eye, were so popular that the Kabbalah Centre, where the stars go for instruction, tried to patent the string, sold for $26 to $36. The U.S. Patent and Trademark Office declined that application.

Go into any large bookstore in America and you'll find several books on regional ghosts and haunted places. Ghost hunters and ghost busters work all over the country. E-Bay sells haunted dolls and teddy bears. One week's auction offered a haunted tuning fork, a haunted milking stool, a haunted gravestone rubbing, a haunted blanket, and a haunted bathtub.

Magic also penetrates our lives in ways that are quite mundane. It's at the car repair shop when the engine stops pinging as soon as the mechanic appears and begins to ping again only when you pull out onto the street. It's in the beauty salons when hair that spikes about your head like a scarecrow's coiffure turns supple and silky on the day of the appointment. It's at the restaurant when diners arrive only after the waiter sits down with his own plate and smokers' food comes only after they've lit up.

You've heard of voodoo economics perhaps? Money magic is the most pervasive of all. Of course it would be, since money itself is the ultimate magic, a piece of paper that can do everything. Everyone wants good money magic, a way to win the lottery, gambling luck, an unexpected check in the mail, but the money magic of everyday life is more often bad. Win some money, get a bonus, have a little inheritance, and a major appliance will go out, the kid will get sick, a tire will go flat. Once you're as poor as you were before the money arrived, life returns to normal. It's as though there's some kind of balance sheet that makes sure we stay at exactly the same level of prosperity all the time.

These are matters of life's proceeding that hardly need to be commented on. They're so common that they show up in jokes, and no one looks bewildered or wonders what's being talked about. Trot out all the scientists you want, arm them with a million statistics. It won't do any good. We know these things.

I often heard people talking about inanimate objects as though they were alive and powerful. This can opener never works for me, someone might say, or the bus always comes early when I'm running late. Or I always have to kick the machine before it will start. Or this computer only works for Mark—it hates the rest of us. Or it never rains when you've got an umbrella. No one is serious, you say? Maybe not, or maybe they're whistling in the dark. It doesn't matter which because language creates reality. What we name is what we notice, and that's another argument for the inherent strength of magic. We've been programmed to ignore as much of it as we can, and still it pops up.

Theater people are notorious for their magical beliefs. Take *Macbeth*, for example. According to lore, witches who were displeased with Will Shakespeare's treatment of them in *Macbeth* cursed the play, and ever since it has been bad luck to mention the name Macbeth or quote from the play while in the theater. Instead, it is called The Scottish Play. Absurd? Here are just a few of the misfortunes that have occurred around The Play. In its first performance, Shakespeare was forced to play Lady Macbeth when the boy who was to have had the part died of a fever. In 1672 an actor playing Macbeth is said to have substituted a real dagger for the fake and killed the actor playing Duncan as the audience watched. In 1775 Sarah Siddons, playing Lady Macbeth, was nearly attacked by a disapproving audience, and in 1926 the actress Sybil Thorndike was nearly strangled. A riot during an 1849 performance in New York City was spurred by a mass demonstration in favor of an American actor involved in a feud with the British actor playing Macbeth. Twenty-three people died. During a performance in 1953 Charlton Heston's tights were accidentally soaked in kerosene, caught fire, and burned him badly. This is merely a sampling of the misfortune around the play.

Now take a look at the magic of sports. Baseball players spit into their hands before picking up a bat. Bowlers wear the same clothes for as long as a winning streak lasts. Rodeo riders put the right foot in the stirrup first. Tennis players avoid holding two balls when serving. Michael Jordan wore shorts from his alma mater, the University of North Carolina, under his uniform. Hall of Famer Wade Boggs would eat only chicken the day of a game. If these things seem silly, forbid the players their magic and see how seriously they take it. Little Leaguers learn such thinking from coaches and parents, who might be expected to oppose such gross superstition but in fact go right along with it.

Sports fans are even worse. When the Red Sox were in the World Series, I heard a new story of magical influence every day. One story made it to the *New York Times* and was written by a science writer who believed that the Sox could win only if he ignored their games. He called it obeying his lizard brain, meaning, I supposed, that he was reverting to something prehuman in himself, but he was wrong. Relying on magic is utterly human.

People are quick to believe that a losing player or team is jinxed. The New Orleans Superdome has been exorcised a number of times by voodoo queens and nuns. Fans also turn to magic for help in winning. The Brits, the Swiss, the Dutch, and the Australians stick pins in voodoo dolls to help their teams win at soccer and rugby. When the Philadelphia Eagles were in the playoffs for the Super Bowl in 2005, the *Philadelphia Inquirer* put out a hex sign to go on televisions during the game and a magical chant from a Wiccan priestess that was to send good energy. When the Eagles and the Patriots were ready to face off, a journalist in the suburbs consulted a voodoo "witch doctor" and a Druid priest in New Orleans, and the Internet's religion magazine, Beliefnet.com, republished a column with seven rites to make the Super Bowl America's national pagan midwinter rite.

Magic also lives in the homes of America. I heard dozens of tales about ghosts flitting around in houses, most often seen, sometimes heard, and other times merely experienced as a cold feeling or objects that moved about in strange ways. Whole families sometimes accept the existence of these apparitions—human and animal. People are also quick to believe certain houses are haunted in malevolent ways. Think that's not true? Try to sell a house where someone has been murdered.

And who upholds this kind of nonrational thinking? The family, of course. Parents begin teaching their children the importance of enchantment before the babes have left their cradles. The most beloved holidays are replete with magical trappings: the Christmas tree, the Easter egg, the Valentine Cupid, the Halloween witch. Almost all holidays have pagan progenitors, and most people know it, but that doesn't diminish their enthusiasm one whit.

The first stories parents tell their little ones are of magical enchantments, fantasy tales in which witches cast spells and orphan girls have fairy godmothers. They are wise to tell such tales early and often, according to some of civilization's best thinkers. Myths are so vital to citizens of a republic that they ought to be the beginning of literary education, Plato believed. Myths and fairy tales are "models for human behavior" that give meaning and value to life, said Mircea Eliade, whose studies of such stories are classic works. Children deprived of fairy tales may be stunted in psychological development so that becoming secure, well-functioning adults is much more difficult, according to psychologist Bruno Bettelheim, who believed the stories speak a language that matches children's inner worlds better than any realistic story ever could. From the lessons of fairy tales they learn to deal with their fears and aggressions. In unconscious, deep-seated ways, they learn that life will have hard challenges that they can triumph over and that shrinking from such difficulties will restrict life to less than it ought to be, wrote Bettelheim. Good wins in the end, effort is rewarded, and evil is punished—if not by other humans, then through magical laws that support right decisions and valiant efforts. All those lessons give children a sense that life will work out well for them, that it is destined to.

"Our positive feelings give us the strength to develop our rationality; only hope for the future can sustain us in the adversities we unavoidably encounter," Bettelheim wrote. People who don't get enough fairy tales in their childhood are likely to revert to magical thinking as teens or young adults in an attempt to get the psychic balance and sense of purpose that these stories impart to the unconscious mind.

Could that be why so many people are taking up magic now? Maybe. The good doctor had another theory. He thought that in times of great stress and insecurity people revert to the kind of magical thinking that is common in childhood and primitive cultures. For him, quite obviously, belief in any kind of divinity or force that benefits humankind is deviant, childlike thinking.

Philosopher and psychologist William James wasn't so sure about that. He suspected that powers and forces not yet acknowledged by science might be active on the earth. He thought that belief in things greater than ourselves could have definite benefits, especially for those he called the sick-minded, among whom he counted himself.

The healthy-minded person looks at life with optimism and is able to hold his own against the ills of the world, clearly understanding himself to be separate from most of them and able to chart his own course, said James. Following Bettelheim's thinking, we might say that the healthy-minded person has internalized the heroes and demons of the magical (or unconscious) world and found his place among the strong, the beautiful, and the wise. Whether his actions and attributes actually place him in such company isn't nearly as important as whether he thinks they do, because it is his belief in himself that makes him healthy and effective.

James's sick-minded person, on the other hand, needs the second birth promised by religious life. He is depressive, fearful, too sensitive, morbidly fixated on illness, death, and failure. He needs a new outlook so that he can forge through life with hope and confidence. He looks for something outside himself, some transformation. It is for him that religion may be vitally important—and a true path toward fulfillment as a human being—says James. As we shall see in the stories that follow, the same might be said of magic, especially in a time when the authority and truth of religion are under siege.

Parents are also wise in telling their children magical stories because such stories introduce children to enchantment, a state of being that serves us in all sorts of practical ways. Without enchantment, it's hard to create, hard to learn, and hard to have the kind of hope that keeps life fresh. It is even hard to do science.

Sociologist Mark A. Schneider defines enchantment as encountering events or objects "so peculiar and so beyond our present understanding as to leave us convinced that were they to be understood, our image of how the world operates would be radically transformed." Adults seek to be enchanted by things that are real and "at the same time uncanny, weird, mysterious, or awesome." That sense of mystery and awe compels students to learn and scientists to experiment. It caused me to keep looking at the magical community even when I wanted to look away.

To become enchanted is a valuable skill, more essential than it has ever been before. To understand the inner truth of a person who is radically different from you, to penetrate a belief that seems preposterous, to grasp a faith that violates everything you've held dear, you must become enchanted. It's the only way. It's not difficult. Look into the wide eyes of a laughing baby, let yourself fall into that innocence, and for a breathless moment you can be taken over. People are enchanted every day—by a baby, by a flower, or by the sound of their own voice speaking ideas they didn't know they had. But to become enchanted by that which frightens or repels you— that's less common and perhaps even more vital.

We've never needed that type of enchantment more than we do right now. We live in a time when we are being asked to encounter, appreciate, and accept people and ideas that are utterly foreign to us. We are told that we must stop labeling the stranger as strange, as odd, as less than we are. The fate of our world, stocked with bigger and bigger bombs each day, may depend on it. The happy habit of declaring ourselves the "true" people and labeling outsiders the "other," of calling our ways good and other ways evil, has been with us since we crawled out of the cave. Now we are being forced to consider and to accept or reject more and more people with ideas and values that are completely contrary to what we have always believed. The demands are coming faster and faster in human relations, in religion, and in science.

It's no accident that scientists are on the frontiers of the new. They seek to be enchanted often—but only briefly, Schneider writes. As soon as they understand what has enchanted them, its power is explained and therefore taken away. For them, that is the victory. They have proven that the enchanting thing is as mundane as everything else in the world. Like anything else that has been dissected, it is then dead. The great benefit of dissection is that anything is much more useful once its parts are understood and can be manipulated for other uses.

One of the most poignant stories of how science giveth and science taketh away comes from Georgia's Sapelo Island, among a people called the Geechee. They were an isolated people, and thus disenchantment came later for them than for others. It started when scientists with the Marine Institute of the University of Georgia came to the island and became friendly enough with the local people to learn their lore, according to *God, Dr. Buzzard, and the Bolito Man.* The Geechee told them about a ball of light sometimes seen in the swamps called the jack-o'-lantern and about a spirit called the hag that visited people during the night.

"The scientists took away all the mystical, magical things about the jack-o'-lantern by saying that what we saw as a floating ball of light was something that naturally occurs over a low-lying damp area," wrote Cornelia Walker Bailey. "What caused that glowing effect was gas, they said, and that's what we'd been looking at. It was never a jack-o'-lantern at all. And we said, 'Aah, that's what it is.'

"Once the scientists explained it, nobody ever saw a jack-o'-lantern again. Because once you put magic to a spotlight it disappears. When you explain it away it goes away. It's never there anymore. So Cousin Charles Walker, who got hopelessly lost following that mysterious ball of light when I was a kid, was the last person on Sapelo ever to see the jack-o'-lantern.

"Then the scientists explained away the hag, the one that sometimes would fly from Raccoon Bluff to Lumber Landing and Shell Hammock and ride three people all in one night, and then the old people would say, 'That hag was *busy* last night.'

"That was probably a case of poor blood circulation, the scientists said. Your blood was circulating in your body poorly. 'Who the hell they think they are?' Grandma said. 'What do they know about the hag?'

"The teachers at school also started telling us there wasn't any such thing as the hag, and the kids my age looked at each other and said, 'Gosh, everybody is saying the same thing. There's no such thing as the hag.' While all those thoughts were whirling around in our heads, the hag went, 'Uh-oh. Time to go. Too many people coming over,' and it flew away. All of a sudden, the hag didn't come visit anymore. Nobody had the sensation of being in bed and waking up with this *heavy weight* on top of you, being ridden all night by a mysterious hag and being so tired in the morning you couldn't move. It was just *gone*.

"But where did the hag go? Did it fly off somewhere where there was less modern know-how? Was the hag ever coming back? And did that many people have poor blood circulation? Adults and children alike?

"Soon the old people said, 'Chile, I remember when the hag would come ride me all the time. Things sure change.' It was the beginning of the end of magic as we knew it on Sapelo and nothing would ever be the same."

Most of us can mourn that loss with the Geechee people and, at the same time, agree that there wasn't really a hag or a jack-o'-lantern. Right? They're better off now. Right?

But the scientists aren't just changing the Geechees' perceptions of the world; they're changing ours too. Author Russell Shorto claims that we have a little scientist living within us who is constantly keeping tabs on the rationality of ideas, testing and weighing to make sure that whatever we accept fits the scientific model. Every time science explains a little more of the world to us, we incorporate that knowledge and use it to process events around us. Some of the most exciting new research on the brain tells us that what we perceive to be happening around us and to us, even what we remember about our past, may not be true at all.

As William James noted, science is "callously indifferent" to the experiences that make up the lives of most people. Life is personal and romantic, he wrote. Premonitions, apparitions, omens, visions, dreams, answers to prayers, miracles, and other "unnatural" events are woven into our lives in ways that are almost below our consciousness. Because human beings are helplessly committed to making meaning out of what happens to us, and these things do happen to us, it's hard for us to resist the sense that "events may happen for their personal significance," as James put it. Forswearing such connections may not be to our benefit at all. To accept that transcendence is imaginary, that epiphany is delusional, is to accept a state of spiritual impoverishment that hasn't been required of any other human beings.

We do not want to be irrational. That would be among the worst of modern sins, but the corporeal and the ethereal are often indivisibly mixed in our experience. We know, also from our experience, that the rational, measured-out, logical model is not always sufficient when dealing with life's realities. This insufficiency can sometimes have a lofty spiritual import and sometimes be quite practical and everyday. Enchantment is an example. Any husband who has given his wife a quick solution for her problems only to see her become angrier knows this. "I need you to listen to me," she may say. She doesn't want a rational formula to ease her distress. She won't be happier if he gives her statistics on how many other women feel as she does. She wants him to become enchanted, to enter so deeply into her distress that his view of the world is changed and the insult of easy answers is no longer possible. Enchantment always causes complications. He is wise to resist, as she is equally wise to press for a true connection and nothing less.

Enchantment frightens us for good reason. Whether it's enchantment of the ordinary kind or the magical kind, it may very well change us, and we may not be able to return to our old selves, to our old certainties and our easy understandings. Magical people seem to fear that less than the rest of us. They want to be enchanted and are quite willing to be changed forever as they go deeper and deeper into realms beyond everyday understanding. Most of us wouldn't mind a little more magic ourselves, if we could slip in and out of it. We too want to leave the drab realities of work-a-day life, to experience the transcendent, to revel in endless possibility. But most of us have lost any belief in good magic. All that's left is a vague sense that evil is afoot and ready to draw nearer. The only magic most of us believe in is the scary stuff.

*M*any of the magical stories I heard as I traveled featured friendly visitors, spirits of the known dead coming back to comfort the living, happy coincidences, and fortunate omens, but a surprising number were of malevolent spooks and eerie happenings. Two acquaintances told me they suspected their suburban houses of harboring a bad spirit. Both have teenage daughters, traditional attractors of such beings. Two sisters told of the night when a cold, controlling being came into a hotel room, demanding that one of them go with him; the other sister held on to her sibling and refused to give in to him. A pretty young divorcée talked of the night she awoke to feel that something had crept into bed with her. She felt a hand smooth her hair and she saw the bedcovers move.

A woman whose background was born-again Christian told of reading a book on voodoo until deep in the night. She fell asleep and then awoke to see half-human, half-animal figures roaming about on the landing outside her bedroom door. She had never seen or imagined such beings. The book had not included them.

"I was not asleep," she said. "I was completely awake. I know I was because I reached out to touch the wall beside me."

"What did you do about the creatures?" I asked, knowing that she had left the religious assurances of childhood beliefs far behind.

"I called on the blood of Jesus," she said, her voice going high with emotion.

"Good idea," I said. Old habits die hard, which is sometimes for the best.

Then she went to sleep, and the next morning she told her husband.

"Those sound like lwa," he said, referring to voodoo spirits; he then described what she had seen. The next week she saw a voodoo exhibit that also pictured exactly the figures she had seen. She put the voodoo book away and hasn't read anything like it since.

I heard about black women who burned the hair left in their brushes and a Jewish woman who wrapped such hair in toilet paper, taped it up, and flushed it down the commode. They feared that if the hair wasn't disposed of properly, birds would find it and build nests, which would cause those who'd lost the hair to have headaches or go crazy.

Bad magic makes the newspaper all the time. In the town where I live, four friends on their way to a family reunion were killed. A man crossed the center line in his car, going the wrong way, and hit them head on. The next day a friend was quoted as saying, "There were a lot of bad signs before they left."

A father whose son had been killed in the war on Iraq remembered their last conversation. "He told me this was his last mission before he comes home, and I told him not to say that," the father said. "I didn't like those words, 'his last mission,' and I told him to call me when he gets back.

"But he will not call me now."

I thought, how terrible that we poor humans, so menaced through all our lives, feel not only helpless but as though some chance remark, innocently released into the air, might draw bad fortune, like Tolkien's eye of Sauron, piteously searching for us through the night.

Sometimes bad magic is disguised as good magic. A plane crashes, and the guy who missed the plane because his car had a flat tells reporters that God saw fit to save him. If you put a God-tagline on it, it's more acceptable, but it's still magic. The reporters are thinking, *What did God have against all those other schmucks?* but they don't ask that question. They would be insulting God, ruining a nice story, and disillusioning thousands of readers who think there's a good chance God or intuition or whatever might do the same for them. Editors do not like that kind of reporter.

But the worst thing is that people seem all too ready to believe the bad magic and much less able to trust the positive. I did hear positive magic stories, but watch the quality of this one and you'll get an idea of the fix we're in. Whenever one of my Catholic friends loses anything, she prays to Saint Anthony and she always finds it. So one day her cousin called her to say that she had lost a diamond earring. She knew it was in the bedroom, but she had been looking for hours and she couldn't find it.

"Pray to Saint Anthony," my friend said. "It always works."

The woman did pray to the saint of lost things. Then she started looking again. She flipped the top bedsheet up in the air, and out flew the earring. My friend laughed as she told the story and said, "But the trouble now is that she will think that Saint Anthony found the earring for her."

"Didn't he?"

"No, of course not."

"I thought you believed in it."

"Of course I don't," she said, laughing more.

"Then why did you tell her to do it?"

"Because it always works."

Is that religion or magic? Does it matter? Is there a difference?

One Christmas a Philadelphia lawyer listened to a few of my stories over wine and cookies and then said, "Aren't you afraid?"

I replied solemnly, pausing between each word so that she would not miss my inference, "No. I am not afraid. I do not believe in it."

She looked a bit abashed, which isn't an easy thing to make a Philadelphia lawyer do. What was she frightened of? Nothing, I'd bet. And everything. All the things that may lurk just outside the light. She had plenty of company. Never once did anyone in the mundane world say of my magical investigation, "Wow. You'll find out how to assemble good spirits." Or, "You'll attract good fortune." Or even anything as crass as, "You'll win the lottery." They predicted no good fortune. But plenty of bad.

As talk of bad magic kept popping up all around me, I realized that I had lied to the Philadelphia lawyer. I too was captive to such thoughts, and I did not know how to undo the spell. Many of us believe that innocent actions can bring evil crashing down upon us: too much good fortune, ignoring the "signs," a wish or a brag unwisely spoken. We can toss off a psychic's promise of good fortune, but let the fortune-teller predict death, and a chill will fall over us. It is as though we're trapped in a Brothers Grimm fairy tale that is grim indeed.

Good magic does descend on us in a willy-nilly fashion, in occasional visitations, in blessings that we desperately try to connect with a certain color or pair of socks or food that we've eaten, but it can't be counted upon. It can't be controlled. It does not rush to our aid when we say certain words. It exists mainly in the world of fantasy, in holiday tales and children's books. Most of us have lost any hope of being able to summon a force for good. We don't even try. We'd be afraid to. At least, the celebrities with their red wrist cords to deflect envy and the women wearing evil eye charms have an antidote for the bad magic aimed at them. The rest of us duck and dodge.

I am about as fearful as a person can be and still get out of bed every morning. You've heard of the coward who died a thousand deaths? That's me and not only me. Everyone I've loved, pets included, has also died many times. Died, been buried, and well grieved at least a dozen times a week. It only takes a second or two. I can go right on peeling potatoes, mopping the floor, snipping the heads off withered dahlias. I've been doing it so long that I don't pause for more than a mumble or two.

My husband says he's going to the store for milk. He's dead from a car that crossed the line. He's taking the dog for a noonday walk. If they're not back in twenty minutes, heat stroke has killed the Lab. He's too heavy to carry home, so my husband is sitting on the curb next to the dog's body wishing I'd think of them and bring the car. I'd like to encourage my friends to visit, but they won't survive the trip. The only safe people are the ones I don't like.

As for myself, staying home cuts the odds in my favor, but anything could get me. Cancer, stroke, toxic tomatoes. The other day I was standing at the top of the stairs with my back to them and I thought, *What if I backed up and fell down the stairs. It might kill me.* So I didn't. But I could have. One absentminded moment and I'd be gone. I've had some absentminded moments. Who wouldn't with all the death that's floating around?

I can't easily accept the idea that my thoughts change reality. My thoughts are all too dreary, which only goes to show just how big a lie I told the Philadelphia lawyer. I needed the magical people far more than I wanted to admit. They are the only ones who still have a technology of the sacred that can summon good magic and forestall bad magic. The rest of us don't even believe it can be done. They not only think it can be done but think it can be done better and better. I quite obviously hadn't absorbed the lessons of fairy tales well enough to believe myself safe in the world. If I wanted to be free of my irrational fears, maybe some irrational magic, a little of the dog that bit me, would be the solution. I needed some irrational belief in the good, the kind of belief that Bettelheim said healthy adults absorbed from childhood fairy tales. I couldn't go back to childhood, but I could go forward into magic. Hard-core magical people believe without doubt that the power of magic is available to us and that others can learn to use it. Luckily, they were just the people I was going to see.

3.

America the Magical,
I Sing of Thee

hat I should be surprised to find so many Americans talking about magic had something to do with my own background. I was raised Southern Baptist in the days when it was a fairly mild, stripped-down version of Protestantism, long before Christians became millionaires writing about gentle Jesus coming back to napalm unbelievers. If anyone in our church had whispered such bloody fantasies with such loving detail, we'd have slid to the other end of the pew and piled our songbooks up as a barrier.

My surprise also has something to do with my ignorance of America's occult history. I thought magical thinking was way, way in the past, back in Egyptian days, back to the Romans, important to the Celts, but after that it began to die. In fact, belief in magic has always been around. It just hasn't always made the history books. Until the 1970s, few historians paid it much attention. The European and Salem witch trials are the exception, and it took a lot of killings for that to happen. But witch trials are only part of the story.

Dabbling in the occult was, is, and always has been as American as the Pilgrim Fathers, more so even. In 1776, only 22 percent of the colonists in Massachusetts were Puritans, and even the Puritans practiced magic.

"Colonial Americans were, in fact, more likely to turn to magical or occult techniques in their effort to avail themselves of superhuman power than they were to Christian rituals or prayer," writes religion scholar Robert C. Fuller. Most of them practiced a variety of magical practices such as astrology, divination, fortune-telling, and folk medicine.

Church membership at the start of the Revolution was 17 percent, a figure so low that some scholars suggest that schoolroom pictures of early American Puritans going to church ought to be joined by paintings of drunken revelers. Seen together, they would give a more accurate understanding of America's heritage. Boston's taverns were probably fuller on Saturday night than its churches on Sunday morning.

When Frenchman J. Hector St. John de Crèvecoeur wrote about America in the late 1700s, he called religious indifference an American trait, along with selfishness, industry, litigiousness, and good living. The further inland he traveled, the less religious he found Americans to be. Even Christians didn't let their faith curb their opinions; "general indulgence leaves everyone to think for themselves in spiritual matters," resulting in what he called a "strange religious medley." Much the same might be said today.

People who came to America then, as now, were dreamers, adventurers, oddballs, and freethinkers. Many of the early settlers were criminals. They were people stout enough to believe that they could prevail against the wilds with nothing more than force of will. Some were joiners, but many were not. In short, they were perfectly constituted for transgressive thinking, and magic has often been that.

As early as 1690, the Reverend Cotton Mather complained that Puritan Massachusetts was plagued by "little sorceries." People used whatever was at hand—sieves, keys, peas, nails, and horseshoes—to tell the future and to keep enemies at bay. Salem's witch trials began when adolescent girls put an egg in a glass of water, a popular way of divining that Increase Mather, father of the more famous Cotton, had warned against in 1684. A 1760 booklet called *Mother Bunch's Closet* directed young girls to summon their future husbands by writing, "Come in, my dear, and do not fear," on a slip of paper, putting the paper in a pea pod, and laying the pod under the door. The next person who entered would be the husband. "Dumb suppers," at which no human was allowed to speak, were held on Halloween night to show the faces of future husbands and to summon spirits of the dead. Mirrors might be used, as they sometimes are today, for seeing the future spouse and for bringing back the dead.

The highly placed also practiced occultism. John Winthrop Jr., the governor of colonial Connecticut and an alchemist, owned magical books from the library of Elizabethan England's great magus and mathematician John Dee. Ezra Stiles, the president of Yale College, was an alchemist. Other alchemists, mostly Yale and Harvard graduates, continued to practice the art in New England until the 1830s. In 1773, Massachusetts judge Samuel Danforth offered Benjamin Franklin a piece of the Philosopher's Stone, which was supposed to turn base metals into gold. Franklin wasn't interested. He, George Washington, and other founding fathers were Freemasons, an organization that used magical symbolism and initiation ceremonies aimed at individual transformation.

In the 1740s, in Pennsylvania's utopian commune of Ephrata, patients were promised 5,557 years of life through medical alchemy. In 1765, a broadside against the Stamp Act claimed that a hex had been put on the Philadelphia commissioner handling the stamps. If he continued to distribute them, he would endure rheumatism, pox, and gout, claimed the pamphlet's author.

Not only did God-fearing, churchgoing Puritans use magic and pass it down to their children, often with no sense that they were doing anything wrong, but Puritan doctrine itself unwittingly fostered such practices. The Reverend Jonathan Edwards, one of America's earliest theological geniuses, believed that God's "emanations" were like celestial light that transformed those who received it and made them capable of perceiving "images or shadows of divine things" all about them in nature. Magical people, who were often called "cunning folk" in those days, have similar ideas about the omnipresence of divine things, the ability of humans to discern them, and the need for some special talent or spiritual gift or training in order for these things to be revealed.

Edwards, who is best known today for his sermon "Sinners in the Hands of an Angry God," also had some part in the First Great Awakening, which swept through America in the early and middle part of the 1700s. This advent of revivalist preaching, with its emphasis on personal, ecstatic experience, seated the proof of divine presence firmly inside the individual, empowering experience in a way that would continue to grow within American religious life. "The Great Awakening popularized a rhetoric of liberty, a conviction that true authority rested in personal conscience rather than in established authority," writes Fuller.

The Puritans had another idea that made magic attractive. Nobody could ever know if they were predestined to be saved or to burn in hell. Even being concerned about your eternal fate could mean that you weren't among the elect. God was in charge but distant. This kept the Puritans in a constant state of insecurity.

Today, also, God is distant and salvation is shaky. As one scholar has quipped, science has taken God away and given us an ape as his replacement. We too are insecure. The Puritans' problem was too little information. Ours may be too much. Magic was an antidote, then and now. It can reveal the future and protect from calamity. It can discern and disarm an enemy. It can bring punishment to evildoers and good fortune to the adept. It can connect humans with divine will and wisdom. If it works, of course, which is a whole other issue.

Much of the magic in America was brought from Europe and Africa. Later, other forms of magic came with Asian immigrants. Native Americans, of course, had their own forms, and the new arrivals often blended Old Country magic with whatever they learned from the Indians. America itself was thought to be a magical land. The magician John Dee called it Atlantis.

Immigrants also brought magical tools with them. Divining rods probably came with early German immigrants, and by the 1790s European Americans everywhere were using them to locate water, ore, buried treasure, and lost items. Americans are still divining, or dousing, or water witching, as it's often called. So many people use sticks or wires to find things in the earth that classes are taught all over the country.

Another early magical tool was the chain letter, which became popular among the Pennsylvania Dutch and by 1725 had an English version. This letter, which was supposedly written by Jesus, promised that those who carried it could not be damaged by guns or swords, but anyone who did not copy and pass it on would be cursed by the Christian church. Chain letters with promises and curses are still common, of course, with the Internet having given them a whole new life. Spell books that purported to teach good magic and instructed readers on how to contact and control various spirits were passed down within families. One such collection, called *Der Lange Verborgene Freund* (The Long-Lost Friend), was compiled in

1819 and 150 years later was still being carried into battle by recruits from Pennsylvania who went to Vietnam.

Religion and magical thinking are so intertwined that scholars still argue over where the dividing line is. Some Puritans would open the Bible to a random page and cite the first verse their eyes fell on as a way of getting divine guidance about their eternal fate. Many spells and invocations ended with "in the name of the Father, the Son, and the Holy Spirit." In some instances the Bible was also used to determine criminal guilt or innocence.

Today the Bible is often used in magical workings by people who claim it's the best spell book ever written. Christo-magic is common in Pentecostal and Holiness traditions, although they would not call it magic. Saint magic is popular among Catholics. Hoodoo, an African American magical system that also calls on Jesus and the saints, is outside-the-church Christo-magic.

Even when they oppose magic, religious crusaders sometimes aid it. Their fierce opposition gives magical workings publicity, credibility, and a fearsome cachet that they would never otherwise have. Early Dutch and German American traditions told of grimoires—magical books so powerful that people who started reading them would become entangled in the words like flies in a web. The book would hold them fast unless they began to read it backwards to the place where they first started or until a Christian healer released them. The idea surfaced again during the American Satanism scares of the 1970s and 1980s when anti-cult investigators were so frightened of occult books that they warned it might be dangerous to read them and recommended synopses or overviews as safe substitutes.

Religion and magic have always intermingled and at the same time repelled each other. Religion tends toward supplication, whereas magic sets forces into operation, commands, and demands. It relies on the power of objects, of symbols, of numbers, of words, and of human will. It empowers human experience over doctrine. Religious people wait on God; magical people push. Magic cuts out the clergy, dispensing with their role, usurping their power. And instead of telling people that they should not want what they do want, magic tries to help them get it.

In the nineteenth century, Ralph Waldo Emerson and the Transcendentalists helped further push Americans away from depending on religious authority as the only avenue for supernatural power when they put forth three main metaphysical doctrines: "(1) the immanence of God, (2) the fundamental correspondence between the various levels of the universe, and (3) the possibility of 'influx' from higher to lower metaphysical levels."

"As above, so below," is one of the most commonly quoted magical tenets, and once again the idea that God might be within or immanent meant for the Transcendentalists that there was no reason to look to religious authorities. Divine power could be tapped into by anyone who realized it was there and knew how to gain access to it. Walt Whitman was a journalist of little renown until he read Emerson, who fired him up with visions of such magnificence that he became a poet of considerable mysticism. He wrote in his typically robust and earthy style in *Song of Myself*:

> *Divine am I inside and out, and I make holy whatever I touch*
> *or am touch'd from,*
> *The scent of these arm-pits aroma finer than prayer,*
> *This head more than churches, bibles, and all the creeds.*

Between 1875 and 1900, American religion struggled to deal with urbanization, industrialization, immigration, and the depredations of science on traditional faith verities. At the same time, Americans were hearing about religions outside the Judeo-Christian tradition, something that hadn't happened before in a widespread way. The Transcendentalist writer James Freeman Clarke published a book called *Ten Great Religions* that went through twenty-one printings. In 1892 the World Parliament of Religions attracted 150,000 visitors to exhibits about the world's religions. These religions introduced magical concepts that had been quelled within orthodox Christian circles, encouraged dissent from orthodox Christian views, and helped people look within themselves for answers.

Historian Arthur Schlesinger labeled this time "the critical point in American religion." Liberals and conservatives split, as they have today, and people who considered themselves spiritual but not religious could be seen as a definite group for the first time. Philosopher and psychologist William James was among them. James dabbled in occult matters and was convinced that human consciousness has continuity with a wider spiritual universe. The ideas of philosophers Georg Wilhelm Friedrich Hegel and Friedrich Schelling also influenced those who rejected Christianity and tilted toward a magical worldview. During this same time, Spiritualism, the religion founded on the idea that the dead can be contacted, was catching on all over the United States and Europe. One Catholic group estimated their numbers at 11 million—an overestimate probably, but an indication of how big the movement seemed.

On the eve of the twentieth century, as many as 40 percent of American men were involved in fraternal organizations, mostly Masonic, that constructed and performed elaborate mystical ceremonies. A group of Freemasons called the Hermetic Order of the Golden Dawn formed in Britain to recast Masonic ceremonies into magical workings. Among their members were upper-class, well-educated Brits. The poet William Butler Yeats was one of them.

The American fin de siècle surge of magical practice came forth in a variety of ways. Anton Messmer's practice of animal magnetism to heal people was spreading. Paschal Beverly Randolph, a free man of color, taught and wrote about magic techniques that included sex magic. And Madame Helen Blavatsky, who believed she was being directed by mahatmas who had lived in Tibet, founded her Theosophical Society in New York in 1875. Her *Isis Unveiled* is still in print, and at 500,000 copies still selling.

In the common culture, magic also flourished. When treasure hunting swept the country in the late nineteenth and early twentieth centuries, magicians, conjurers, fortune-tellers, and clairvoyants were often asked to consult peep-stones, which were crystals placed inside the seer's hat. The clairvoyant would put his face into the hat and sometimes stay that way for hours before emerging with a message. Almost every New England town still had a witch or wizard. The owners of trading ships often consulted astrologers or fortune-tellers before setting sail. Countermagic was also commonly employed. If cream refused to thicken, a hot rod thrust into the churn was thought to undo the bewitchment by burning the witch. Witch bottles filled with urine and heated in a pan were used to hex those who had placed spells on others.

*W*hen I was a child, I didn't know anyone who lived by signs and omens. I never heard a single person call upon angels for a parking place. Nobody talked of encountering spirits of the dead. Nobody looked for meaning in coincidental events. Nobody talked about what they were *meant* to do, meaning meant by the universe or by some kind of contract they'd chosen before being born. Nobody said, "Be careful what you wish for because you just might get it," as though we were living in a fairy tale where the mere utterance of foolish desires had the power to damn us.

I come from the children of poor people, sometimes poorly educated, but we didn't spread superstition. When we heard it, we laughed. We called it baloney or hogwash. To do anything else would have been ignorant, and that is something we never wanted to be. My family was trying as hard as we could to enter the prosperous, reasonable world that had so long been closed to our kind, but even as we struggled that world was changing. What we would have called childish imagining was taking hold. The latest resurgence of American magic started in the counterculture of the 1960s. By the end of the 1970s, it was already going mainstream.

In 1975, literary and cultural critic George Steiner declared that in terms of money spent, literature produced, and people involved, our culture was the most superstitious and irrational of any "since the decline of the Middle Ages and, perhaps, even since the time of the crises in the Hellenistic world." In that same year, historian Theodore Roszak found himself going to parties where he frequently heard tales that "stretch one's powers of amazement." Somewhat to his own astonishment, he wasn't rejecting them. "One listens *through* them to hear still another intimation of astounding possibilities, a shared conviction which allows one to say, 'Yes, you feel it too, don't you? That we are at the turning point, the *kairos*, where the orders of reality shift and the impossible happens as naturally as the changing of the seasons.'" Some of those tale tellers became New Agers, and if that had been all there was to the spread of magical thought, magic might not be so important today.

In the 1980s, magic went even more mass culture. A deluge of self-help programs and positive-thinking seminars that could have been taken straight from the philosophies of the ancient magi began a fundamental shift in our concepts of who we are and what our relationship to reality is. Most people didn't make the connection to magic, of course, but the gospel of positive thinking says that a person's intentions, his will, and his inner reality can change what happens around him. That's purely magical.

Such thinking seemed utterly pie in the sky to me when I first began to hear it. I remember arguing vehemently with a cheerful salesman who was flirting with me one night. Our budding love affair never left the bar because I was so contemptuous of his soft-brained thinking. You can't *think* your way to success, I told him. You have to work your way there, against great odds, with constant awareness of your weaknesses and frailties. In fact, believing you will triumph is the surest way not to, I believed, although I was too canny to say that outright. I was Calvinist to the core, completely out of step with my times. What I didn't realize in my dismal pride was that I was operating out of the selfsame magical idea, but at the opposite end of it. I believed only in bad magic. To him optimistic thoughts were empowering; to me they were dangerous.

Next, magical thinking showed up in the explosion of self-help programs. The idea that progress is always possible is very American and is often linked to Puritanism, but the modern strain is built on a different base than the older versions. With the new kind of self-help we're still trying harder, but it's no longer because we're God's unworthy creatures. It's because we're uncovering our inherent potential, our inner wisdom. We're becoming all we were meant to be. That's magical. Every bit of that is magical thinking. Magical theory, unlike doctrines that stress the inadequacy and weaknesses of humankind, teaches that people have strength and knowledge within them that is hidden and must be uncovered by their own efforts.

Magical ideas have also gone mainstream in more obvious ways. Today half or more of Americans believe in psychic or spiritual healing and extrasensory perception. One-third believe in haunted houses, possession by the devil, ghosts, telepathy, extraterrestrial beings who've visited the earth, and clairvoyance. All these numbers are higher than they were in the 1990s. Belief in astrology is also up. In the 1930s only 6 percent of people believed in it: in 1985 the number was 47 percent. Some of the change can be attributed to near-death experiences, which have increased as medical technology has been able to bring more and more people back from the edge of death. According to Gallup, 8 to 13 million Americans report having had such an experience. Of people who come close to death, 34 to 40 percent report otherworldly experiences. People who aren't dying when they're expected to are also exerting influence that might be considered magical; 55 percent of doctors report that they have seen results in their patients that they consider miracles.

Magical ideas are also getting new respect from social researchers. A recent study found that 65 percent of kids have an invisible friend, a doll, a stuffed animal, or another object that they consider a living friend. Many keep these friends long after they stop admitting it to their parents, and they often have multiple friends. The researchers were surprised by the number of forms that such friends take. Some are tiny, whereas others are huge; some are ancient; and some are human, whereas others are not. Researchers were also surprised to find that the kids who have imaginary playmates are often popular, well-adjusted kids with plenty of human friends. One researcher wondered if magical friends help children in real life by giving them safe ways to practice their reactions, think out their feelings, and communicate their emotions.

Today magical, mystical beliefs are so strong in the general population that some people believe a great magical renaissance is beginning. I heard two magical explanations for why that might be so. One was from magician and psychologist Robert Masters, who writes that five hundred years ago, when Christians were making a great business of torturing and killing anyone who didn't agree with them, the old gods and all their friends—elves, fairies, gnomes, angels, and so on—decided to withdraw from the world. In the year 2000, they agreed, they would come back and check out the situation. If the climate seemed more hospitable, they might stick around. Some of the entities reneged on their agreement and started drifting in early, which is the reason goddess worship took off in the latter years of the twentieth century, Masters believes.

Another explanation came from a channeler in North Carolina who has been giving messages for a group of spiritual adepts for many years. These wise spiritual beings say that a window between the worlds opened in the year 2000 and will stay open for fourteen years or so. Whatever consciousness humans grab on to during that time will be what they'll have to work with for a long, long time, say the masters.

But it isn't only magical people who see a shift toward the non-rational. Scholars see it too. Two historians, one from Alabama and one from Brigham Young University, wrote a scholarly book about the history of Western magic called *Magic, Mystery, and Science*. The new theories of physics and the trends of postmodernism are shifting toward a new era for occult practice, write Dan Burton and David Grandy. "We hope this book will help readers prepare for that era," says the last sentence of their introduction.

What's going on?

Globalization. Immigration. The collapse of faith in science. The migration of Eastern religions to the West. And maybe something else, something more personal, more basic and utterly unscientific. Maybe soul hunger is to blame.

Sociologist Max Weber believed that the world was being deadened by scientific notions. "As intellectualism suppresses belief in magic, the world's processes become disenchanted, lose their magical significance, and henceforth simply 'are' and 'happen' but no longer signify anything," he wrote. "Science elevated us far beyond anyone's dreams and at the same time demoted us. We went from being the glorious reason for creation to being a side product of mindless accidents."

Mathematician Blaise Pascal saw a universe of "eternal silence" coming in the seventeenth century, and he was filled with dread:

> When I see the blind and wretched state of men, when I survey the whole universe in its deadness and man left to himself with no light, as though lost in this corner of the universe without knowing who put him there, what he has to do, what will become of him when he dies, incapable of knowing anything, I am moved to terror, like a man transported in his sleep to some terrifying desert island, who wakes up quite lost with no means of escape. Then I marvel that so wretched a state does not drive people to despair.

We've gone further than Pascal could have imagined. A few months before his death in 2004, Francis Crick, co-discoverer of DNA, promised a reporter from the *New York Times* that his research into consciousness and the brain would lead to the death of the soul. "The view of ourselves as 'persons' is just as erroneous as the view that the Sun goes about the Earth." He predicted that "this sort of language will disappear in a few hundred years. In the fullness of time, educated people will believe there is no soul independent of the body, and hence no life after death." His co-researcher, Christof Koch, had some doubts about whether human beings, already "cast out of the world of meaning," were ready for such elucidation.

I suspect that Crick, like so many other scientists, completely misunderstood the inclinations of people who want mystery and meaning in their lives. While his research might lead the rest of us to give up hope for our souls, magical and spiritual people won't, but neither will they fight science. They embrace science, even as they give it their own spin. When scientists proved that life evolved from a long chain of being, they said, "How could anything so complicated have occurred without a guiding spirit? Impossible." When scientists showed that the brains of people with spiritual leanings and visionary experiences behave differently from the brains of people without such ideas, the magical people said, "We knew it. The brain is hard-wired to pick up the hidden knowledge that's all around us. We must recover our abilities." When the new physics told of light that changes from waves to particles depending on the observer, they said, "See. Everything is connected."

Widespread disappointment with organized religion also plays a role in the resurgence of magical thought. A recent survey showed that half of Americans believe "that churches and synagogues have lost the real spiritual part of religion." One out of every three adults believes that "people have God within them, so churches aren't necessary."

Daniel Maguire, a former Catholic priest who is a professor of ethics at Marquette University, goes so far as to say that belief in the great faiths is collapsing. People are looking for something to replace them, much as they did in the first century as Christianity began to rout paganism. Now it seems to be the other way around. Sociologist Elizabeth Puttick believes that three faiths are competing for hegemony in America: Christianity, Buddhism, and paganism. As former professor of world religions Lin Osborne has said, "People are doing exactly what they ought to be doing. They're creating their own mythologies." By that, he means that they are finding and sometimes making up their own grand stories about what life means and how we ought to act in it. It's happening even within the churches, where 55 percent of people say they entertain some occult belief: trance channeling, astrology, reincarnation, or fortune-telling.

I first saw how far people are going when I was a religion reporter for the *Dallas Morning News* in the mid-1990s. I went to a little suburban apartment where a dozen people were meeting for a ceremony. They were all tricked out in togas and talked in ways that were either poetic or ridiculous, depending on your sensibility. I didn't understand them at all, but I was trying. Finally I said, "Let me get this straight. You're just making it up as you go. You're taking whatever you like from whatever ancient system you want, mashing it together with whatever else appeals to you, and calling it your religion. Is that right?" Labeling their form of belief a made-up religion would have been an insult worth fighting over to most of the religious people I knew, but these folks looked delighted by my perspicacity.

"That's it," they said. "You've got it."

Disillusionment with the answers provided by organized religion is so prevalent and the hunger for spiritual connection is so intense that one out of five Americans identifies as a spiritual seeker. Even many church members call themselves "spiritual not religious." What they mean is that they won't be bound by doctrine. They rely on their experience to tell them what is spiritually valid. If something that seems mystical or magical happens, they don't look to a priest or a rabbi to tell them if it's all right to think about it. Of the 40 percent of Americans who don't claim to go to church, only about one-fourth are completely unreligious. That means that the largest spiritual group in America is the unchurched, writes religion scholar Robert C. Fuller.

Even within the churches, emotional, mystical, visionary experience, not doctrine or Scripture, is rapidly becoming the most important element in religious conviction. It's no accident that Wicca and Charismatic Christianity, at opposite ends of the theological spectrum but both relying on ritual that shakes body and soul, can claim to be the fastest-growing religions in America. Voodoo, Santeria, and other African-based religions that allow followers to be actually possessed by the divinity are also attracting new populations, including Anglos in Miami, New York, Houston, Charlotte, New Orleans, and Philadelphia.

Three of the biggest questions of spiritual belief are Is there Something out there, some force or intelligence, some energy, some creator, some organizer of the physical? Does that Something impinge on us, expect something from us, have a plan for our lives? And can we use this Something for our own purposes, causing it to smile on us, to bless us, to protect us? Religion grapples with all three questions. Magic assumes the first two and concerns itself with the last one.

To repeat the definition of magic I like best: it is the study of the ways in which natural forces, energies, and gods can be compelled or induced to help us. Calling it the technology of the sacred highlights magic's study of ways to focus such energies. This technology may attract the attention of busy gods through sacred geometry, as the ancient Romans did when they constructed temples filled with geometric symbols; it may provide a road map to higher consciousness, as the Kabbalah does; it may harness the vital forces of herbs, roots, and rocks, as folk magic does; or it may pull down power through ritual, as Wicca does. Or it may be as simple as focusing one's attention to notice what's happening. The salesman who believes that making all five lights on the way to work bodes well for the day may not think he believes in magic, but he does.

Some people believe that magical thought dies down and then flares up again, and there's been lots of speculation about what conditions cause a turn toward magic. But it may be more accurate to say that the elites who write history and study trends swing toward and away from paying attention to magical thinking. Because these elite scholars and writers leave records of their thoughts, it appears that magic ebbs and flows, but perhaps it has only moved out of public sight. Roelof van den Broek and Wouter J. Hanegraaff are among the religious scholars who say that the influence of magical thinking in art, science, literature, and philosophy is a "third current" that has shaped Western culture as profoundly as Greek rationalism and Judeo-Christianity have. Northwestern University historian Richard Kieckhefer calls magic a historical crossroads where religion meets science, where popular culture meets learned culture, and where fiction and reality come together.

At the same time that an increasing number of scholars are studying the historical role of magic, thousands of books are being published about how to do magic. Serious journalistic looks at what today's magical communities might have to say to us, however, are rare to nonexistent. It is into that void that we will now step.

Part Two

LESSONS IN LIGHT AND DARK

It puzzles me that transcendent intimations,
once vouchsafed to spiritual adepts and powerful intellects, now seem available mostly to
devotees of dank crankeries.

—HAROLD BLOOM

4.

Looking for Living Dolls, Whack Jobs, and the Lucky Mojo Curio Company

A first order of business was to decide how I would approach my inquiry. I would have to deal with my skepticism, quiet the little scientist within me, or I would never get anywhere. It was altogether too easy to explain away even the strangest of the magical people. Take the vampires as an example. Nobody can say how big this community of mostly young people is, but it is international, numbers in at least the thousands, and appears to be growing. Some consider themselves to be actual vampires who need human blood, but the majority seem to be interested in taking other people's energy.

When one young psychic vampire told me how he discovered his dark nature, I drew up a list of signs. If you always wear sunglasses when you go outside, if you prefer being up at night to being active during the day, if you have low energy and depression, if you're often ravenously hungry and you like your steaks bloody rare, you might be a vampire.

You might also be a typical American teenager, but never mind that for now.

Believing himself a vampire, he thought that he needed other people's blood to live. Later he came to understand that it wasn't blood that he needed but life energy. He could get that energy by being in crowds, at parties, in church rituals—anyplace where people were gathered. If strong emotions were being generated, that was even better. He could also get the energy he needed through touching people in a conscious way.

Psychologize that description and you have a young person who can't relate well to others. He's alone a lot, and that makes him more depressed. He realizes that he can make himself feel better by being around other people. But relationships that involve talking are difficult. So he avoids those. Soon he realizes that merely being in a crowd can buoy him up. Being in a crowded bar, in a mall, at a sports event, can make him feel more alive. If he concentrates his attention on one person, he feels even better. He interprets this as having fed off their energy.

That might be true, or it might be that he has merely stopped thinking of himself so constantly and that is a relief. Fueled by fantasy fiction and computer games, inspired by visions of vampires who were dangerous and fascinating, he can call himself a loser or an immortal vampire. He chooses vampire. He concentrates on that, thinks about it a lot, has dreams about it, meditates, and has imaginary experiences, which he interprets as past life memories. He is affirmed, knows who he is, and knows how to live. Soon he looks on the Internet. He finds other people who feel the same way. They band together, exchange stories, spin theories, and form a group.

Now let's apply sociology. These are odd times we live in. Reacting in odd ways to the loneliness of a society without real community, one in which extended families don't live together and the banalities of television and rock music substitute for human interaction, wouldn't be that unusual.

It makes a neat package. End of story.

So why wasn't I content? I liked being so smart. It made me feel good to have figured it all out, but a person can be too smart for her own good. I'd taken the vampire's story, categorized it, labeled it, and minimized it. I'd done to the vampire what all of us have learned to do to ourselves and to almost any new idea that comes along. Whenever we don't think the way everyone else does, or see what everyone else sees or believe what everyone believes, we reason it away.

It isn't a bad technique, unless the technique starts running the technician. Anybody who does that enough can find that she has stopped heeding her own feelings and stopped believing her own experiences unless they can be fitted into a mold. And once she does that, there's no ground under her feet. Pretty soon it doesn't matter what new information comes in, she's got a slot all ready for it and she never learns a thing but what she already knew.

I'd seen it happen to lots of people. To myself maybe.

By demythologizing the magical people, I'd satisfied the little scientist within myself, but in truth it had been too easy. From the beginning of my investigations into magical culture, I'd sensed that the people I was talking to were behaving within an enchantment I wasn't part of.

For instance, I was told that Salem witch Shawn Poirier could enchant dolls so that they moved. Several of Shawn's friends told me that one. He had enchanted the dolls in the window of a shop called the Crystal Moon. "Sometimes I sit on that bench outside and just watch them move. Try it out," one of the witches said.

I was eager to do that. In the world of magic, you hear lots of stories that lots of people are willing to swear by, but it's pretty rare that you get to see something done that can't be called coincidence. If those dolls moved, I'd relocate to Salem and start studying the Craft.

The next day when the shop was closed, I went to the bench that faces the window and sat down. There were dolls in the window, fairy creatures hanging from strings. Maybe one or two of them moved, and maybe Shawn was the reason, but I suspected a current of air. None of them blinked or moved their little glass heads while I was looking. It wasn't magic enough for me. I felt a little silly at having been so excited.

Who would this be magic enough for? And then I remembered that the man who had most fervently assured me the dolls moved was the fiancé of the shop's owner. He was crazy in love with her, had been since they were teenagers. She'd been married twice before, and he had mooned after her through those marriages and his own. She was a witch. So now he was a witch. They both credited a love spell with bringing them together. That's the kind of man who would sit and watch these dolls swing on their strings and be enchanted. A man bedazzled already.

Another time, a Salem magician told me that an early lesson for his magical students was learning how to blow up clouds. They would stand looking at the sky and pick a cloud to focus on. Not a big cloud, because that would require more power than they had at first. Pick a thin, wispy cloud, he advised them, and send all your energy to disperse it. It's amazing how often those clouds just fly away, he said. I later heard that this is a common practice among student magicians.

I didn't say much about that story, but everything I thought was insulting. Wispy clouds disperse all the time. Even big clouds do. They are insubstantial, drifting with the wind, always moving. They disperse whether you look at 'em or don't look at 'em. The reason I didn't say much was that my interpretation was so obvious that I knew it wouldn't do any good to point it out. He wasn't an idiot. He and his wife run a magical shop and seem to be staying in business. He was well read, had a good vocabulary, was well spoken and apparently sane. So what was going on? Somehow he was analyzing this event in a way that was utterly unlike my own analysis. They all were doing that.

The outer facts of the magical people's lives, the verifiable ones, often made little sense to me. The outer facts of Shawn's group were summed up by Penn Jillette in a *Penn & Teller* broadcast titled succinctly "Bullshit!" After Shawn and his friends, dressed up in witchy gear, sneered at the camera, waved their hands about, and told their life theories, Penn was again succinct. "Whack jobs," he called them, so pleased with his mean-spirited fun that he was practically snorting.

Nobody watching could blame Penn for his assessment based on the observable facts. That's the outer truth of it, and that might be all there is to any of the magical people. But Penn was also giving his audience another message, an inner truth that they could not fail to understand. His ridicule warned listeners that they had better stick to what he and his kind would allow them to believe, or he would have the same kind of snorting fun with them.

Shawn told me that he and his friends hadn't known they were going to be on *Penn & Teller*. But considering everything, he thought they came off pretty well. If someone can call you a whack job on national television and you can feel pretty good about that, maybe you are magic.

*M*y introductions to magic sometimes came in somewhat mysterious ways, which is only to be expected, I guess. One hot summer day when I was in Memphis flogging my book at one of those little tables that sits at the front of the bookstore, a woman came up to me.

"I was in here last week," she said. "I saw this book, and it seemed like I was supposed to have it. Then I saw the sign that said you were going to be here, and I thought that I had to meet you."

"Is this the way you live your life?" I asked, grinning to show that I was a friendly smart aleck.

"Well, yes. It is." Someone interrupted us then, and she walked away. When I looked for her again, I saw that she was standing in another aisle waiting for my attention.

"Who are you?" I asked.

A writer, she said, writing a novel about a woman who uses hoodoo on her lover.

"Hoodoo?"

Not voodoo, which is a religion. Hoodoo, which is an African American magical system that was brought over during slave days and is making a comeback with blacks and attracting whites around the country, she said. A lot of black people won't talk about it. They call it "that stuff," or "that mess," as in, "I don't fool with that mess."

"But ask them if you can have some of their hair," said the woman, who was African American herself. "They'll say, 'No way. I am not giving you a piece of my hair.'"

We laughed.

"I'd like to know more about hoodoo."

It's difficult to get black conjure docs to talk about what they do, she said, especially to a white person, which I am. Practitioners of hoodoo aren't likely to be arrested anymore, but memories of a time when hoodoo could land you in jail are still alive. It's hard to even find such people. White people are beginning to learn the old ways, however, and they will talk. She told me about Catherine Yronwode, pronounced Ironwood, a Jewish woman in Forestville, California, who runs a mail-order supply company called the Lucky Mojo Curio Company.

"You ought to contact her," said the woman.

The next week I was in San Francisco, ninety miles from Forestville. I had a free day. A rental car agency near my hotel was advertising cars for $19 a day, unlimited mileage. So I called Lucky Mojo. A man answered and said to come on out.

When I got to the rental counter, it turned out that all the $19 cars were gone, but I could have one for $35. It was almost twice what I expected to pay. That is often the case in the magical world.

I took it anyway.

"I guess you could say I'm an agnostic about magic. I don't believe in it, but that doesn't mean that it couldn't be true," I told Catherine Yronwode, when we met. It was important to mention my position as an open-minded nonbeliever. Open-minded because otherwise she wouldn't talk to me. Nonbeliever because then she couldn't hex me. I'd read that only people who believe in bad magic can be afflicted by it, a fact that I later mentioned in a carefully off-hand way to Catherine. She laughed and said, "Oh yes. I call that the Alice Defense, after Alice in Wonderland, who was being attacked by cards but didn't think it was happening because everyone knows that cards can't attack people."

"Oh yeah?" I said, feeling testy on that point. "If hoodoo works so well, why are white people still on top? Seems like they would have had all sorts of bad conjure thrown at them. They've sure deserved it."

"Well, I don't know," she said slowly. Catherine, who is most often called Cat, can get ruffled, but not over what you might think. "Maybe people want different things."

She never asked whether I believed or not. None of the magic people did. They don't even like the word *belief*. "I don't *believe* magic works," they invariably told me. "I know it works. From experience." Ah yes, experience. Hadn't they been told that experience isn't to be trusted until the scientists verify it? Perhaps not, or perhaps being a whack job makes you exempt.

Magical people are not much interested in proof. They don't set up double-blind controls. They don't compare the number of times a magical act succeeds to the number of times it doesn't. "Magic will never be proved," one witch told me. To magical people doing it is more important than testing it, and for them the evidence comes with the doing. If I huffed and puffed until the evidence of their magic was blown away, they rarely did more than shrug. Most are too smart to argue the point. They know the world of disenchantment runs on different rules. To understand what they mean is as difficult for a mundane as it would be for a suburban dentist to think like a medieval magi.

Many people define magic as the infamous ceremonial magician Aleister Crowley did. He said it is "the science and art of causing change to occur in conformity with will," which makes magic much more than a spell or ceremonial invocation. His definition is often favored because it allows ordinary physical efforts to be counted as magical acts, and most magical practitioners agree that doing a magical working without any real-world action to back it up may have little impact. They often see magic as a way of bolstering the effect of other efforts. If you want a job, do the magic, Cat tells her customers, but you'll still have to go out and look for a job. Don't expect one to fall from the ceiling. It might, but don't count on it.

I too like Crowley's definition for its broadness. "Causing change in conformity with will" expands magic so that we can question whether what seems mundane actually is. It allows the idea that all sorts of actions can be magical if we have the will to believe they are so. To think that magic is merely something purchased in a spell kit is to undersell it.

To me, magic is a way of thinking, a method of experiencing reality, of changing reality even, that Newtonian science won't allow. It's the belief that human thoughts, rituals, and symbolic actions can affect the physical world. It's an openness to events outside of human comprehension. For most magical practitioners a whole constellation of ideas goes with that. There's future-telling. Often there's a belief in multiple gods, in synchronicity, in a life plan or a contract that was made before birth. There's talk with the dead and with those who haven't ever lived, angels, higher intelligences, astral masters. The idea that otherworldly spirits can be directed to do things that help humans is common. Some magical people believe not only that they can call upon magical forces but that they are actually magical themselves.

When I met the Silver Elves, a fifty-something couple who may be modern America's most legendary elves and have been known as such for thirty years, I mentioned that my psychiatrist neighbor had given me a diagnosis of people who think they are elves or fairies or vampires or werewolves, or anybody else who thinks they can do real magic.

"Schizotypal?" asked Zardoa, the husband.

"That's it."

"We fit that description perfectly," he said. "Except in one way. "We aren't unhappy, and our lives work perfectly well."

They have two grown children, who are gainfully employed and apparently well adjusted. The Silver Elves themselves teach computer workshops at the local community college and are getting advanced degrees in depth psychology.

"Do people you work with know that you're elves?" I asked.

"Oh yes. They know," said the wife, whose name is Silver Flame. "When they introduce us, they always say, 'This is Zardoa and Silver Flame. They think they're elves.' That's how they put it. That we 'think' we're elves." She laughed, a perfectly normal female laugh without even a hint of silvery bells in it.

I don't know why I thought I had to explain my position on magic to Cat Yronwode. I could have saved my breath because she didn't buy it.

"You're not an agnostic. You're a well-mannered atheist," she said.

I didn't care for that description. I'd rather float around in the gray areas of life, moving with the current, sitting on the fence, watching everyone else, and saying little to nothing. Atheist sounded so harsh. So definite. Atheist blew my cover.

But she was right. I was looking for good magic only because I didn't like the hold that bad magic had on me. I wanted to dispel that cloud—even though I could hardly admit that there was one. I wanted to say to all of us bad magic believers, "Just stop it. You're being ridiculous."

I was firm on the difference between good and bad magic. Good magic is magic that helps, and bad magic is magic that hurts. Coming from a Judeo-Christian perspective, the distinction seemed clear. Good is good and bad is bad, and never the twain shall meet. The difference is as clear as God and Satan, heaven and hell, east and west. I didn't expect problems with anything as basic as *that*, and if I'd confined myself to Wiccans, there wouldn't have been any problems. But magical people outside the Wiccan community often didn't share my ideas about what is good and what is evil. In fact, my entire notion of good versus bad, which theologians like to call dualism, was about to come under fierce attack. Many magical people utter the word *dualism* with the utmost scorn. They believe instead that good and bad are all part of a whole, equally valuable even. The gods themselves are combinations of good and ill, I was told.

I picked hoodoo to start my magical search because it is based in a real living community with traceable roots and is an eminently practical form of magic. It employs African folk medicine and magical beliefs, mixed with Native American and sometimes European magical ideas and charms. It uses plants, oils, and roots along with other usually natural elements in mixtures that are thought to have power when put together with the proper intent. Christian Bible verses and prayers are often employed. Candles play a part, and so do written names and clothing or bodily elements such as fingernails or hair. Even footprints are used in hoodoo magic: some spells call for a footprint to be scooped up or sprinkled with magical mixtures.

Hoodoo often employs small flannel bags called mojo bags, tobies, tricks, or lucky hands, filled with herbs and other objects. The magical practice of hoodoo may also be called conjure, root-work, or simply root.

Even though hoodoo has been practiced for hundreds of years throughout the South, it is shrouded in mystery. Few people outside the African American community know about it, and many of them don't know much. Anthropologists often have been stymied when trying to track down hoodoo docs. If you find them, said one white researcher, who didn't have much luck, you'll be doing a service for the community of knowledge.

I also liked hoodoo as a first place to look at magic because it isn't trendy. It isn't New Age. It has a long history handed down from person to person. Although it has elements of religion, it isn't a religion. It is as purely magical as a practice can get, and it isn't practiced only by leather-wearing kids with studs in their tongues. Hoodoo also has an earthy, grounded quality that comes from its having once been the sole recourse of powerless people with desperate needs. One of the first uses of hoodoo was by slaves who wanted kinder treatment from overseers and owners. If any magic really worked, I told myself, this would be it.

It was lucky that Cat Yronwode was one of the first magical people I encountered. We had a lot in common. She is bookish. I am bookish. She spent her childhood reading magical texts. I spent mine reading fairy tales. We both loved those books with the wholehearted passion of lonely children. She was an only child for most of her childhood; so was I. Neither of us was popular with our schoolmates. Cat's vision was too poor for her to enter into most of the games children play. I hated recess more than any other time of the day. I read so much that my family longed to banish my books. Today they hide magazines and put away the cereal boxes so I won't spend breakfast reading instead of talking to them.

One more thing we have in common: Cat's cross-eyed. I could not see that her eyes, such a deep brown they looked black, weren't straight by looking at them, but she said they were, and I might not be the best judge. Bookish, unpopular, odd, cross-eyed.

What's not to like?

Cat knew plenty about magic, which was lucky, because in my first readings about magic I'd picked up some hint of the depravity that so many nonmagical people had warned me about. Magic that uses sexual acts is an important part of many practices because sexual energy is mysterious, powerful, and often thought of as part of the life force that courses through the universe. Some of the sex magic is raunchy stuff, by my standards, but magical people, being mostly broad-minded types, are often loath to declare anything out of bounds. Cat has no such problems, an attitude so rare and refreshing within magical circles that it endeared her to me immediately.

I was horrified, for instance, to find that people still follow the English magician Aleister Crowley, who used his lovers, male and female, but especially female, as receptacles that could help him with magic and then be cast away. His first wife became an alcoholic and was committed to a mental institution after their marriage. He beat one of his consorts so badly that the bones around her eye were shattered. He deserted his children. One man died of enteric fever while at Crowley's estate undergoing bizarre rites that included cutting himself with a razor, killing a cat, and drinking its blood. Another of his male disciples committed suicide.

I was also puzzled by the popularity of Gerald Gardner, who founded modern Wicca in the 1940s. To me he seemed like a mendacious old guy with strong sadomasochistic interests who figured out a way to have lots of naked young women about and call it religion. Cat felt much the same way about those guys.

Many magical ceremonies use the act of sex to raise energy. People in some of the magical religions raise energy with animal sacrifice. Others use chants, prayer, meditation, dancing, ritual, and sex. One of the highest Wiccan rituals, called Drawing Down the Moon, may involve public intercourse between a priest and priestess and include what's called the fivefold kiss, which starts at the feet and moves up the body. Some ceremonies also include tying people up and hitting them with whips.

Living in the suburbs of Milwaukee, not exactly the epicenter of cool, I was somewhat defensive about my feelings toward sex magic. I am apt to be called prim by those of a more libertine bent. I'm touchy about that. I don't have any trouble with people's feet or private parts being kissed or with people running about naked or with people putting sex together with the sacred. Even scourging has a long tradition among religious people seeking to transcend ordinary consciousness. But I'm squeamish about public sex and pain being paired with spirituality, especially when men are making the rules. I know that fertility is a big part of goddess worship, and that goddess worship is often a big part of magic, and that temple prostitutes were common in polytheistic religions, but men were making the rules then too. It's been my experience that anytime men start telling women how sex ought to be, women don't do well.

Once when Cat attended a ceremony of the Ordo Templi Orientis, or OTO, which is the group that follows Crowley's teachings, she objected to the high priestess being nude while everyone else was dressed. What they called a ritual was nothing more than a Baphomet titty show, she said. Baphomet, Crowley's magical name, is an idol sometimes said to represent the devil. When they tried to get Cat to eat what they called a Cake of Light during their Gnostic mass, she wouldn't do it. Their Cake of Light had sexual fluids mixed in, and she didn't want to eat one. The discussion got pretty heated before it was all over. They said she shouldn't have participated in their private ritual if she wasn't going to finish it. They urged her to give up her scruples, but Cat didn't budge. I liked that. Nobody would call Cat prim. Her website mentions that she likes having slow sacred sex, that she hopes to have it at least twice a week, and that she's a steady roller, which is not a term I'd heard before but it's not hard to guess what she means. Cat's website also has some tips on how to have good sex, magical and mundane.

You have to know what you're looking for or you won't find the Lucky Mojo Curio Company. There is no sign on the street, only a dense wall of bushes. The edges of the long drive are marked with posts that have abalone shells nailed on them, facing outward. Their silvery surfaces gleam like pie pans when headlights hit them. Stray too far to one side or the other and the high screech of rose thorns on car paint will warn you off.

The shop is a four-room cottage shaded by a vine-covered porch. The vegetation around it is so thick and tall that the cottage seems to squat, swaddled in the earth's bounty. Inside the cool front room, the shop's curious objects, herbs, magical implements, oils, and images of gods, saints, and goddesses seem dusky and richly hued. Large glass jars of powders, roots, and dried plants stand on high shelves at the back of the room. A golden dragon sits at the front of the shop, a life-sized wizard stands next to the door, and a hundred-year-old skeleton resides in a wooden toe-pincher coffin at the back. Bright Nepalese temple skirts rim the ceiling. The shop is so mysterious and the handmade labels on the products are so beautiful that Disney ordered hundreds of products for the voodoo queen scene in *Pirates of the Caribbean II*, and producers for *Skeleton Key*, a movie about hoodoo starring Kate Hudson, paid Cat to re-create her shop on their set.

The shop's five female employees spend their days behind a long counter mixing and stirring, plucking a pinch of this and a spoonful of that from the hundreds of bags, boxes, and jars about the shop. The smell of herbs and incense gets into the skin of anyone who stays too long. If you order Cat's products, the smell of the shop concentrates inside the shipping box so that when the package is opened, magical fragrances rise into the air, dispersing like the spells they bring with them. The murmur of female voices is sometimes broken by the shrill ring of a telephone or accompanied by the sound of Cat singing the blues. Every candle, mojo bag, or talisman that goes out of the shop is prayed over.

She seemed more like a little Talmudic scholar than the wild conjure woman I'd expected. Her manner was quieter and her mien more serious than I would have guessed. Wearing a long dress and a canvas apron stained from much work, she came toward me smiling. She wears her brown hair as she has for more than forty years, hanging straight, parted down the middle so that the wings of it fall far into her face, narrowing it. She claims to be five-foot-three but seemed shorter, possibly because she wears flat shoes or maybe because she was often bent over reading something to me from a book. When she reads, she often puts her face close to the book, which sometimes causes her hair to fall forward like a child's. She weighs what she has all her adult life, 110 pounds, which makes her pleasantly proportioned, neither matronly nor anorexic. She dyes her hair but never wears makeup.

Her accent is crisp Californian, but her pace is lazy, as though she spent a good bit of time down South, not enough to drawl, just enough to talk easy. Conversation with her is not for the prudish. Talk of vaginas and penises, the various things that might be done with them, the fluids that come out of them, and the problems that might befall them are matters that she treats with perfect candor, which is a good thing for a conjure woman, since her clients are mostly women and their problems often involve love.

Cat's shop was also a good first choice for my investigation into magic because it is crawling with good magic. She has oils for luck in gambling, powders for winning in court cases, tricks to attract money, ways of ensuring protection, mojo hands for reversing hexes, and magic for a hundred other practical needs and just causes. Protection spells are big, money and jobs are often sought. But love is the big one—everybody wants love, and it's harder to get than money.

For that reason, Cat stocks a good number of male and female genitalia toward the back of the shop. She has vulva candles, plump and pouty, and penises in various colors. Penises seem better repre-sented, perhaps because making them function or keeping them from functioning in too many other places is often a concern of hoodoo customers. The candles get "dressed," which is to say rubbed or anointed, with various oils and may have strings bound around them in ways that are supposed to keep the object of the work under a lover's control. Watching how they burn and what the wax does is important.

Encouraging the life force is important not only in magic but in many religions. So there are plenty of magical objects for sex spells. From India come linga or penis stones of the god Siva. These river rocks have red-brown marks at the tip, which represent his love-making with a goddess during her menstrual period. Cat has twenty-three penis amulets from Thailand, including a tiger on a penis and a bunnylike animal penis. She wore a necklace of penis amulets when she married her current husband. Raccoon penis bones hang on a rack in plastic sacks. Stored among the giant glass jars, High John the Conqueror roots resemble testicles and are thought to help restore sexual nature, increase power, and attract luck. They are among the most sought after plants in African American magic. The root is named after a legendary hero who helped slaves endure by playing tricks, making them laugh, and showing them a way to prevail when it didn't seem possible.

During World War II, author and anthropologist Zora Neale Hurston wrote an essay offering the root's power to the country at large. "We offer you our hope bringer, High John de Conquer," she wrote. So "if the news from overseas reads bad . . . listen hard for John. . . . You will know then, that no matter how bad things look now, it will be worse for those who seek to oppress us. Even if your hair comes yellow, and your eyes are blue, John De Conquer will be working for you."

When a woman calls asking for help to bring a lover back, Cat asks questions first. How long has he been gone? Do you know where he lives? Have you had a period since he left? she might ask. If not, the magic has a better chance of working. If it has been two years and they were together four, Cat says, forget it. These are all commonsense matters. As improbable as it might seem, common sense does play a role in good magic, but the lovelorn rarely take Cat's advice. So when the case seems hopeless, she compromises and tells the customer, "I'll sell you products for three weeks, and then you're going to want to come back and want to do it for three months, and then when it doesn't work, come back and I'll tell you how to get over him."

Cat wouldn't tell me how much her business earns, but customers order from all over the world. About 85 percent of her customers are black. I signed up for her Internet hoodoo class, which has more than four hundred students, about 50 percent white. She now has a second class and about five new students a week join. When she first began writing about hoodoo on the Internet, people didn't know what she was talking about. Now her site gets eleven thousand unique visitors a day.

Cat was also a good first choice in my search for good magic because she was pointed toward all that is idealistic and noble-minded before she was even born, and, at the same time, no one in her life was anywhere as noble as they could have been. She calls herself a red-diaper baby because her parents were ardent Socialists. Her father was an artist who went to work in the ship-yards to avoid being drafted. He faked being an engineer and was soon employed as one. His obit called him a petroleum engineer although he never finished high school. Her mother, who came from Munich in 1932 fleeing Hitler, is now in her eighties and writes horror stories. One is about a town where all the people except one woman are turning into dogs. The woman notices that everyone's teeth are getting longer.

Her father left the family when Cat was five. He sometimes invited her to visit, but he never took off work. Instead, he locked Cat in the house. She had learned some Russian at the Berkeley elementary school she attended, and she knew sign language. So when her father left, she escaped and went about town pretending to be a deaf-mute Russian. If she saw dead birds, she picked them up, then skinned and mounted them. An odd child.

Her mother was a librarian at U.C.L.A. and her parents owned an antiquarian bookstore. One of the library patrons was Aldous Huxley. He was so blind that Cat's job was to make sure that when he signed for his books the paper was under his pen. She followed Henry Miller about the shop and went home to play with his dog Skippy. Her first social protest was when she was in the sixth grade, against Woolworth's refusal to let blacks eat at its lunch counter.

Some of her magical books were those collected by her German grandfather. One, which she still owns, is a collection of German folk customs and magical beliefs. The pictures so enthralled her that she begged her mother to translate. They struck a deal. Cat would baby-sit her sister for fifty cents an hour, and her mother would translate the book for fifty cents an hour.

Cat has been so lonely at times in her life that even now as she's going to sleep she sometimes hears a sentence that makes her sigh with despair: *Nobody likes you.* If it comes out of nowhere, and it usually does, she suspects that it's part of a magical attack. She might get up and do something to counter it, such as lighting a candle or making some brushing motions with her hands. At the least, she repositions her body. If you don't do that, the thought will sink in unimpeded and take root, she said. You never want to let that happen.

I liked Cat's story. Magical attacks aren't in my experience, but bad thoughts are. It seems to me that I can recall every mistake I've ever made, every embarrassment I've ever suffered, every failure to be kind or generous or smart enough. When such memories worm their way into my perfectly happy life, they feel like an attack. So. Cat's tips on how to ward off such thoughts were more than I could have hoped for: an easy cure for the bad magic in my mind. I'd use them, and if they worked, I might believe in magic.

Magical attacks are pretty mainstream in hoodoo thought. One of the saddest I read was about a man who did some little thing that displeased a conjure woman. She was a thin-skinned old bat who scared all the children. So she "threw down" on the guy, said that he would never have another home and would wander for the rest of his days. His house burned down the next week, and he never was able to get another. He went from friends to relatives to living at the side of the road until the day he died. Mean old biddy. Somebody should have put a roach in her food.

Cat's exposure to hoodoo began early but in an indirect way. Her parents hoped that their child would become completely American. To that end they gave her three record albums for her fifth birthday. One was *Dust Bowl Ballads* by Woody Guthrie, and another was *Negro Folk Songs and Spirituals* by Leadbelly, and the third was *The American Songbag* by Carl Sandburg, which was mostly murder ballads. Those gifts began her lifelong love of rural American music and led her inevitably to one of America's great gifts to music, the blues.

Hoodoo is a big part of the blues. Ma Rainey's "Black Dust Blues," for instance, is about a woman who is angry because Ma stole her man. "Lord, I was out one morning, found black dust all round my door," begins the song. The singer starts to get thin and has trouble with her feet. "Black dust in my window, black dust on my porch mat. . . . / Black dust's got me walking on all fours like a cat." This song deals with what's called "throwin' down" on someone. In African magic, the feet are thought to be a particularly vulnerable place for evil to enter. So "laying a trick" might involve throwing magical powder where someone would walk over it. Socks or shoes might be sprinkled with hoodoo dust. In a love spell, socks might be tied together.

In the "Aunt Caroline Dyer Blues," the Memphis Jug Band sang of a famous Arkansas conjure woman:

> *Aunt Caroline Dye she told me,*
> *"Son, you don't have to live so rough,*
> *I'm going to fix you up a mojo, oh Lord,*
> *so you can strut your stuff."*

She may be promising him good luck, but gambling hands are among the most popular mojos. So she might be telling him that he will be able to win with her help.

Spells to attract love are common in hoodoo, but in this one, recorded in 1928, the spurned woman seems out for revenge. Jim Towel sang,

> *A gal for me had a great infatuation*
> *She wanted me to marry, but she had no situation*
> *When I refused, she near went wild,*
> *Says, "I'm bound to hoodoo that child"*

> *She went and got a rabbit foot, she buried it wit' a frog*
> *Right in the hollow of an old burnt log.*
> *Right on the road where I had to walk along*
> *Ever since then my head's been wrong.*

One of the most famous hoodoo-blues stories is told about the great guitarist Robert Johnson, who was said to have met the devil at the crossroads and sold his soul in return for his talent with the guitar. When Johnson was poisoned after drinking from an open bottle being passed around a bar, he'd broken one of the primary rules of hoodoo, which is never drink from an opened container. A woman who wanted to gain love and control a man by exciting his passion beyond all reason might have put some menstrual blood in the drink. An enemy might have put any manner of potion inside: a charm that could make snake eggs hatch in his belly, a powder that would cause him to go mad, an extract that would make his legs swell up and cause his hands to shake. But in Johnson's case, breaking the open bottle rule had even more dire results. According to the story, a jealous husband had poisoned the drink. Johnson died that day.

There are two problems with that story about the crossroads. One is that it didn't happen to Robert Johnson, Cat told me. It happened to a guy named Tommy Johnson, and who knows who he was? Not many people, which calls into question the whole deal about making pacts with the devil. The second problem is that hoodoo pacts with the devil don't involve selling your soul and going to hell. During a crossroads ritual, a black man does appear. Some people call him the devil, but most people in hoodoo call him the god of the crossroads. He usually grants a physical skill and taking it does not mean that the person's soul is going to be damned.

It was music that led Cat to the first conjure shop she ever visited. Shops in Berkeley didn't carry the music she liked, so one day when she was not yet a teenager she took the bus to Oakland, where there were many African American shops. She went into one and began to look at small bottles with strange labels. She was particularly intrigued by one called Essence of Bend Over floor wash. The name made her want to laugh, but she was too polite for that. So she asked the shopkeeper what it was. It's something that people put in their mop water to help sweeten other people's temperaments, he said.

"Why would anybody want to do that?" she asked.

"Well, some people work for other people."

She wanted to buy some, but he shook his head.

"No. You're a young person. You want magnetic sand. You want to attract attention." And so she bought some and used it to attract the attention of a boy she wanted.

When she was fourteen, Cat heard a deejay say that a rain dance was needed to make the California drought end. So she pulled out her magic books, enlisted the aid of a friend, went up on the roof of her house, and did a magical ceremony for rain.

"While we were up there, I swear to God, the clouds came in over the bay. This white fog came right over our house, and I thought, *My God, this really works,*" she said.

Cat left home while still a teenager. Like thousands of other young girls in the 1960s, she became a street hippie. She worked carnivals doing various tricks, metal bending, fortune-telling. She learned plenty of ways to make magical beliefs work for selfish ends. She learned to do what's called cold reading, which means that the psychic is working from a script and from good guesses about human nature. Cat eventually learned such little-known facts as that most men of middle age have had at least one life-threatening accident. Most beautiful women have never been sure of their beauty. Most people believe they're smarter than their bosses. Many women have one breast larger than the other. She could have made good money doing cold reading, but she didn't want to make her money that way. She learned candle scams, which involve making a candle smoke excessively so that the client thinks some bad luck needs to be protected against, and pigeon drops, which involve getting the customer to bring money that is switched to blank paper before it's given back. But she never did those things.

She learned astrology. When her first child was born, she did the baby's chart, which indicated that some kind of terrible trouble was ahead. The baby died of sudden infant death syndrome. Experiences like that, where she could see something unpleasant in the chart but was helpless to do anything about it, caused her to back away from astrology.

She did all the things that hippies did then—took drugs, had lots of sex with various people. She was arrested for growing marijuana and spent three months in jail. For a number of years she lived in a Missouri commune called the Garden of Joy Blues, which had no running water or electricity. She loved science fiction and comic books and folk magic. A lot of magic was going on during the 1960s among people who liked science fiction and comic books. Cat was among the groups of magicians and neo-pagans who laid the foundations for the burgeoning of magic that began then and continues today.

As it had one hundred years ago, an influx of Eastern religious ideas helped open people's minds to new ideas, but fantasy literature of all kinds would also play a part that has only grown with time. One that fired the imaginations of millions, J. R. R. Tolkien's *Lord of the Rings*, was published in paperback in 1965. Within a year American college kids were wearing T-shirts that said FRODO LIVES and GO GO GANDALF. What developed within the magical community came from something of a misunderstanding, a pattern we see again and again in the beginnings of magical groups.

Tolkien was a devout Catholic who loved ancient mythology and hoped that his rendition of a great mythical world and the battles fought there between good and evil would return such stories to adult consideration. Although his stories don't mention deities or have any theological system, they demonstrate Christian teachings and virtue in heroic terms. For many years he described his great trilogy as simply a story, not a sermon, not a lesson.

But by the end of his life he was defending against what he feared was a new paganism that had caught fire among his fans. His fears have since been realized. The influence of his work among neo-pagans and magicians has spread far beyond anything he might have imagined. Many people who believe themselves to be otherworldly creatures began thinking about such things while reading Tolkien. His books also spurred others to write fantasy and science fiction, which fed into games and fan clubs, which inspired more magical activity. Ursula Le Guin and Marion Zimmer Bradley created make-believe worlds that others took seriously in the real world. Vampires had Anne Rice and a host of other authors. H. P. Lovecraft also captured the imaginations of readers.

Magical people often talk of their favorite authors as spurs to imagination and fictional characters as models that open them to possibilities. Some believe fiction is more than that. Writers and other artists are communicating with the universal unconscious to create new myths, they believe. Belief, ritual, prayers, evocations, even the retelling of stories activate unseen forces that are perceived only on the unconscious level at first. Artists bring these very real beings and potentialities into the light where human attention and intent vitalize them.

*C*at had many good magic stories to tell me. To improve her singing she once did a crossroad working, which is a spell that's done at the juncture of two roads. She wanted to be in a black gospel group, the competition was tough, and she didn't have the voice for it. After she went to the crossroads, her singing was better, and she got into the group. She once undid a hex that had caused her to sicken. She did a New Year's prosperity spell that increased her hoodoo business 150 percent. It took months of talking and listening to her before I heard these stories because she rarely brags about the magical events she has brought about. One time she did boast a bit and it cost her.

A visitor to the shop began telling stories of his good fortune through magical means. She chimed in with her own. As soon as he left she realized she had bragged about magic, which wasn't good. The punishment fell on her Mojo Car, a 1994 teal blue Ford Escort station wagon covered inside and out with thousands of sacred, magical, and lucky figures: Godzilla, Jesus, the Virgin Mary, Buddha, the Statue of Liberty, Glinda the Good Witch.

She and her husband, whom she calls her Lord of Cars because she doesn't drive, were cruising through town when a woman paused to stare at the Mojo Car, and at just that moment the engine blew. The woman came over to apologize.

"I admired it too much. I'm so sorry."

Despite all the magic Cat could bring about, she wasn't immune to the kind of bad magic that the rest of us fear. In fact, she believed it more wholeheartedly than we mundanes, and it got her, just like it would get anyone else, which was not at all what I'd hoped to find.

If I hadn't offended Cat Yronwode during our first meeting, I might never have heard the best magic story of them all. I'd offended her by asking her if she really believed in hoodoo. She was so obviously well read and analytical. She wasn't the least bit flighty or ookie-wookie-spookie, which made me wonder if she really believed these outlandish tales of magical power. I meant no offense, but sometimes being a reporter and being offensive can't be pulled apart, no matter how politely you phrase the question. Later she complained that I'd implied she was a charlatan, but at the time she replied mildly, "I know that it has worked for me."

As an example, she told me that she had done magical work to bring her husband to her. She used lodestones, which are magnetized pieces of magnetite, often used in love work because they attract each other, and she prayed to the Hindu god Siva one April. Before the month was out a man named Tyagi Nagasiva, nicknamed Siva, who lived on Ironwood Drive in San Jose, called to say he wanted to visit. Because she had prayed to Siva and a man named Siva showed up, and because the street Ironwood is pronounced like her last name, Yronwode, Cat felt she had received magical signs affirming that he was the one. So they married. That was five years ago, and they are married still.

This was exactly the kind of good magic a lot of folks could use. She had the evidence to back up her claim that it worked—a good husband—and I agreed with her that the result was unusual, so rare and wonderful that it was indeed good magic. I believed magic brought them together, not only because they were so suited but because she summoned him, didn't go out and get him, just waited for him to arrive. They knew each other vaguely through the Internet but had never met, never talked on the phone even. During that first conversation she worked up his astrological chart as he talked and decided that having sex with him might be a good idea.

When she did the spells, Cat was edging up on fifty. She was not a woman who would go out of her way to have a facelift, work out at the gym, or wear provocative clothes to attract a man. All she would do was to be absolutely herself, which is the best way, of course, but not always appreciated in dating situations. She had two boyfriends, but she was ready to trade them in for one husband. She lived in a small town, worked much of the time, had ideas that weren't shared by a whole lot of people, and was strong-willed enough to give most men the trembles. Siva is also fourteen years younger than she is. A number of the magical women I met had younger consorts, something you don't see much in the mundane world, and all of them were nice-looking guys.

Siva is a tall, thin man with plentiful facial hair, which is exactly the type of man Cat likes. They have a neo-Tantric relationship, which means they consider their relationship a sacred part of worship. He calls himself her devotee. Each morning Cat and Siva begin the day by telling each other their dreams and then praying to each other, either by having sex, which they regard as prayer, or by facing one another on a prayer rug. That they should be always kind to one another and honest is part of their practice. That they be monogamous is part of what she insisted upon. He reveres her as the Goddess and likes to call her Sri Catyananda. Part of his dedication is to be of service to Cat doing humble tasks: dusting the house, carrying feedbags for the chickens, putting out cat food for Kitty Boy Floyd, the half-wild cat who visits only long enough to eat.

Siva doesn't own a Laz-E-Boy, doesn't watch sports, and doesn't drink a lot of beer. He also knows a lot about computers. Cat having nabbed him was magic worth considering. It went beyond mere luck and beyond coincidence. Seemed pretty peachy to me.

Then Cat mentioned Siva's blood pact with Satan. She said it fondly, as though having such a pact made him only more adorable. So much for peachy. A magical person would have been interested in exploring why this man of such dark energy would be the answer to her prayers, but I was not even close to magical yet. I wanted good magic, not bad. If Siva was a follower of the dark side, that was bad, end of discussion, which meant I missed my first chance to move beyond the simple notions of good and bad that were helping to hold me in place. I would see Siva again, however, and the lesson would still be pending.

5.

Newton's Alchemy, Hegel's *Grimoire,* and What Civilization Owes to Magic

Even before Cat's fine young husband disappointed my early hopes by turning out to be a blood-pact Satanist, I knew that bad magic is as wily as a virus. It can survive anything. It can pop up anywhere. Cat said one reason so many Americans still believe in the winds of ill fortune is that bad magic was hearty enough to make the trip over the ocean. I've noticed the robust nature of trouble in many contexts. Good always seems to be puny and late to arrive. I can't count how many stories of suffering and worry I've heard that ended with God finally coming to the rescue. Nobody ever asks why it took him so long, but I can't be the only one who's wondered. Have you ever heard anyone say, "And finally the devil showed up"? No. He's always on the spot, raring to go, got the tools ready. If anybody was hiring, he's the kind of guy they'd go for.

I should have known all about the power of bad to sneak its way into good. It wasn't reasonable of me to expect so much of the good witches of Salem, but I did. Perhaps that was because the magic of Salem reached out to me even before I got there. I'd called ahead to set up interviews and talked to one of the witches, a woman named Gypsy who owns a magical shop. When I said that I wanted to write about magic, she replied, "Oh you do, do you?"

Then she directed me to wait until the night of the new moon and light three white candles. I was to sit before them and say, "May this be for the good of everyone concerned." I liked the idea. So I did it. The light of those candles turned everything in my tatty, cluttered old study beautiful. The room glowed with the warmest light I'd ever seen. I was so charmed that I lighted the candles again a week later just to bask in the aura, but it wasn't the same, and it never has been since. Gypsy said the glow was the Goddess showing up and being amplified by all the other people calling on her that night. Maybe so.

I went to Salem early on in my hunt for good magic because witches, often called Wiccans, are the best known of the magical people and probably the most numerous. The 2000 U.S. Census puts them and other pagans at more than 300,000. When other types of pagans are added in and counted on a worldwide basis, some people say the number might go up to a million. Numbers for any of the magical people are hard to come by because they don't organize well, often don't join groups, and may count themselves as adherents of many systems at once.

I was especially attracted to Wiccans because they are adamant about doing only good magic. They like to say that all acts of pleasure are the Goddess's rites, an idea very different from the notions I had grown up with. The God I knew didn't have much use for pleasure. In fact, whatever people liked, he seemed not to like. Jesus wasn't much better. He was kinder, but his directives to me always seemed to be about giving up what I wanted so that someone else could have it. Jesus seemed to be on everybody's side but mine.

If this Goddess the witches liked so much was being worshiped with every act of pleasure, she would grow in power every time people laughed together, and if the laughter turned mean, she would say, "Come away with me to a better place." She would thrill when a baby lifted its arms and someone who loved it picked it up and felt that sweet weight of a little trusting body. She would be around during good sex, and we ought to back away from bad sex just as fast as she would. She wouldn't mind a bit if when a sermon or a lecture or a "good for us" message bored us, we decided to have an ice cream sundae instead of listening. And what's more, when caring about the pain of others felt as though it was simply too much to bear, she wouldn't reproach us for being callous but would say, "Take a break. You can care again later."

This goddess sounded fine, especially when paired with the witches' other rule. Do what you will, they say, providing it harms no one. Whatever you send out comes back threefold is another rule. Using magic to override another person's will is completely verboten, which means you can't even do a love spell with a specific person in mind. Some Wiccans won't do healing spells for sick people unless the person agrees to it first. These tidy rules do have a downside.

With regard to the Wiccans, one vampire told me, "They're the Jehovah's Witnesses of the magical community. Totally sure that they're right." The Wiccans are also much maligned in the magical community as being too white light. Fluffy bunny magic, it's sometimes called. Their insistence on ignoring the importance of the dark side is a dangerous distortion, according to some magical people. Those two problems are the selfsame problems that Christianity or any religion that aims at being completely good has always had.

They go with aspirations of high holiness like fat with cheese, but I was too desperate to affirm the good for such depressing truisms to have any appeal to me.

The story of the Wiccan movement's beginning is a wonderful illustration of just how hard it can be to know what's right and true with regard to spiritual matters. Wicca began in the 1940s with a retired English civil servant named Gerald Gardner. Twenty years earlier, a writer named Margaret Murray had claimed that witches persecuted during the Inquisition had participated in a pre-Christian fertility cult with a female deity. Later scholars discounted her stories as having been built on the accusations and confessions extracted from witches under torture. Gardner, influenced by Murray, claimed that an old woman named Dorothy Clutterbuck initiated him into a coven that had existed since the persecutions, often called the burning times by neo-pagans. Later Gardner published stories of contemporary witch covens.

No one in the movement but Gardner ever met old Dorothy. In later years many began to doubt that she existed. Doreen Valiente, an English witch initiated by Gardner, wrote that she found Clutterbuck's birth and death certificates, but whether the old woman was part of an established coven, as Gardner claimed, is still in dispute. There is also evidence that his *Book of Shadows*, the grimoire, or magical book, she was supposed to have given him, was written by Gardner himself, perhaps with the help of Aleister Crowley.

Wiccans often tout their religion as one of the few with a sense of humor, although some witches are dreadfully self-important, especially about their lineage. An increasing number, however, are unconcerned with the literal facts of their group's beginnings. Even if the stories were fabricated, the truth of the teachings and the vision they present still hold, say practitioners. Margot Adler, author of *Drawing Down the Moon*, calls the founding of modern witchcraft the Wiccan myth. "Many have observed that myths should never be taken literally. This does not mean that they are 'false,' only that to understand them one must separate poetry from prose, metaphorical truth from literal reality," she writes.

Plenty of bad has been said about Wicca founder Gerald Gardner, beyond the claim that he was a liar. Frances King in *Ritual Magic in England* writes that Gardner was "a sadomasochist with both a taste for flagellations and marked voyeuristic tendencies." With such tendencies, it might seem especially ironic that he helped ignite a turn toward feminine spirituality, which is still growing. It has inspired millions of women to question male dominance in religious ideas. This emphasis on the feminine has quietly spread to mainstream churches and become the subject of wide academic study. Part of the reason is that Gardner's witches' religion attracted brilliant, dedicated women and was gaining adherents just as the modern feminist movement began. His story may not have been factual, but his timing was impeccable.

Witches are heavy into ceremony as a way of bringing forces together. As technologies of the sacred, their ceremonial circles may be even more important to them than spell work. Wiccans do both high and low magic, which is one of the most basic divisions in magical thought.

Low magic, sometimes called practical magic, is the easiest kind of magic to grasp. It is about transforming the physical events in the world around us. Low magic is usually about performing spells that affect people and events. It might employ gods and goddesses, spirits or angels, and it might not. Low magic and folk magic are often synonymous, although folk magic is more focused on the idea that there's an energy or power, sometimes called virtue, present in the physical world to be drawn on. Hoodoo is low magic. The aims of low magic are generally practical. But the belief behind it is quite lofty: that everything is connected—the elements of the earth, the celestial bodies, animal, vegetable, mineral, and human—all are connected and all are able to interact with one another.

Low magic generally works on two principles. The first is the idea that anything that resembles something else will affect the thing it resembles. For instance, make a doll that looks like someone, and whatever happens to the doll will happen to the person. The second kind of magic works on the idea that anything attached to a person continues to be part of that person after it's detached and will affect the person no matter how far apart they are. That kind of magic might use hair, toenails, blood, footprints even.

All magical people reach far back to former times for their wisdom. That alone is an unusual way of thinking in our modern age. A distinctive feature of modern times is that humans have stopped believing that wisdom comes from the past and they look forward to the future as the site of superior understanding. Modern thinking has made experience and age matter less, and there is now a sense that humans are getting better and smarter all the time. Instead of revering past wisdom, we see it as quaint thinking that we moderns have far surpassed. Magical people, in contrast, seek wisdom by looking backward, further into the past even than the major religions of today.

Such a focus usually makes people conservative in their outlook, but magical people have always been bold. And why wouldn't they be? Loosed from the constraints that have historically limited humans, they believe themselves to be empowered beyond human imagination. Some think of themselves as divine. Others believe they can command the divine. High magic, which concerns itself with transforming oneself spiritually, makes these claims most emphatically, to such a glorious degree that its practitioners have shaped history, ancient and modern. High magic aims at contacting divinity, usually through secret rituals and ceremonies. It is sometimes called white magic or the Great Work, which is often taken to mean forging a link between the human soul and divine presence. Astral travel to other realms, meditation, and dream work are important practices.

During the Renaissance, high magic underwent a great resurgence and was a vital factor in mankind's "reawakening." It inspired science, art, religion, and philosophy by holding out a vision of mankind that was more glorious than anything Christian Europeans had ever known. It informed the thinking of many eminent men, among them scientist Sir Isaac Newton, German philosopher Georg Wilhelm Friedrich Hegel, and another genius whose name has been largely lost to popular history, John Dee.

This Renaissance resurgence of high magic, called Hermeticism, assured humans that "through his intellect man could perform marvelous feats—it was no longer man *under* God, but God *and* man," writes the historian Peter J. French. The stars were believed to be living entities that shape human destiny and can be influenced by humans. Even God's angels might be manipulated to help mankind. In describing the powers of the magus, Pico della Mirandola wrote, "To him is granted to have whatever he chooses, to be whatever he wills."

The revival of Hermeticism marked the dawn of the scientific age, writes French, because it unleashed a driving spirit for power. High magic inspired men with the notion that they could compel nature, force it to serve them in ways never dreamed of before. Where they had once pursued knowledge for its own sake, now humans would conquer the mysteries of the universe because they could grow rich and powerful by doing so. At the same time that Galileo and Kepler trafficked in horoscopes, alchemy fostered a trial-and-error method of experimentation that, coupled with dogged persistence, would soon evolve into the scientific method and yield much more than gold. Magic was the template of science, writes science author James Gleick, citing Friedrich Nietzsche, who asked, "Do you believe then that the sciences would ever have arisen and become great if there had not beforehand been magicians, alchemists, astrologers, and wizards, who thirsted and hungered after abscondite and forbidden powers?"

Built on the writings of a mage, or magician, called Hermes Trismegistus, Hermeticism reached Italy in the middle of the fifteenth century. The Renaissance was in full swing. Humanism, with its ideas about the autonomy and power of mankind, was gaining sway, which dovetailed with magical thinking quite well. As the influence of theology began to wane, admiration for science rose and with it interest in everything Greek and Roman, including classical texts. These developments set the scene nicely for Hermes Trismegistus, which means Three Times Great.

He was thought to be an Egyptian sage who had lived during the time of Moses and incorporated the Jewish leader's wisdom. The Hermetic texts include a creation story in which man was once God and can again become God because divine powers are still within him. In this story, man is immortal and can understand anything—in fact, he is called to understand everything. It is through man's understanding of God that God is able to understand himself.

One reason the Hermetic texts, often called a corpus, excited people of the Renaissance so greatly was that they were so old. They seemed to foretell Jesus's life and to be the text from which Plato learned most of his teachings. Without those attributes, the corpus would have been given far less attention. The writings' date of origin, however, had been misunderstood entirely. Later scholars realized that the corpus was written, not by a sage named Hermes, but by a number of people, all anonymous, using the same pen name. It had come into being two or three hundred years after the birth of Christ, which meant that the information about Jesus wasn't prophecy but history. Likewise, the ideas of Plato were copied from the Greek philosopher five hundred years after his death, not the other way around. The realization that Hermes Trismegistus probably didn't exist and that Hermetic wisdom was built partially on the wisdom of others and on history robbed the teachings of their main claims to legitimacy.

We've already noted that the Wiccan movement's beginnings are also shrouded in falsehood and misunderstanding. This is true of other magical beginnings as well. As a result, one of the hardest turns to make in understanding magical people—and in understanding many spiritual truths—is coming to grips with the difference between lies, fantasy, and mythical or greater truths. The same might be said of the major religious traditions, and has been said, much to the fury of the more fundamentalist faithful. It is almost as though humans need some grand vision, some story greater than what ordinary life provides, in order to understand mysteries beyond what we see every day. We seem to need symbols and drama to fire our imaginations. A simple rendition of the facts, as true as they may be, simply won't do the job.

Scholar Karen Armstrong sheds some light on this problem and gives us another way to analyze the value of a story when she notes that modern people and ancient people regard spiritual stories very differently. When modern people demand that religious stories be factually true, they are confusing two ways of looking at the world, *logos* and *mythos*.

Modern people, writes Armstrong, tend to look at everything through *logos*, which is the old word for reason, as though that is the only method of inquiry. But in the premodern world people believed that there was another important type of knowledge that could not be understood through *logos*. It could only be understood through *mythos*, which is something like the deeper meaning found in a poem or a great novel.

Logos helps us determine practical matters. It guides us in eating, working, and traveling. It governs science. One of the ways our modern dependence on *logos* shows up is that we are utterly unable to credit anything that isn't accessible through *logos*, that isn't factually true and understandable in a factual way.

But when we want to understand the meaning of things, to get at the higher truths, we must use *mythos*. It looks into the deepest regions of our minds, into that which is timeless and unchanging. *Mythos* might have been what my Methodist friend was talking about when she said that of course she didn't believe that vampires are real, but then again, yes, she did. She had some feeling about the value of that old myth, but not being a poet or an ancient seer, she had no words to express it.

In *logos* it is the literal truth of a thing that matters. In *mythos* "what really happened" doesn't matter at all because the kind of truth being sought is beyond facts. Today, as the great stories at the heart of all religions are being discredited because scholars are proving that the stories didn't "really happen," some people are experiencing a crisis of faith. In the ancient world that doubt would not have arisen. It was *mythos* that mattered most.

If we were to reclaim the old ways, would we have access to a kind of wisdom that human beings need in order to fulfill the highest hopes of their humanity? The magical people appear to think so, or perhaps they believe the old stories are completely factual. Whatever we believe about Hermetic origins, the magical systems did fire the imaginations of some great men.

*A*mong the geniuses inspired by Hermetic alchemy in the sixteenth century was a queen's counselor named John Dee. A philosopher and Hermetic magician, he linked magical ideas to the newly emerging discipline of science. During a time when mathematics was suspect as a dark art, Dee was renowned throughout Europe for his studies of mathematics, navigation, mechanics, and geography. Without his wisdom, England would have fallen behind in exploration and Britain's empire would have been a much punier realm. His library was the greatest in England. He was, in short, one of England's most learned and respected men.

For a while his magical abilities were also valued. As court astrologer, he selected the day for Queen Elizabeth's coronation, and when an image of the queen was found with a pin stuck in its heart, it was Dee who was asked to reverse any magic turned against her. Many people bragged of the feats he was able to perform, and all was well until Dee began to receive messages from angels. He was convinced that angels had wonderful things to impart and that establishing a connection with them was a holy undertaking.

To do it he needed the help of a rather shady character named Edward Kelley. Kelley received the messages, and Dee wrote them down. Although he never claimed to see or hear the angels himself, Dee believed in them and consulted them in many things, including in his last geographical venture, which was aiding the colonization and conversion of people in Atlantis, his name for America. The angels' messages and language came to be incorporated into what is known as Enochian magic and are used today.

At one point Dee and Kelley claimed that they had turned base metals into a pound of gold. That feat attracted the attention of a Polish royal who financed their experiments with much of his fortune;

he finally gave up, however, after years of having gotten no gold. Dee returned to England, but times and his reputation had changed. He was branded a sorcerer, and his angelic conferences were described as "execrable insanity." The attacks against him were so severe that his many true achievements were eclipsed.

When witchcraft-conscious James I succeeded Elizabeth, Dee was so anguished by the things said about him that he petitioned the king to try him for sorcery so that he could clear his name. He offered "himself willing, to the punishment of Death: (yea, wither to be stoned to death: or to be buried quicke: or to be burned unmercifully) If by any due, true, and just meanes, the said name of *Conjurer*, or *Caller*, or *Invocator* of Divels, or damned Spirites, can be proved." Note that he only denied commerce with evil spirits, writes French. He was not tried, but when he was out of the country, a mob did attack his home and burn his library. Dee died at eighty-one, a poor man with a sullied reputation.

Newton, the greatest scientist of them all, was not only a secret alchemist but, "in the breadth of his knowledge and his experimentation, the peerless alchemist of Europe," writes Gleick. His ability to transmute a magical substance called quicksilver, better known to us by its chemical name mercury, was so successful that he was slowly poisoning himself by smelling and tasting it. The secrecy of alchemy, the code names its practitioners used, and the grandeur of its aims, which were not only to turn base metals into gold but to purify oneself spiritually, fit well with Newton's view of himself as the new Solomon.

The alchemical aspect of Newton's life was well hidden until 1936, when a trunk of his papers was auctioned at Sotheby's in London. Economist John Maynard Keynes, horrified at the thought that three million unread words of Newton's thought might be lost, bought as many of the manuscripts as he could and tracked down others later. In them he found the father of modern science experimenting and writing in the ancient language of magical thought. Newton wrote of ethereal spirits and used the alchemists' code name for mercury, which was the "serpents." He often communicated his thoughts in the highly poetic, symbolic, and sexualized way of the alchemists, writes Gleick, so that in referring to his experiments he would talk of male and female semen, of the Serpents around the Caduceus, the Dragons of Flammel, and a secret fire pervading matter. Like magical people of today, Newton believed in a meaningful, connected universe. He rejected the idea of "inanimate brute matter" and instead believed that spirits and forces animate everything and are constantly in relationship.

The manuscripts in the trunk so impressed Keynes that not long before he died he said, "Newton was not the first of the age of reason. He was the last of the magicians, the last of the Babylonians and Sumerians, the last great mind which looked out on the visible and intellectual world with the same eyes as those who began to build our intellectual inheritance rather less than 10,000 years ago."

But inspiring science was not Hermeticism's only triumph. Its contention that humans are part of God and are expected by God to become as God also inspired a new boldness in theology. Hermetic doctrine stated that God created humankind as a part of himself that was sent out into the world to experience and reflect, then return to God, thereby completing the Creator. Through intellect, humans could reach the wisdom of God for themselves without intermediaries. A somewhat similar idea about intermediaries was being spread by a new Christian doctrine called Protestantism, but Hermeticism promised man that he could reach far greater heights than Christianity seemed to aspire to.

John Dee and other religious Hermeticists believed that the breach between Catholicism and Protestantism could be healed and that a religion of love and unity could reign. This would happen through the rediscovered *prisca theologia*, the one true theology that cuts across cultures and was revealed by God to man in the remote past. Such unity of spirit and purpose had been undreamt of until that time. Carl Jung, who studied alchemy, echoed it in his theories of the universal unconscious. Joseph Campbell's studies of similarities in mythological stories bolstered it. Romantic writers were inspired by it when they yearned for and wrote about a return to nobler, more enlightened times.

Philosophy was also affected. Centuries after Dee's death, Hermeticism fed the thought of Hegel. Some believe Hegel actually was a Hermeticist, which is saying something quite controversial because Hegel is one of the greatest philosophers of the modern age, and Hermeticists were followers of magical ideas that came from ancient, shall we say, unenlightened times. Many of Hegel's admirers choke on the idea that he was otherworldly at all. Look him up in the dictionary and you will find that his philosophy is described as a method to make the final truths of religion scientific. The idea that he might have been a practitioner of magic runs thoroughly counter to anything scientific and is deeply offensive to some of his followers. But one scholar, Eric Voegelin, is so convinced of it that he calls Hegel's *Phenomenology of Spirit* a grimoire that "must be recognized as a work of magic—indeed, it is one of the great magic performances."

Hegel and all philosophers of his and our time have been forced to react to Plato, Aristotle, and another German giant, Kant. Immanuel Kant believed that humans aren't able to think well enough about metaphysical matters to figure out the truth of reality. Hegel took a breathtakingly bold stand against that notion. Surpassing

Plato and Aristotle, who believed that humans are in the process of finding truth, Hegel declared that he had found it. And he seemed to say that if we follow his blueprint, we too can possess it, writes scholar Glenn Alexander Magee. Like the Hermeticists whose work filled his library, he believed that although the events and objects of life appear to be unconnected, they are actually woven together in an unseen pattern of meaning.

One influence on Hegel and on modern Hermetic thought was a shoemaker named Jakob Böhme, who had a mystical vision in 1600 that came to be important in magical development. This vision inspired him to reinterpret Christian ideas in such a way that they fit with Hermetic ideas. He wrote, "You need not ask, Where is God? Hearken, you blind man; you live in God, and God is in you; and if you live holily, then therein you yourself are God." Furthermore, he believed that since we are natural beings, our contemplation of nature is a mirror. Nature is also the thought of God. So we hold up a mirror to God. "Thus, through our human understanding, God is fully actualized: He achieves self-awareness and closure."

How did an uneducated shoemaker know such things? Hegel believed, as the Gnostics and as Böhme did, that all knowledge is inside us, part of the great interlinking, waiting to be revealed. From this came Hegel's concept of speculative philosophy, which he also called mystical, and the idea that it takes both imagination, or mystical knowing, and reason to reach the truth, writes Magee.

High magic mystified me. It would take a year of study before I would begin to understand what the high magicians were talking about, which might be one reason why my first Wiccan ceremony didn't go too well, but there was also another reason, a more personal one.

6.

A Cold Wind Blows
on Gallows Hill

The first public witches' circle I ever attended was at Salem's Gallows Hill on Halloween night. I didn't have high hopes for it. Wiccan circles are formed to keep bad forces out and to concentrate sacred energy into what they call a cone of power. It was unlikely that I would be around when a ritual summoned the power of the cosmos. If it did, I probably wouldn't notice. Whenever a group starts working itself up, something in me balks. Sometimes I want to emote, but I can't. Once I could.

It was in a Pentecostal church, which is similar to magical groups in that it relies strongly on experience to affirm belief. My aunt is a passionate believer in the Pentecostal way, which includes speaking in tongues. Converting me was among her goals, and one summer it almost happened. The music was rousing, the preaching was strong, and waves of emotion came rolling through the congregation. I was so taken with it all that I urged my parents to come to the church with me.

My dad sat in the pew neither smiling nor frowning, just listening. I watched his face. Then I looked at the preacher, hopping around, banging the lectern, shouting loud enough to make spittle fly. I'd once been tossed whichever way he threw me, but with my dad beside me everything seemed different. I could see how the preacher was doing it. I heard the false notes, the manipulation, the scare tactics, the promises that couldn't be backed up. Stripped to its bones, his sermon left me unmoved, and that's been the case ever since with regard to religion and excessive emotionalism. I just don't do it, can't do it, and don't want to do it.

The Wiccans' march to Gallows Hill on Halloween is a candle-light commemoration of the nineteen alleged witches who died in Salem three hundred years ago. They march through the lovely Old Town part of Salem where brick streets and little shops housed in buildings more than a hundred years old make it easy to imagine that you're living in a time long ago. If magical energy is concentrated by what humans do, Salem ought to be jumping with it.

Not only does the town have a monument to the people who died after the witch trials, all sorts of magic shops, and many, many magical people, but one of its stellar attractions is the Peabody Essex Museum, a multimillion-dollar facility that houses idols, ceremonial costumes, and magical implements brought back from around the world during the 1700s. Not all of the town's best people are entirely happy about the messiness that witches and pagans bring to Salem with their magic, their fortune-telling, and the influx of tourists each year at Halloween. Disputes between the witches and the town establishment were particularly high the year I was there. The differences between the two sides could easily be seen.

Old Town had been all but taken over by costumed witches and wizards, pagans in medieval garb that could sometimes have stood a good washing, and businesspeople capitalizing on the town's spooky history. Kitschy museums of magic and horror abound, along with fun houses that feature various kinds of gory death. Step inside the cool, high-ceilinged Peabody Essex, where even the air is purified, however, and everything changes dramatically. The blue bloods who volunteer at the museum are immediately evident. The hair is shorter, the women's makeup hardly visible. No raven tresses and kohl-rimmed eyes, and not a tattoo in sight. You might never suspect that both sides of Salem, magical and old money, support magic in their own ways. Inside the museum is historical magic from faraway lands, kept under glass in hushed and well-lighted rooms, while outside new magic with all its tacky contradictions, popular appeal, and flamboyant hucksterism flourishes. The two hardly meet.

For the march to Gallows Hill, I purchased a really great witch's hat, my first ever. It was black, of course, with silver stars, purple ostrich feathers, and a long trail of net. I wore lace-up boots and an ankle-length velvet opera coat with a swirling skirt. I looked so much more dramatic than the real witches that I began to fear I stood out as a poseur. When a hip-looking witch complimented me on my get-up, I said sheepishly, "I don't think the real witches wear this kind of thing."

"Real witches wear whatever they want to wear," she said.

But the hem of my coat was catching on the hooks that held my bootlaces so that I had to stop to untangle it every half-block or so. The thin soles of my boots didn't protect my feet from the uneven pavement, and they hurt long before we reached the hill. Eventually we arrived and waited for the circle to form. A little girl standing behind me chattered with excitement.

"Everyone will stand in the circle, and no one can break the circle. If they do, it will be bad. Last year some people did that, and it got real cold. The gods didn't like it," she said. Luckily this night was warm.

At last the ceremony started. It was, as promised, a taste of eternity. People chanted, waved swords, and sang for so long that I wanted to whimper. My feet throbbed as I shifted from one foot to the other, standing on my toes so my heels wouldn't sink into the soft earth. On and on it went, people in the middle performing their sacred rites, me wishing that some god somewhere, anywhere, would tell them to shut it off. Finally, I sat down, a glum lump of velvet in the dirt. With my big hat and collapsed body, I looked like the Wicked Witch of the West in her last moments. People frowned. I frowned back. Anyone who wanted me up would have to hoist me. Behind me four people lost patience entirely, broke the circle, and left. I longed to do the same. By the end I was shivering and too bored to care about anything. As I limped away the little girl tugged on my velvet sleeve.

"Did you see it? Those people broke the circle and it got cold, just like last year. I told you."

She was right. A cold wind did come up after the people walked away. Strange. On another night I might have thrown my peaked hat in the air and yelled, "Blessed be," but I was hungry, my feet hurt, and it was about a mile back to Old Town.

"Yeah, yeah," I told the kid. "You're right. Gotta go."

Wiccans don't charge for magic, which has shielded them from some of the bad reputation magic has for being the tool of charlatans. Like Christians who would never charge for prayer, they believe charging would be wrong, a bad use for magic. They will, however, charge five dollars for a polished rock, three dollars for a little bag of herbs, and nice-sized prices for contacting spirits through readings. They also charge to teach magic.

Hoodoo docs charge up front. Once when I asked for work from a hoodoo woman in Savannah, she told me that she would charge $750. A guy on St. Helena Island, South Carolina, the son-in-law of the area's last Dr. Buzzard, now deceased, wanted $500. I wasn't trying to kill anybody. I wasn't even trying to make somebody love me. All I wanted was a little mojo bag to keep me from being so afraid to travel. Finally, I went to Cat, who tch-tched over the prices. Then stopped herself by saying she wouldn't like to criticize what other rootworkers were doing. She suggested that I do the work for myself since I was in the hoodoo class, but I knew root-work required talent and I was fairly sure I didn't have any. No talent. No experience. No faith. No good mojo. I also liked the thought that she or her staff pray over everything they sell.

"I want you to send me something," I said.

"What do you want?"

"Whatever works. Send me everything that might help."

The next week a package arrived in the mail. Inside I found a red flannel mojo bag with an evil eye pinned to it, Safe Travel oil, a seven-day candle dressed with oils, a Saint Christopher icon, and some Psalms to say as I lighted the candle. The supplies cost me $53. Strangely enough, they did make me a little less afraid. For a while I actually felt some equanimity regarding life's perilous nature. I don't know why. Maybe it was because I'd taken steps to help myself instead of rolling over to hideous fate like a dog showing its throat. Or maybe it was the mojo.

Sometimes money isn't enough for serious magic. A hoodoo woman in North Carolina told me she did some work to heal her dog when he was close to death. For it to succeed, she had to give up something she valued highly. So she took her best hiking boots to the trash pile and threw them in. The dog got better.

Mary Ann Clark, a Santeria priestess and doctor of religious studies in Houston, shared stories of two women who were helped by her religion, which is a combination of Yoruban, Bantu, and

Catholic spirituality that developed in Cuba and the Caribbean. One was in danger of having a premature baby. The other was plagued by depression. Both did Santeria rituals and were blessed in the way they wished to be. But they didn't convert to Santeria. If they had such good fortune, I asked, why didn't they?

Perhaps because too much is required, the priestess said. The orishas, or Santeria gods, give, but they may also ask a lot in return. Sometimes they want a live animal sacrifice. Sometimes they require that those who are going to be initiated beg for the money that the ceremony requires.

The Silver Elves told me elvin spirits also like sacrifice, but killing isn't called for. They are more likely to be impressed with sacrifices that parents make for their children, which is not to say elvin spirits are always utterly noble. They also like money. "Money has juice," said Zardoa Love, the Silver Elf husband.

Cat's shop is filled with offerings of thanks for answered requests. Each benefactor has favorite things. One likes pound cake, another wants rum, another prefers money, and others like cigarettes. Don't ever forget to give the saint or the divinity what you promised, she tells her clients.

Sometimes the fee for magic comes in having to deal with the consequences—the old "be careful what you wish for" problem. Once Christian Day, a friend of Shawn Poirier, the Salem witch, was all hot over a guy. Late one night he came to Shawn for help. Shawn didn't want to do it, but when a friend is desperate and the absinthe is flowing—absinthe is a big drink among magical people—and it's deep in the night, things happen. Out of patience, he finally said they would visit the loved one in his dreams, which is a common magical action. They did, and while there they did some things that anybody would be willing to wake up for. The next day the guy called Christian to say that he'd had some incredible dreams and wanted to go out.

Christian soon tired of the new love, but the aroused one wasn't ready to quit. When Christian came back asking Shawn for a spell to make his new boyfriend go away, Shawn shook his head.

"I got him for you. You're going to have to get rid of him."

Everything has its price. Nothing is free. And good magic is hard to find, as was about to be demonstrated to me yet again.

*M*y first private magical ceremony looked more promising than the public circle. It was a coming-of-age ritual for a Salem girl. Despite my aversion to ceremonies, I love the idea of having sacred, celebratory ways to mark life's transitions. I'm convinced such ceremonies are one of magic's great gifts to the modern world.

On the night of the girl's ceremony, Shawn the Witch was presiding in his living room, which was resonant with Boris Karloff–type music booming from the big-screen TV. Shawn and some of the women witches had long straight hair of a color that can only be called dead-black. Anybody who wanted to smoke in this house was welcome to. There wasn't a plaster angel or a ceramic fairy in sight. No pink either. An étagère in the dining room was filled with Dolls of the Living Dead: little white-faced ghouls with blood dripping from their mouths; nuns with fangs; sweet curly-haired darlings with white eyes, still in their display boxes.

Shawn Poirier's group prides itself on being old-fashioned witches, the kind who do magic at the edge of the forest, have people visiting them in the dark of night, and don't give a flip about lineages. Only, of course, there isn't a forest anywhere near. Shawn lives in a yellow house in a neighborhood with narrow, car-lined streets, where houses nuzzle the curb so closely that they seem about to topple and stand so near to one another that there's hardly room for driveways. His is set apart by a giant lighted pentacle in the front window. Many people come to this house for help, the witches assured me. "Every clock in the house is set at a different time," Shawn said. "That's because people come at all different times. And every time is right."

Shawn is a tall, heavy-shouldered, handsome man with a goatee that the devil might envy. He also has a formidable widow's peak. He always wears black. His accent is East Coast rough, Burt Lancaster just off the docks. As he talked his hands moved languidly through the air, silver rings catching the light. One hand held a cigarette; the other twirled a piece of shoulder-length hair. His delivery is also Lancaster, purring beguilement, right out of *The Rainmaker*, that lovely tale of loneliness, hope, and chicanery. Once a tongues-speaking Pentecostal, he uses plenty of Bible verses and poetic phrases.

One year, he told me, he went to summer camp and wandered into the forest alone. He met some fairies there and fell asleep, as everyone knows that a person who meets fairies does. They gave him special powers and took something in return. They took his ability to love any other person truly and deeply. So he became a powerful magician, but he's always lonely. The only reason he is invited to parties is so that he will do magic, he said. Everyone watches him and expects something. Psychic work is his specialty. Sometimes he longs to be nothing more than a regular guy, he told me.

Good magic wasn't easy to find, even in a town full of witches. On the night of the coming-of-age ceremony for the girl, Shawn, who was wearing dramatically ruffled shirt cuffs that showed his many silver rings off to good advantage, waved his hands about as seven of us stood in a circle, watching with somber expressions. The kid, a nice-looking, clean-cut girl wearing a turtleneck, stood in the center.

First Shawn commanded the spirits, gods, and goddesses to attend us, which made me jumpy. The school of God-summoning

I'm from is more the begging brand. *Please, please, please, please, Jesus. We are filthy rags before your magnificence. Maybe if you could maybe turn your most glorious countenance toward my most unworthy . . .* but never mind. Call me anything, just call me, as they say. Given what's been going on with faith, no one could blame divinity—be it a he, a she, or an it—for showing up no matter how the invite is phrased.

So Shawn commanded the forces of the universe, and then he turned his attention to the girl, telling her how she would be strong and fearless, how she would bow to no man and they would all obey her will. I was liking this, and so were the other grown-ups. Then the mother witch announced that she had chosen two other witches to be her child's godparents. I think she said godparents. Seems like it would have been something with a bit more flash, fairy godparents, maybe, but it wasn't. In any case, they gave the girl blessings, likened her to some valiant animal, hugged her, and then waited.

When the new godfather witch looked deep into her eyes, she looked back and said, "You have the heart of a jackal." He smiled a bit feebly. What to say? Jackal isn't a compliment, even to a witch. It was a bad moment. Nobody spoke.

Finally, she said, "I don't even know what a jackal is." The circle laughed. Happy again.

Afterward, Shawn was saying how much the witch family meant to the kid and how many good times they'd had and how much magic they'd done. She said, "Can I go find the cat?"

To me she said, "My dad's Catholic. I live with him a lot of the time."

Shawn reminded her that he once did magic for her slumber party. She said, "I don't remember."

"Yes," he said. "You remember."

"No."

"The time we levitated your friend?"

"No."

"Yes. We all gathered around and put our fingers, just the tips of our fingers, under your friend."

"Oh," she said.

The witches' coming-of-age ceremony seemed to indicate that good magic of life-changing import isn't so easily created. At least not for kids. Adults? Maybe. They are more easily impressed.

My second Salem magical lesson came from a high priestess of the Cabot School of Witchcraft. Laurie Cabot is known as the Official Witch of Salem. Cabot was the first woman in town to adopt black robes, thick black eye makeup, and wildly teased black tresses as everyday attire. She made a vow to the Goddess in the 1970s that she would never take the robes off. People would spit at her as she walked her two daughters to school, according to one story that has made her a local legend. Cabot has been teaching witches how to be magical ever since and has a national reputation for it.

Soon after I arrived I was browsing in a witch shop owned by Laurie Cabot's daughter. A midthirties woman from New York State came in with her husband and young son. As she was paying for a couple of fairy dolls, the New Yorker mentioned to the talkative clerk that she would like to know more about witchery. The clerk promptly offered to teach her, saying that she had been taught by Laurie Cabot herself and now that she was of high rank, she took a few students each year. She didn't charge anything, she said, because it was a labor of love.

When the customer left, I told the clerk who I was, and she told me a good story about how her husband had died and how she had fibromyalgia and was in constant pain but wouldn't give in. Witchcraft kept her going and kept her in contact with her dead husband. His visits were pretty lively, she said, leering a little to let me know he was a ring-tailed hooter, dead or alive. I liked that. So I leered back.

I asked if she would teach me too, and she said she would. I'd have to be willing to return to Salem several times during the year for seasonal rituals, she said. Between rituals, she would send me lessons about the history and the science of magic. In a year and a day, I'd be a real witch.

People flood into Salem all year long for the workshops offered by the Cabot coven mates. I considered myself lucky to have found one who would bring me into the mysteries. She gave me her number, and we agreed to get in contact. About a month later I called. She was eager to begin, but first I'd have to send her $75. I put the check in the mail and bought plane tickets to Salem. She cashed my check, but my witch lessons never arrived.

I later found out that a lot of local witches seem willing to take their chances with the threefold rule, which says they will get back whatever they put out threefold. I heard dozens of stories about backbiting, cheating, threats, even some illegal behavior. Helen Gifford, a columnist for the *Salem Evening News* wrote, "Just mention the word [*witch*] in this city and—poof—a controversy appears." Money has been at the heart of all the witch wars, she wrote. "When they sell us spiritual counseling for $75 an hour, offer to teach us about their religion for $600, try to hawk pendants and love potions and crystals—are they practicing a serious religion or running a business, which is just like any other business?"

Witch wars are common throughout the magical world. When the witches don't like something or someone, they might make a witch's bottle to turn spells back on the sender or even to attack another witch. The bottle is put it in a freezer. A good part of Salem's witch community has run out of freezer space, one witch quipped.

Maybe my expectations for Salem's good magic were too high. I'd had higher hopes for the Wiccans than for any other magical group. Anybody who knows anything about them says they are a loving, nature-oriented bunch of gentle people who seek to do only good. Cat says Wicca is Christianity with a goddess. I don't know that she means it as a compliment, but I took it as one. That upped my expectations even more, but I guess it shouldn't have. I know quite well that Christians also talk a better game than they are able to live. So do we all perhaps.

7

Maleficia du Jour: Served Hot, Cold, and Cash before Delivery

*E*verywhere I looked I found elements of magic that so repelled me that I wanted to give up my search altogether. Hoodoo, as just one example, is full of *maleficia*. A person can be caused to sicken, suffer, and die in many ways. For instance, bury a photograph with a piece of the victim's hair. The person will rot away as the items do. Nail a photo of your enemy on a wall, shoot at it with an unloaded gun, cursing as you pull the trigger. Think evil thoughts of the person for the rest of the day. On the third day he will be dead. Put earthworms inside a fish. Fry it and serve it to the victim. In three days her intestines will be full of worms. To make a pregnant woman suffer a long and difficult labor, take a snail from its shell and iron it into her husband's underwear. The birth will go at a snail's pace.

How could anything good stand alongside so much aberrant, willfully malicious, behavior? I'm not saying there wasn't plenty of good to fasten onto in magic. The magical idea that everything is connected, with humans at the center of it all, able to marshal forces that science barely dreams of, is a delicious idea. And not just because of the promised power, although I do like power, but because it means that we aren't genetic mistakes but part of a whole, a plan with an array of spirits and wonders all around us. The Hermetic assurance that humans have a powerful, exalted place in the eyes of God and a vital role in completing his work is a dazzling call to greatness. Feeling much like those Renaissance magicians must have, I thought, *What could we do if we worked within that power?* Always supposing that we did it with a pure heart, of course, and that seemed to be the rub. The hearts of many magicians didn't appear to be so pure, or even striving for it.

Newspapers tell of drug dealers all over the country hiring magic workers to help them. The press only hears about the ones that don't work out, of course. In one particularly embarrassing failure, a Santeria practitioner in the Bronx was arrested when police charged that she had aided drug dealers by asking her spirits when it was safe to deliver drugs to certain locations. Cops, tracking the dealers from one place to another, had been laughing at her and the spirits for six months.

I talked to a male voodoo practitioner who told me that he might charge $50,000 to protect drug merchants. His deities think what he's doing is perfectly all right; they approve, in fact. This guy, who works out of Florida, wouldn't let me use his name. "My customers might not like it," he said. Another magic worker vouched for his reputation as a man of power but pointed out that his customers would be difficult for me to locate, and probably surly if found. I wondered at the price. Mary Ann Clark, the Santeria priestess in Houston, doesn't do such work, but the size of the fees didn't sound improbable to her.

Strange powders and dead animals are so common in the Miami state courthouse that a special voodoo squad goes in to clean them up. In Miami federal court, a prosecuting attorney recently complained that although he doesn't like restricting anyone's religion, his cleaning bills were becoming exorbitant because of the Santeria dust regularly sprinkled on his chair.

Some of the best reasons not to do magic are the people who have done it. The promise of power can lead to paranoia and delusions of grandeur. It can also cause people to dwell on avenging slights when they would be better off forgetting them. It can cause people to imagine that others are responsible for bad fortune or illness when in fact they are responsible themselves or no one is responsible. I saw temptations toward all of that in my research, and many people succumbed.

Aleister Crowley, considered by many to be the greatest modern magician, had many extraordinary mystical experiences, among them hand-to-hand combat in the desert with an evil spirit. He called himself the Beast and 666, as a way of identifying himself with the anti-Christ. He accomplished great treks through wilderness and climbed mountains, but he seemed to have little love for his fellow humans. He beat the servants who carried his luggage during his expeditions, refused to help rescue fellow mountain climbers who were in danger of losing their lives, and betrayed almost everyone who loved him. He had grand ideas about himself and all that he would accomplish, but few of them came to pass. He ended his life in poverty, having spent his inheritance and earned little more, and without having achieved the following he expected.

Other magicians have been similarly unlucky. As author Colin Wilson noted, a rapid ascent to fame and power and then a slow descent toward infamy and poverty is a common path. Count Alessandro Cagliostro, a famous eighteenth-century magician, died in prison. Gregory Rasputin, the Russian magus of the late nineteenth and early twentieth century, went down in history as the man who wouldn't die. Assassins poisoned him, shot him, battered him with an iron bar, and dropped him into the river through a hole in the ice before he finally died. Giordano Bruno, a sixteenth-century mage, was burned at the stake. Pascal Beverly Randolph, the nineteenth-century American Rosicrucian and sex magician, killed himself.

Hoodoo docs have suffered too. South Carolinian Roger Pinckney writes of Dr. Bug, who gave young men a potion that would make their hearts flutter and get them out of the World War II draft. When two men died on their way to the draft broad, Dr. Bug was tried and pled guilty. Out on bond, the conjure doc was so disheartened that he took to his bed and died. Dr. Buzzard, the original holder of that name in the Carolina lowlands, also helped men avoid the draft but was never convicted because no one would testify against him. High sheriff Ed McTeer, a white man who did hoodoo rootwork himself, went after Dr. Buzzard and pulled him into court for doctoring without a license—"an occupational hazard of root doctoring," Pinckney notes. Dr. Buzzard was convicted and fined $300; like his colleague, he was so distressed by the defeat that he retired to bed. Diagnosed with stomach cancer, he died soon afterward.

An English magician during World War II believed himself to be so magically strong that he could walk unharmed through bombs falling during the London blitz. He was wrong, and one of the bombs killed him. A brilliant young Californian aerospace engineer and magician named Jack Parsons was thought by many to be Crowley's successor. Instead, he was killed during a chemical experiment in 1952.

Some of the tenets of the Nazi and Italian fascist parties were fostered by magical thought, particularly ideas about racial superiority. Heinrich Himmler, head of Hitler's SS, was said to have used severed heads to communicate with ascended masters. A so-called

realm of the dead was underneath the dining hall of the headquar-
ters' castle, writes Peter Levenda. It included a well in which coats-
of-arms that represented leaders of the SS would be burned after
they died, and the ashes worshiped. SS members were discouraged
from celebrating Christmas and attending Christian ceremonies.
Instead, they celebrated the winter solstice with sacred fires and
invocations of Teutonic deities.

Although once interested in the occult, Hitler later turned violently against all such practice. His deputy führer, Rudolf Hess,
continued to believe in the occult and convinced himself that he was
destined to talk the British into making peace. A German astrologer
working for the British told him that a German-English organization
known as The Link was going to overthrow the Churchill government and would meet him in Scotland on October 10, 1941, according to Levenda, with the help of the Duke of Hamilton. Hess, a pilot,
flew to Scotland by himself and, decked out in various occult symbols,
parachuted into the arms of the Brits, who promptly arrested him.

*I*t wasn't only people I didn't know who were talking about
scary stuff. *The Lucky Mojo Hoodoo Rootwork Hour*, a telecon-
ference with Cat and a Florida rootworker named Christos Kioni,
was generally about love spells or luck or other positive matters, but
not always. Every Wednesday night at nine, I'd dial up, turn off the
lights, crawl into bed, and listen in the dark. Sometimes when they
talked about dirty tricks people could pull or rootwork's power to
cause mischief, I'd get a shiver. Cat would maybe tell about some
old root doc who put foul stuff in a bottle, shook it, hung it up in a
tree, and let it swing there for as long as the rope lasted. The object
of the work would have aching joints or money troubles or be
forced to wander all his days, whatever the conjure doc had ordered

up. Only when the rope broke would the work be lifted, and only if the afflicted one had lived a good life. After such a story, I'd sometimes hear other hoodoo workers sigh happily and say, "That's good. Oh, that's real good," like Shakespeare's witches hanging over the cauldron.

The first time I called into *The Lucky Mojo Hoodoo Rootwork Hour*, I listened through headphones while cleaning the miniblinds in my study. As I dusted, climbing on the desk, crawling over furniture, I may have huffed a little. The next week everybody was talking about the heavy breather who had freaked them all out. Maybe somebody was doing bad work on the class, someone said. Enemies were certainly about—other conjurers jealous of their success or angry Christians.

Or maybe somebody too dumb to mute the phone, Cat's co-host Christos Kioni offered. I should have confessed, but I resisted knowing the truth. The evil lurking at the edge of space had probably just been me, out of shape, clumsy, trying to get a little housework done. I hoped no one had put out a curse on the heavy breather.

Cat doesn't always censure what others might call black magic. One of the students in our online hoodoo class told of having evoked spirits to deal with an official who menaced his family. The work involved sacrifices of chickens and was aimed toward the official's car. Not long thereafter, the official had an automobile accident that disabled her. She gave up her job, and the threat to the family went away. Others in the class congratulated the student on such a strong result. When one student suggested that trafficking with such spirits might be dangerous, Cat's response was "Some people like to play on the wild side. To each his [or her] own." A few days later, however, she noted in a separate post that those who seek to benefit others are the rootworkers who grow strongest.

Her shop is filled with supplies that can put a hex on anyone. She stocks graveyard dirt, which scares plenty of people. Needlessly, she might say, since African Americans think of spirits as benevolent, and the most common use for the dirt is to connect with protective spirits. Graveyard dirt is also combined with other ingredients, such as sulfur and ground-up vermin, to make goofer dirt. It's bad stuff that can be used in spells that aim to kill people. She also has black candles. I was shocked that she stocked such items.

"I won't kill anyone," she said. "I've had people ask me to, and I tell them, 'If you want someone killed, you'll have to do it yourself.'" She doesn't do any work for others anymore, but she sells supplies and advises people.

"What about black magic?" I asked, and then began to clarify. "Not black. I mean dark. I mean harmful magic. Bad magic. You know what I mean." Trying not to sound racist was twisting me in knots.

She nodded. "I know what you mean."

"Okay. I'm trying to ask if you have any problem with that."

"I trust that it's justified," she said mildly.

The word *justified* is important in hoodoo conjure work. Rootworkers often say Psalms and other Bible verses over their work. But in their prayers for power and destruction, they always remember to say, "If this be justified, Lord, let it come to pass." Then it's the Lord's call, and the rest of us are merely his instruments, which is a cozy place to be. It beats going to war in the name of God or killing because God has been insulted or bombing school buses because his temple has been defiled or any of the other reasons I'd heard for abusing others in the name of God. The hoodoo method, setting natural forces into motion and then appealing to God for a decision on whether it's a go or not, is a bit like prayer with a barb.

The conjurers also may refuse work that they don't think is justified, and some who refuse to do any bad work at all are called "lady-hearted." But what's bad and what's not is always up to interpretation. I suspect that if they're convinced someone is being unjustly punished or wronged, even lady-hearted workers might feel free to help. The St. Helena Island hoodoo doc told me that a large part of his work was for people in prison. The original Dr. Buzzard, generations back, also specialized in jailhouse work. He was said to have a flock of buzzards at his command that would descend on the jail and free prisoners.

To determine what's justified, conjurers listen to the person asking for the work. They also often do some form of divination. It might be Tarot or I Ching or throwing the bones. I don't know whether divination works, but I do know that listening to one side of any story may not tell you what's justified. Hearing both sides always complicates up the situation. I never talked to or heard of hoodoo docs seeking the other side of a story. They rely on their judgment, divination, and the discretion of Jesus. Maybe those three tests are enough. One more test when a hex is in question comes from Luisah Teish, a priestess of the Yoruba Lucumi tradition, which is another name for Santeria. "Hexing is appropriate when you seek to stop an abusive action for which you would be willing to receive the same punishment if you committed the same crime."

Conjure docs often favor turning bad magic back on the sender as a way to deal with enemies. That punishes whoever bears them ill will without hurting those who they suspect but who might be innocent. A North Carolina rootworker, Adele, told me that she does reverse work once a year that's aimed at anyone who seeks to harm her. Then she watches to see what happens. Sometimes people she hasn't suspected have car wrecks. One man's house burned down. Not only were they punished, but she then knew who was working against her.

When I expressed my misgivings about bad work, Cat reminded me that everybody doesn't love everybody and everybody doesn't do everybody else right. Poor people have always turned to religio-magic for healing and justice. Some of her clients have thrown down on drug houses, trying to get pushers out of their neighborhoods.

Does it work?

"That depends. It might, or it might be that the drug dealers were doing the same thing."

Cat's ideas began to shift my thoughts about the clear-cut nature of good and evil, which softened me up for a harsher challenge that was to come.

*A*nimal sacrifice is part of many magical practices, and needless to say, I don't like it. Wiccans don't do it, and I never heard of Western high magicians doing it—except Crowley, who had a cat killed to prove that his magical power could keep it still despite its terror. He also crucified a frog once. I doubt that many hoodoo practitioners kill animals today, but old stories often included examples of people cruelly killing frogs, cats, and bats in order to use parts of their bodies in magic.

Among practitioners of African diasporic religions such as Santeria or voodoo, however, animal sacrifice is still important. These kinds of sacrifice aren't for the expiation of sin, as were Christian and Judaic sacrifices. Sometimes in African belief systems sacrifices give the gods payment or food for the magical actions they are asked to perform. I also heard people say that animal sacrifice was one way among many of bringing the energy of life into the ceremony.

Wiccan circles' cone of power is supposed to focus and intensify energy. Candlelight is a form of energy that sends intentions out into the world. High magicians in one Hermetic ceremony I watched concentrated on holding the energy of specific deities within themselves as a way of keeping those gods' power present during the ceremony.

Defenders of animal sacrifice say that anyone who eats animal flesh has no ground for complaint since animals killed for food are often treated much more cruelly and killed with less regard than are sacrificial animals. Defenders also say that animals killed during ceremonies are killed quickly and eaten afterwards. According to U.S. law, they cannot be killed slowly or cruelly. Those are good defenses and usually stop the criticism, except among vegans and vegetarians, who have a different ethic. But I am not one of those, and I don't like criticizing other people's religious beliefs. I planned to ignore the issue of animal sacrifice altogether. Then I read a diary recording a trip to Haiti by a group of Americans who wanted to be initiated into voodoo.

The diary gave details of a chicken sacrifice. It was not quick and easy, as such sacrifices are often said to be. They broke the chicken's legs and pulled out its tongue. The diarist defended the Haitians as living in a different county, with different circumstances, following an old tradition. She was being taught by an old man of great stature in his community, and she trusted him, believed him to be in close touch with gods and magic forces. Nevertheless, she was so upset about the chicken that she cried. The same evening I read the diary, I began a book about urban voodoo, which touted the great strength that comes from giving up puerile Christian notions about good and evil. The two accounts were not a good combination. I read them as I was about to go to sleep. They disgusted me so much that I threw the urban voodoo book across the room.

"I will not torture chickens," I muttered toward the blank wall of my bedroom. "I don't care how many gods promise to aid me. I don't care how many mild-eyed old men steeped in an ancient wisdom say it's right. And I'll keep my ideas about good and evil too."

I snapped off the light, punched my pillows, and slouched deeper into the bed. I raged for a bit, still mumbling angrily as I tossed about. Then I fell asleep, and the magic began.

I dreamed that I was in a prison common room where men were lined up and being killed one by one. A woman walked down the row stabbing them repeatedly with a small knife until they were dead. None of them struggled or fought back. Watching with me was a dark-haired young man, dressed in dark pants and a white shirt, who loved me. He left the room, and the woman turned to me.

"You've been found guilty," she said. "I have to kill you now."

"You're going to stab me with that little knife?" I asked. "Oh no. That's going to hurt."

"No. I'm going to give you injections that will cause your body to go numb. First your hands and feet will lose feeling. Then as I give you more shots, the numbness will reach your heart and you will die."

She began the injections, and I slumped over onto a school desk, unable to move my hands or feet. Paralysis was moving up my body when the young man walked back into the room.

"She's innocent," he said.

"Okay," the woman said, as though she didn't care one way or the other. "I'll stop giving her shots, and she'll be fine."

I awoke feeling horrified at such a bloody dream, and then I began to laugh. No one reared as I was in the Southern Baptist church could fail to know that the young man who declares you innocent in the face of judgment is Jesus. I hadn't been to church in a long time, and few people would identify me as a Christian, but who should come roaring to the rescue at the first assault from pagan beings and occult powers? Jesus himself. Maybe he dropped down from heaven, or maybe I'd dredged him up from the core of my being. Either way, I was surprised and glad to see him. I called my mother that morning to tell her the dream. I knew she was fearful about my investigations in the occult world. Hearing that Jesus was on the case would comfort her.

In truth, it had comforted me too. The Baptists believe once saved always saved, but I hadn't counted on it. The dream made me wonder if I had strayed as far from Christianity as I'd thought. It seemed to affirm a core of goodness, strength, or innocence within me that could withstand any occult evil that might be thrown my way. It seemed to say that I could count on that inner knowledge, which was a lot like what Hegel and the Hermeticists believed. They thought that humans are created out of God, you'll remember, and so are part of God with the truth right there. They also had a position that seemed to speak to my struggle over the separation of good and evil. They thought that neither side is likely to have the corner on truth and that generally a synthesis of opposing ideas, taking some from each, will reveal the whole truth.

I didn't take the dream to be an endorsement of living sacrifice, especially since it appeared that I was about to be one in the dream. I took it as an assurance that I didn't have to be afraid of occult powers. They wouldn't "kill" me. My core beliefs would stand up. I could let them be challenged, even modified, without fearing that I'd lose the essence of the morality I valued. My dream wouldn't stand up to scientific scrutiny, but I'm not a scientist. I'm just an ordinary Jill trying to get by. I believed the dream's message, and it gave me courage.

Was it a message from Jesus? Who can say? But let me tell you what happened next, and you can make your own decision. That afternoon I picked up the urban voodoo book again. As I sat on my front porch I read something new to me. When voodoo spirits, or lwa, take possession of believers, the first sign may be that the believers' hands and feet become immovable, exactly what had happened to me in the dream. The woman had given me injections, and my hands and feet were paralyzed. That part of the dream couldn't have come from deep inside my mind. I *hadn't* known it.

I put the book down and sat still, moving only my eyes, scanning the empty yard. "What is going on here?" I whispered to the sunny day around me. No one answered, which was good. If someone had, I might have run into the house, shut the door, and never come out again, which wouldn't have made me safe at all since everyone knows that spirits can come through walls.

The first lesson from Cat had blurred the lines between good and evil. This second lesson gave me courage to push on. The third lesson mixed everything up so completely that my ideas of good and evil may never recover.

The first time I met Cat's husband Siva, the blood-pact Satanist, he hardly spoke, which is not unusual for him. He is a quiet man. His hair is dark and long. The first tier of his beard is shorter than the rest and bushes out. The longer part, which hangs far down onto his chest, is sometimes plaited by Cat into tiny snaky braids. Tall enough to stand like a spectral presence above every crowd, he always wears black. Sometimes he adds a gray knitted watch cap. He answers questions carefully in a soft voice that belies his rather fierce appearance. Anyone who watches his eyes will see that he is often amused, frequently delighted.

Cat and Siva have their differences. She primarily does low or practical magic. He does all kinds of magic, but high magic is a strong interest for him. She claims magical results regularly; he believes as little as possible. Their house is full of her collections: Christmas ornaments, ceramic Easter rabbits, old labels, posters, jewelry. The main sign that he lives there is one altar on the porch with images of the devil on it. Her favorite deities are Jesus and the Hindu god Siva, chiefly because they are thin men with good bodies and facial hair. Jehovah she refers to as the baby-killer god, mainly for his actions when the Israelites wanted out of Egypt.

Jesus also gets her allegiance because of hoodoo. Unlike voodoo or Santeria or other African-based religions, hoodoo does not usually employ African deities. It uses African magic and medicinal lore but usually not African gods. Hoodoo is Christian through and through. In some parts of the country it's Protestant and in others it's Catholic. If you try to take Africa out of hoodoo, it's not hoodoo anymore, and the same is true if you take the Christianity out. Although she is Jewish, Cat doesn't hesitate to end any particular rootwork with the words, "Do this in the name of Jesus." Anybody who can't get along with Jesus can forget rootwork, she said.

Siva considers himself a monk of the goddess Kali, who is often associated with destruction. He seemed clearly on the dark side, but that doesn't always mean what I thought it did. His blood pact with Satan, for instance, is in support of the wildness of the earth. For magical people the dark is often identified with the female, with the moon and the tides and the silent forces of nature. It is sometimes used as a way of calling up intuition and the unconscious. Goddesses are often identified with the night and sexuality. The annual sojourn of Persephone in the underworld is talked about as a necessary going into the dark for spiritual growth. The dark is also accepted as a necessary balance to the light. So that even when dark things are identified with bad actions or feelings, they are honored as part of human experience.

Siva's full name, Tyagi Nagasiva, is one he took as all monks do when they consecrate their lives. Tyagi means one who renounces. Kali gave him the name Nagasiva. He was inspired by reading Catholic monk Thomas Merton's writing, especially *The Silent Life*,

and studying the lives of monastics in history. A contemplative, sacrificial way of life appealed to him. Being a monk did not forestall
his marriage.

Kali first came to him one night when he was walking to the bus
stop. She didn't give her name. He only heard a voice. He thought
the voice might be coming from nearby trees. He has reverence for
trees and has done pilgrimages to visit some that he considers especially holy. When he asked if the voice was coming from the trees, it
said, "You can believe that if you want to." He has no holy book to
elucidate his relationship with the Goddess, but he believes that she
often speaks to him. He writes down what she says and has compiled other writings about her, especially those written by devotees.
Those serve as his holy writ. She is not, however, a very directive
goddess. She often gives him another perspective and then refers
him back to his own understanding, which the Hermeticists would
say is an excellent place to look for direction.

He is also a member of the Church of Euthanasia, which has
four pillars: cannibalism, abortion, suicide, and sodomy. By the time
I read that, I was wondering if Cat's magic wasn't an example of
needing to be careful what you wish for. I questioned a longtime
friend of Cat's about Siva. "All I know is that he's very kind," the
friend said. Kind? Cannibalism and suicide? Kind?

On his website he publishes a compilation of other people's
explicit tips on committing suicide. The guide recommends the action
and commends all those who absent themselves from the planet
prematurely. When popular media have fastened onto the site, he
has been vilified and demonized, but Internet communications have
often been from people grateful for the information. He is also
sometimes told that he ought to kill himself, which he says he would
do if he weren't serving the earth. The material is horrifying,
instructive, and sometimes funny in a sick way. He describes it and

the Church of Euthanasia as Dada-esque. "It's a method for catalyzing a change of consciousness in the human species," he said.

The original Dadaists were a social-political movement that specialized in doing absurd, radical actions. Dada artists included Salvador Dali, Max Ernst, and Marcel Duchamp, who shocked the world by making a urinal into art. It takes more to shock the world these days. Siva is up to the task.

Before I talked with him, I was becoming convinced through my Internet readings that Siva was a weird individual, rather nasty and perhaps a bit crazy. He is the Satanic Outreach Director for the Church of Euthanasia. It pleases him to refer to himself by the acronym SOD, which seemed an apt term to me too. The most famous Satanist in the United States is the late Anton LeVey, who was a rather nasty guy himself, and it seemed from Internet evidence that Siva might be carrying the Satanic label in the same outlaw tradition.

Bestiality is among the practices Siva supports but doesn't practice himself. I knew that Siva and Cat owned an adorable Portuguese water dog, which looks like a heavy-boned, somewhat short standard poodle. "Do you have sex with your dog?" I asked.

"No," he answered, but when she humps his leg he doesn't stop her. "If it can be shown that there are animals that want a greater degree of physicality, then I would be in favor of that."

Oh.

He also has not helped people kill themselves and has not eaten human flesh, except a hangnail or two of his own. He thinks cannibalism might be a better way of respecting the dead than letting them rot in the ground. "My aim is along the line of *Soylent Green*. So we can have the splendiferous experience we all want when we die, and we can chose how we die." *Soylent Green* was a 1973 movie set in 2022, when food was made from human corpses.

His support of masturbation, sodomy, and bestiality is part of his allegiance to no-growth. The earth is being harmed by the number of humans on it. So the fewer the better. As a measure of his commitment, he had a vasectomy while still a young man.

He puts in many hours each day and far into the night on the computer, cataloging material, linking people with magical information, and entering into discussions in which he jabs at those with opinions he deems too strong or underchallenged. This is part of his dedication. He began his occult life interested in sex, drugs, and rock 'n' roll, things that at that time were hidden and unknown to him. The dark, transgressive nature of the magical world was its primary draw for him. Two decades later it still is. Only now his sex is restricted to his wife, and in addition to rock 'n' roll he's likely to be listening to the Memphis Jug Band because that's the music his wife likes. At forty-two, Siva may have tamed down some, as most of us do when we get older, but his essential commitments are the same.

He thinks transgressive behavior that is condemned by society is valuable for humans and for the society as a whole. It reminds people that there are values other than those being supported by authority. "It's important to protect the wild, even in people."

Sometimes his methods shock people; others turn away with no response, and some are compelled to follow up on his thinking. I told him I thought he was strange. He replied that a lot of people did. I wasn't sure how spirituality and his bizarre contentions linked up. The word *spirituality* is being used in so many odd ways that I don't know what it means half the time, I said. To me being a spiritually mature person means behaving in a certain way, I said.

He agreed.

So I challenged him. "What ways?"

"More patient, more engaging, more able to be with things that might be difficult for others, more kind."

"That's what I think," I said. When Siva evokes anger and attack, it's part of his discipline to reply gently and with patience. Like Jesus.

At one point in our conversation about spirituality, we began to talk about Buddhism. I said, "They talk about getting rid of the self. I don't need that. I need to find a self."

And he said, "I do too."

What was this? I was agreeing with a Satanist about the most basic spiritual questions. Then he told me that he also considers himself a Christian.

One night when he couldn't sleep he picked up a Bible that he kept by his bed and began reading the teachings of Jesus. He came across the story of the young rich man who came to Jesus asking what he ought to do to be a follower. Jesus said sell all your goods and give to the poor. The young man went away saddened. This is one of the most perplexing and hardest Scriptures, I think. I've mentioned it to many stalwarts of the faith, and most of them say Jesus didn't really mean it.

But Siva, who had taken a vow of poverty along with his other vows to Kali and had already given away his clothes, did take the verse seriously and devised a ritual of his own to dedicate himself as a Christian magician, using what he calls the Christ formula. Part of that dedication is to be like Jesus in telling people things they don't want to hear. Also like Jesus, he believes himself to be part of the Great Martyrdom Cult, which is a label he coined himself. Present-day Christians helped him form his ideas about the Great Martyrdom Cult by patiently answering his questions and then attacking him because he didn't agree with them. "It was like they gave me the formula and then gave me the opportunity to use it," he said.

The Great Martyrdom Cult, which may be a group or individuals who've lived through time, opposes societal repression, rouses people up, and rescues important parts of human experience by mentioning things and performing actions that society considers abhorrent, as Jesus did. When he ate with publicans and sinners, he was violating some of the most important taboos in Jewish society.

The more I talked to Siva the more I respected the seriousness of his position. He is dedicated to his Internet work and has become renowned and sometimes reviled for it. He limits the amount of time he spends earning money so that he will not forget his more important commitments. His gentleness testifies to his sense of what the spiritual life ought to produce. Once when Cat was telling me about a party where a drunken woman had tried to seduce him, she said, "Siva, tell her that story."

"You know that I won't," he said quietly.

"Okay, then. I will," said Cat, who proceeded to do just that.

At another time I heard him tell of having brought the Curse of Allah down on an unknown person who had stolen his bike. At the same time, he asked that whatever happened to the other person would also happen to him. When Cat questioned him on the idea that he would share the punishment, he said it seemed like the right thing to do.

"You're so tenderhearted," she said, the same fondness in her voice that I'd first heard when she told me of his blood pact with Satan.

Siva's picture of Jesus wasn't a new one to me. My concepts of who Christ was have changed radically three times in my life. The Jesus I knew as a child was the savior who came to keep us from going to hell. He was concerned with sexual sins, lack of faith, Bible reading, and churchgoing. The Jesus I knew as a young woman was radically different. He was concerned with the poor, incensed by injustice, and censorious of people who made a lot of money and kept it for themselves. The Jesus Siva experiences was one I didn't meet until I read the writings of Marcus Borg, a professor of religion at Oregon State University.

Siva's story sent me back to Borg's writings. I wanted to know if Jesus and a Satanist really were as akin as Siva said. I had no doubt that Siva offended common morality in all sorts of ways. Was Jesus equally offensive? Borg calls him a subversive sage who undermined conventional wisdom. When he chose to defend the prostitute, befriend the tax collector, and touch the sick, he chose compassion over purity, a serious matter in his culture. Purity meant that one was like God. Impurity meant that one was siding with the unclean or ungodly. Doing that undercut all that the culture depended on to define itself. When Jesus was called Lord, Savior, Messiah, he challenged the Romans and the uneasy balance Jews had with their rulers. When he refused to conduct his healing ministry in a settled, organized way, he challenged the patronage system, which was a critical stabilizing factor for a country with many poor and a tiny number of very rich, writes another scholar, John Dominic Crossan.

So, according to some respected Christian scholars, Jesus challenged power in every way: economically, religiously, and politically. He also let women speak, listened to them, and defended them when they stepped out of line. So add sexually to the ways he challenged power. The threat he represented was so dangerous and repugnant that it got him killed, and nobody spoke up for the idea that he was innocent. When I asked Siva why he acted as he did, he replied that he was speaking truth to power, the same directive that is so often given to Christians.

I'd taken Siva to be the epitome of darkness, and he wouldn't have minded that title a bit, I suspect. But the more he talked about darkness—or as he would put it, the wildness of Satan—the more I agreed that it ought to be protected and the more vital it seemed not just to him but to me and to all of us. I wasn't converting to

Satanism, but I'd finally seen real value in the magical people's refusal to embrace dualism.

As a result, an utterly unexpected change occurred in how I looked at the world and myself in it. I didn't become hedonistic and immoral, as I had feared, at least not any more than I already was. I didn't do fewer good deeds or more bad ones. I didn't use my new perspective to excuse my own bad behavior at all. Doing such things never even occurred to me. Instead, I began to see my good deeds differently. For instance, usually if I was giving away money and liking myself too much for my generosity, or being kind to someone I didn't really like and resenting it, my "evil" feelings would ruin everything and I'd completely discount the idea that my intentions were good. If I tried to do any kind of good and it backfired, I'd blame myself and plunge into mourning and remorse as though I'd known that the bad result was going to happen. I didn't think of it consciously, but I must have reasoned that good and bad are utterly separate and I wanted to be good. So whenever I wasn't purely good, I flipped into feeling completely bad.

Those tendencies made life quite difficult. They caused me to despise my own best efforts. They also contributed to a kind of cynicism that journalists are all too prone toward. My attitude was pretty close to the bad magic that I'd started out trying to defeat. What I mean by that is that my dualistic ideas damned almost everything, like a curse that no amount of courage or goodwill or even virtuous action could dispel. Why? Because the magical people had been right in refusing to separate bad and good as utterly as I did. Good and bad intermingle, and because they do, I could never find the purity I wanted, not in myself and not in anyone else.

Once I accepted that idea, I stopped beating myself up so much. Whenever I tried to do good and something bad came from it in addition to the good, I said to myself, *There's the dark side*. I began to see the intermingling of light and dark in other situations. When a special occasion that everyone had looked forward to turned out to be a letdown, I thought, *There's the dark side of anticipation. That's how it is*, I would think, and, *It's okay*.

It felt as though I had gone from reasoning as a child to being an adult. It gave me a different perspective on Christians, who are so often accused of being hypocrites. There are a million dark sides to the good intentions of spiritual striving. None of them deserve to be excused or accepted, but none of them invalidate the effort either. Good and bad don't cancel each other out. They intermingle. Maybe the best any of us can do is try to increase the amount of good and decrease the bad.

What that meant for my magical investigation was that I no longer felt compelled to make the magical people's behavior and ideas live up to a Judeo-Christian or even a community standard. I hadn't given up the idea that such standards have value, but I had broadened my perspective. I could look at the magical community for what it was: the usual intermingling, a little stranger sometimes, but reliably mixed. Most important, with the help of Cat, Jesus, and Siva, I stopped wanting to bolt every time I saw something that was so ridiculous, evil, or wrongheaded that it seemed to invalidate what the magical people were saying.

"Take the best and leave the rest," a Spiritualist once told me. I scoffed, thinking that she was trying to excuse her lack of accuracy. Now I realized that her admonition had greater value than I realized. She was saying that you ought to look for the good, you can depend on it, and you ought to claim it. What would happen if we did that, I wondered?

Before we ended our conversations, realizing that Siva knew quite a bit about elves, vampires, fairies, and other magical creatures, I asked him if he knew why people thought themselves to be such entities. His explanation was the clearest and most reasonable one I heard. He suggested that they might be people, like himself, without a strong personality or sense of ego. Perhaps they hadn't been allowed to role-play enough in their early life. Fastening onto a role of great magical intensity might be a way of finding some self worth being, he said. That made perfect sense. Two people whose lives were most strange and confusing to me fit his theory and were about to give my new perspective on light and dark a good workout.

8.

The Vegetarian Vampire and the Wooden-Headed Death Puppet Have Something to Say

*I*n our first conversation Mistress Tracy, Queen of the Vampires, told me that as a child she liked to wander around jabbing things with a stick.

"Things?" I asked.

"You know how it is. You see something dead and you poke at it," she said. I didn't know how that was, but I made encouraging sounds and kept listening.

Tracy Devine is a sanguine, or blood-loving, vampire. She is not immortal and not the kind who kills people by biting them on the neck. She doesn't bite people or animals, living or dead. She's vegetarian. The two fangs permanently implanted on her incisors aren't thin enough to pierce skin even when they've been freshly filed, and perhaps she isn't quite savage enough. Vegetarians aren't generally known for their ferocity.

She does like tasting the blood of her lovers. "What's more intimate than that?" she asked.

I went to meet Tracy on a dark September night. When Shawn the Witch and I arrived at her isolated New Hampshire house, orange Halloween lights glowed in the windows. The yard was filled with a hearse and pickup trucks—hers, her boyfriend's, and two others. A magical stone sat at the side of the doorway. It protected the house. Out back were horses, a pig, and geese.

We climbed steps toward the back door, knocked, and were admitted by Tracy's boyfriend, Jeff, a tall young man whose head was shaved except for long silky tufts of black and pink at the top and back of his head. We entered a room decorated with a crepe paper banner of skulls and orange jack-o'-lantern lights. A string of red-veined eyeball lights lay in a tangle on a side table. Through an open bathroom door, I saw a black shower curtain with a skull and crossbones. Most of the dining room was taken over by two huge wood-and-chicken-wire crates for Tracy's dogs: a greyhound rescued from a racetrack and a Doberman. The greyhound had limpid eyes and dark raised scars on its flanks. Pickles the Snake lived upstairs.

A tablecloth imprinted with jack-o'-lanterns covered the table. On a shelf above the table were glass jelly dishes shaped like hens. Tracy collects chicken art as well as bones. It's something we have in common. The chicken art.

Shawn pointed to the end of the living room where a human skeleton hung from the ceiling. Next to it was a rocking horse that Tracy's four-year-old daughter rode. Oddfellows, a Mason-like group, once used the skeleton in ritual ceremonies. Animal bones and skulls also sat around the living room. A brass pot contained what appeared to be human bones—a hand, a femur, and other parts

I couldn't identify. Shawn put the pot on the table and invited me to root around in it. I did. Then I washed my hands.

Tracy is a tattoo artist. Figures, doesn't it? Blood. Pain. Something that lasts forever. The paintings around the house were hers too: Tracy with outspread cape, hovering over a sleeping village; Tracy and Shawn in a medieval town square, a whirlwind around them; Hannibal Lecter in his mask, carrying a girl who might also be Tracy. Hannibal is one of Tracy's heroes. So is Michael Myers, the killer in the Halloween slasher movies. Her daughter has watched all the Halloween movies. She loves Michael Myers so much that she calls him Uncle Michael.

Tracy relishes these examples of dark energies, but it did little good to ask her why. I did, and she almost invariably said, "They're cool." Her answers didn't speak to the question, but when I applied Siva's ideas about the Great Martyrdom Cult, her life spoke for her. The GMC, you will remember, is made up of people who are impelled to live out roles that oppose society's values. Siva thinks their impetus comes from an unconscious compulsion to serve the balance of light and dark that gives life its wholeness. Psychiatrist and author James Hillman might say they are propelled by their daimon, which was Plato's word for fate, or the soul's imperative. Either way, members of the GMC serve to remind people of those parts of themselves that the community wants to abolish. Jung called it the shadow side. Freud called it the id. Siva likes to call it the depths.

As we continued to talk, Tracy told me that she had little mercy for whores, strippers, and other people who "have no class." The fictional killers who get rid of them are her heroes because they rid the world of people who don't contribute anything good to it. Michael Myers kills horny little teenagers who shouldn't be out doing nasty things anyway. She's joking, kind of.

One of the attractions of being a vampire or a werewolf, or Mr. Hyde for that matter, is that you don't have to justify dark passions. You can just have them and express them. No shame. No need to restrain your thoughts.

"I like animals," she said. "It's people I don't like." *Dumbo* is one of her favorite movies. She always cries when she watches it.

Tracy was wearing a dress that was fitted in the bodice, with a long overdress slit up the front. She wore no makeup that I could see. Her face looked almost scrubbed. She had a high forehead topped by a fringe of very short bangs combed straight down, a pale face, and small teeth, except for the fangs, which were odd but not unattractive, and smaller than I expected. Her hair was fuchsia and black, long and mostly loose, with several small ponytails. Shawn said the ponytails were to curtail the mischief of spirits that might fly into all that long hair.

She often wore a deadpan expression that she used to good effect playing straight man for her own jokes. Her delivery and her accent were a little like Carla from the television show *Cheers*. Shawn said she protects her alabaster skin by carrying a parasol in the sun, preferring darkness, as all vampires do, but Tracy, who has a surprisingly down-to-earth side, wouldn't go along with such glamorization.

"*Look* at me," she demanded, holding out a pale arm. "I'm just like my dad. He bubbled all up in the sun."

She is a witch as well as a vampire. Both palms are tattooed with pentacles that she uses to send and receive energy. She also has a pumpkin tattoo. She grows pumpkins in her garden, carving runes and other ancient symbols on them so that as they grow the magic grows. "Then you make a pie, and the magic goes inside of you," she said.

She also constructs a scarecrow each year that is magic.

"You bring it alive by your actions, and by thinking of it the whole time you're stuffing it and trying not to think of anything else," she said.

"That's how you do a spell. You're putting life into whatever you're doing, you're breathing life into it. At the end of the spell, you send the energy. It's a scientific fact that energy is matter, and if you concentrate hard enough you can send it."

"It's the scientific mind-set," she said, like a kid proving a point. "I watch *Nova*."

Witches believe everything is alive. When any of the vehicles they own begins to stall, Jeff is wont to begin cursing the machine. Tracy stops him.

"It'll hear you, and then we'll never get home."

Tracy describes herself as having been a normal kid. In junior high she started to think that she'd like to look like some of her heroes in rock bands. She dyed her hair white and began dressing in leather and metal and in torn clothes. Kids started to call her names. A less determined girl might have conformed. Tracy started wearing even more bizarre clothes.

She was vague about how the vampire phase started. Her attitude paralleled many magical people's. They often say, "It's just something I discovered I was." Tracy is strict about how a vampire ought to act. No nasty costumes are allowed at her ball. "Sexy is all right, but not gross." She won't tattoo hookers or strippers. If she's tattooing a guy who starts talking about having gone to a strip joint, she presses harder. She pushes until he hollers.

Here's the part of her story that made me wince: Tracy's daughter is named Carrion. Carrion, as in roadkill. Carrion Abigail. The child's grandmother cried when she heard the name. If you're a goddess in some mythic tale of cosmic meaning, naming your child Carrion is all right. But New Hampshire isn't Mount Olympus.

There's a photo of Carrion on the table. She's a pretty little blonde. Pink is her favorite color, and she takes dance lessons.

"I didn't name her Carrion because it's dead meat. It's a pretty name. If she doesn't like it, she doesn't have to use it. She can call herself Abby. Or Carrie. Or Carrie Ann. I don't care. Just so long as she's happy," said Tracy, who usually calls her daughter Boogie because that was the first word that made the baby laugh.

"Do you mean 'boogie' with one *o* or two?" I asked. "Bogey as in bogeyman or boogie-woogie?"

She shook her head as though to clear it. "Boogie as in your nose. I was getting a boogie out of her nose and she laughed."

Oh.

"I have a picture to show you," she said. She went to the back of the house, and when she returned she handed me a black-and-white, eight-by-ten photo of Carrion at about six months old. It's a fall day and the child is naked, sitting on the ground surrounded by fallen leaves. Her legs cover any part of her that might make the photo pornographic. Tracy, the moralist, would never show salacious photos of her child.

The baby is looking directly into the camera. She's smiling. Her skin glows in the light. I looked at the photo for a long time. The leaves are dry enough to crackle. The soft baby flesh seems real enough to be warm.

"Some people look at that photo and never see what's behind her," Tracy said.

I hadn't seen it. Maybe the brain doesn't want to see all that the eye beholds. Posed behind the baby, nestled into the leaves, was one of the skeletons. Its bony grin was clearly visible.

There was Boogie, the most precious thing in the world to Tracy. Soft and glowing with life. And behind her, behind this little girl named Carrion, was the fate that awaits every living thing.

As a young child, Tracy understood something about the world, something that all of us probably understand and then spend the rest of our lives trying to forget. Poking with a stick at those dead animals, she saw the great mystery and wonder of our short moment here. And she never forgot.

She was smart enough to know that what she had to say wouldn't be listened to in the world at large. She found that out when she dyed her hair white. So she decided to embody her ideal of power and elegance and life that never ends. She decided to live it, to turn herself into a symbol of it. I don't know if she thought about it that way. Probably she just did it.

"Who wouldn't want to be a vampire?" she said. "You're powerful and strong. You're elegant, and people look up to you. You never get sick, and you never die."

Golden Dawn mage William Butler Yeats might have understood what Tracy was doing. "We cannot understand the truth," wrote the mage and poet. "We can only embody it." Shamans of ancient traditions might have also understood. When Black Elk of the Oglala Sioux had a vision of sacred horses, he was told that his tribe must enact the scene in a horse dance. It took energy and time and resources to do it, but they did it because acting out the vision would give it power and help make it reality.

Tracy said it in her own way. "My dad taught me to write my name large."

He had died of emphysema four years earlier. One of the photos on her wall is of her as a little girl with him. They've caught a fish that's almost as big as she is, and he's holding it up between them.

She gestured toward the shelf in the dining room where his ashes sit. "He wanted me to scatter him, but I haven't been able to yet." For a minute she seemed about to cry. "That can of ashes used to hold me on his knee."

Then she gave us a tight little smile and changed the subject.

Ken the Quaker Mortician and Myrna the Death Puppet were not quite as strange as Tracy, but they were close. I met Ken for the first time at Shawn the Witch's house during a ceremony.

It was late September, a time the witches call Mabon, which is their Thanksgiving feast and the beginning of the Season of the Witch. We were in the backyard of Shawn the Witch's house. Spooky music was coming from loudspeakers at the house. Shawn's aboveground pool loomed behind us. Flanking an arrangement of pumpkins and hay bales was a chain-link fence. We were the only ones out. The neighbors were inside, watching TV or hiding from us. The night air was cool, and the fire's flitting shadows licked over our faces, bright and then dark.

The ceremony started when Shawn's roommate Teisan handed us each a sprig of lavender to increase our psychic abilities. We rubbed the lavender between our palms, sniffed it, and tossed it into the fire. The harvest was in and death was in the air as all of life prepared for the long winter, Shawn said.

He told us to kneel before the fire and declare some part of ourselves that we wanted to let die. We must drop our masks, he said. He went first.

"Here before my friends and family, I am vulnerable," he said. He wanted to let his bad temper die. He wanted to let go of his fear.

He wiped his hand over his face like a man in grief. "I am so afraid that I'll be hurt."

Jen Cosgrove, a neonatal nurse and single parent, talked of a hard year. She was grateful for the lessons and happy to let the year go. Jacqui Newman, who is a hereditary Strega, or Italian witch, wanted money troubles to die and her psychic business to flourish. Teisan wanted to drop the mask of coldness that he wears and show others the vulnerability inside himself. At the end of each confession the speaker sealed the deal by yanking strands of hair and tossing them into the flames. I could hear the hair pop as it let go.

When it came time for me to speak, the circle of figures around me was dark and still. As I sank to my knees before the ceremonial fire, the flames' light was so bright that I squinted. Everything else disappeared. The witches were silent, waiting for me to speak.

I said I wished to let the past die. I meant the silly, selfish, foolish moments that float around in my head and can make me flush twenty years after they happened. But I didn't say that. I also wished to stop being afraid. I could have named all the ways I am afraid, but we didn't have all night. As I rose from my knees Shawn whispered, "So mote it be," which is a witchy version of amen.

I sat next to a harmless-looking guy with short brown hair named Ken Glover, often called Ken the Quaker Mortician because he is one. That night he was alone. Usually he brought Myrna the Death Puppet, who is his license to be "a bit naughty," so naughty that Shawn's invitation specifically excluded the puppet.

"She's like a little grim reaper," Ken explained. "She channels for death."

Ken is unfailingly polite, soft-voiced, considerate. He speaks slowly, precisely, without any inflection, a little like Hannibal Lecter, Shawn said. To me he sounded more like Mr. Rogers.

Myrna, in contrast, is rude, caustic, and mean-spirited. Her voice is high-pitched and whiny with a Brooklyn accent. Ken makes no attempt to disguise his mouth movements when it's Myrna's turn to talk, I was told. Myrna is part of Ken's comedy act, during which she does psychic readings for members of the audience.

"You've made death into a comedy routine?" I asked.

"Yes. That's what I've done.

"I told this one guy that he was going to be in a car accident. He was not wearing his seat belt, and he'd have a car wreck. I said, 'You're going to bleed to death because your head is going to go through the windshield and your head will bob up and down until the glass cuts your carotid.'

"Then Myrna said, 'But don't worry. It won't be your fault, and you won't be cited.'

"Once I told this woman, 'You're going to live to be very, very old, and everyone you know will be dead and you won't know anyone.'

"And Myrna said, 'But don't worry. You won't know who *you* are either.'

"And people laugh. They think they shouldn't but they do, and I love that. That's the place I like to bring them."

"Why do you like to do this?" I asked.

"It's the only joke I can tell," he answered.

Myrna's predictions about death have not come true as far as Ken knows. But she does bring up things from people's lives. Myrna told Shawn that he would die in a fire started by a candle left burning in a bathroom.

"But don't worry," she told Shawn. "You won't burn to death. The smoke will kill you."

Shawn's home did burn once. He wasn't in it, and no one was hurt, but that reality gives extra edge to the prediction. Ken told him what he always tells Myrna's victims, "That doesn't have to happen." If they're careful, they can avoid that fate, he says. They still have free will. And now they've been warned.

Ken has been thrown out of at least one party, and he's often told to leave Myrna at home. Jacqui hates the puppet, calls her a potato on a stick. Teisan stays as far from Ken as he can. "He gives me the willies," he said.

Myrna scared me too. I didn't want to hear what she might tell me, but I had to meet her. I couldn't resist. It took a while to arrange, but a month later we met for lunch. Restaurants are my least favorite places to meet. They're too noisy, and it's hard to take notes while you eat. But people like them. This time I had already eaten so my hands would be free to take notes. I ordered iced tea. Ken ordered soup. Myrna was in her black carrying bag. Gently Ken pulled her out, smoothing her dress. We both looked at her.

Myrna has a carved mahogany head with hollow sockets for eyes and a slight smile in the void that is her mouth. Some people think she was carved out of casket mahogany, but that's not true. For hair, Myrna has one piece of rope with unraveling ends that wave wildly about her skull. Her clothes are made from a black shirt that Ken got off a guy he met on the dance floor. She carries a sickle, which she sometimes uses to sip drinks when at lunch.

Her head is large compared to her body, which is a stick underneath a robelike black dress. Not a bad-looking puppet. She could definitely star in a nightmare. No way would I have said anything bad about her hair or her big head. I looked at her for some time, but she didn't speak. Ken put her away.

We talked for the next two hours. Early on I asked a question he must have answered a million times. Why mortuary work? He said he'd taken a computer aptitude test that indicated he could be either an engineer or a funeral director.

"Funeral director seemed like it would impress people more, but later I found out that lots of people who take computer aptitude tests get funeral director."

Ken believes that being a mortician protects him from dying too early or too painfully.

"Since I clean up after death, I've thought that death would give me a certain amount of favoritism." Some morticians become overly cautious and fearful, and in that way Myrna helps him.

"Whenever I think of death, I'm not thinking of dying but of something that Myrna can say about it," he told me. Without Myrna, he wouldn't be able to give prophecies. "If someone asks how they're going to die, all I get when Myrna's not with me is, *You're going to stop breathing. The same as everybody.* Myrna's my id," he said. And maybe something more.

Ken built the original Myrna with his friend Richard. Ken first saw Richard across a bar. There was a certain smugness about him that Ken liked. "He was probably trying to look sexy."

Ken said to a friend who knew Richard, "Introduce me."

The friend said, "You don't want to meet him. His T cells are 17. He's dying."

Ken said, "Introduce me."

At the end of the evening Ken told Richard, "I'll call you."

"Don't call me. I may be dead. Let's make plans."

The next week Richard was in the hospital, but he didn't die. He lived a few more years, and they spent a lot of time together. Cutting humor was a big part of their friendship. "I hope you die," Ken would sometimes snarl at Richard after particularly funny insults, and they would laugh. Richard's humor was a lot like Myrna's. It's love disguised as cattiness, Ken said. "It's a warning. Change or prepare to die."

The last time he saw Richard was before Ken left on a trip to Spain.

"I had to walk out of the house and not look back because I didn't want to upset him or myself any more than I was," said Ken. "It was very painful. I never saw him again, and that always left a tremendous hole in me."

And how does being a Quaker fit with Myrna? Being a Quaker is about centering down, about being a voice for God's spirit, said Ken. So maybe there's a connection.

"You don't think Myrna is God speaking, do you?" I asked.

"No, I don't think that," he said. But she might be Richard.

Myrna has never told Ken about his own death. "I've never asked, and she's never said," he said. "I never will ask."

At the end of lunch Ken picked up the bag that held Myrna and smiled at me.

"Myrna didn't get to tell you anything about your death, but that's okay," he said. "And you know why? Sometimes you don't need to know. And the other thing is that sometimes you're not meant to die until it happens. There's no predestination. Sometimes you just live your life."

"So you mean sometimes Myrna has nothing to say?"

"That's right."

"Because she doesn't know?"

"That's right. You're probably not taking any risks."

"Not if I can help it," I said, a big understatement.

I left Ken still not understanding him or his audiences. Who would find such stories funny? And how could this man who seemed so kind get his yucks in such a crass way? How does a man spend Saturday night scaring the wits out of people and then go to a Quaker church on Sunday morning where all he does is sink into himself and listen for God?

He had assured me that he wasn't on medication and had never been. "Mental institutions?" I asked. No, he said.

I pondered Ken's story for weeks. I looked through my notes and thought about everything he'd told me. And finally I got it.

One story gave me the clue.

"I was at a party one time, and someone said, 'Read for David over there, he's a jerk,' but they used more colorful language," Ken said. "I happened to know David. He was a neighbor of a friend of mine, but David didn't know this. So I set about doing a reading that would really zing him. I asked, 'Is there someone here drawn to know how they're fated?'"

Ken imitated David's gravelly feminized voice. "Yeah. I want to know. How am I going to die?"

"I see snow. It's two, three in the morning, and it's cold and crisp, and the snow is swirling around the street lamps, and when it falls it's very quiet, and you can almost hear the ice cracking. It's that beautiful hush. I see you on a little stone path."

Ken explained to me, "He has a little stone path going to the street. I must have been aware of that because I'd been by his house."

Then he resumed his story. "I see you walking out to the street. I hear a scraping noise. A scraping noise. It's a snowplow, and it's coming into a cul-de-sac."

Then he did David's gravelly voice: "Oh, my God, I live in a cul-de-sac. Oh, my God."

"The driver of the snowplow doesn't see you, and he runs into you and knocks you down. You can't get up."

"Am I going to die? Am I going to die?"

"No, I think you're going to be all right. He just knocked a lot of snow on you. It's just as well. That will keep you warm until you can get up. You're okay. You'll be able to get into the house in a little while.

"Oh no," Ken continued, "I hear something coming. It's the snowplow. He's coming back, and, oh no, he's broken your legs. Now you can't get up."

Ken's victim started saying, "Oh no. Oh no. I'm going to be plowed to death. I'm going to be plowed to death," which was a double entendre because they were in a gay bar.

"And people are laughing," Ken said. "It's sounding really crass at this point. He's having a hizzy.

"And then I said, 'I see you in the house.'"

"Did I get in the house?" David screeched.

"No, it's earlier. You're on the phone. Did you call the city and make sure they come around twice? Why did you do that?"

"Yes, I did that."

"Why did you do that?"

"I wanted to make sure there was a parking place for the Cadillac."

Then David asked, "How can I avoid this?"

And Myrna replied in her Brooklyn nasal tones, "It's July. Buy rock salt while it's still cheap."

The story was over. Ken didn't laugh. He never laughs, but he looked pleased in his deadpan way. I asked, "What happened to the guy?"

"He had a nervous breakdown, and he did a really bad thing. He hit his father and he had to move out. He had to move into the Y right down the street from me, and I had to avoid him every time I went out."

"But he didn't die from a snowplow?"

"No. He moved into a place where he didn't have to have snow plowed. He didn't even need the rock salt."

Ken hadn't spelled it out, but I'd always known that he was gay and his comedy was performed in gay clubs. One of his jobs was at an AIDS resource center doing prevention work. At the time we talked, Ken was thirty-two. During the worst of the AIDS crisis, when no medicine helped and people were dying by the thousands, he had been a kid just coming into his own sexuality. Now he worked primarily in an AIDS outreach center. I looked back through my notes. They were full of terrible ways for people to die. But nobody died of AIDS. Nobody wasted away terribly, weakening with one horrible affliction after another.

There it was. Die violently. Die with great suspense. Die in weird ways that no one can foresee. Of course they would laugh until they couldn't sit up. It would be impossible not to, no matter how guilty you felt. Sitting in a dark bar, sex thick in the air. Take another drink. Anybody might raise his hand, volunteer to be the goat. It would all be so tense, so frightening, and such a huge hysterical relief. And who better to give you that release than Myrna, channel for Richard, the man who once sat across a bar looking so sexy, of whom it was said, "You don't want to meet him. His T cells are 17. He's dying."

When I first met Ken and Myrna, I thought they were just out to terrify people for laughs. A lot of people saw him that way. Like Siva the Satanist and Tracy the Vampire, Ken hardly defended himself, thereby fitting into Siva's Great Martyrdom Cult well. Like some great scary prophet of Jehovah, Ken held up doom as a warning. It had seemed at first that Ken's allegiance was to fear and death, but that was the surface truth. The inside truth was that life or light or the good, whatever you want to name it, was calling Ken, and through Myrna, the potato on a stick, he was answering. Weirdly, yes, but it was an answer.

Here it was again—a paradox that I didn't have a name for. Maybe it was nothing but good intentions, startling me because they weren't clothed in the high-toned talk that usually accompanies noble motives. Outsiders wouldn't call good intentions and good magic the same thing, but old Crowley might. Remember his definition of magic as "the science and art of causing change to occur in conformity with will." Will. Intention. They seem close to the same thing. What Siva was doing, what Tracy represented, and what Ken hoped would happen when he used Myrna to warn party boys, it all seemed like good magic to me. I'd hoped for more, but this was good, and I was glad to find it.

Part Three

MIRACLES AND WONDERS

Connect, only connect.

—E. M. FORSTER

9.

What to Do When the Mother of God Comes Calling

*I*f I really wanted to know about hoodoo, I would need to talk with African American rootworkers, Cat told me. Hoodoo's combination of African magic and Christian ideas is an oral tradition handed down from generation to generation since slave days. It has a Catholic flavor in Louisiana and a Protestant flavor in other parts of the South. As blacks intermarried and mingled with Native Americans, it sometimes picked up elements of Indian magic. When they moved during the Great Migration, it sometimes picked up elements of magic practiced in the eastern and northern United States. Each hoodoo doc taught things his own way, and although there have been white people who practiced the magic, it belongs to African Americans in a way that it can never belong to anyone else. It's their heritage, running through their blood, showing up in their dreams, speaking to them in a voice they understand better than anyone else.

"You'll have to go into black neighborhoods," Cat said.

"I can do that," I said, miffed. I'm afraid of disease, afraid of death, afraid of bad magic, afraid of airplanes, afraid of terrorists, but I am not afraid of black people, and I was touchy about somebody thinking I might be. I was raised in the South, and I sound like it. Southerners who leave home sometimes face assumptions about who they are—conservative, prejudiced, reactionary, stupid. To be fair to Cat, I also look like a white woman from the suburbs, because I am one, and white women from the suburbs are often afraid of black people. But I am not. Not even white women from the suburbs are only what they appear to be.

Cat was reluctant to give me names of rootworkers. She said I could find them myself if I wanted, but I kept hanging around, and finally she suggested I call Dr. Christos Kioni. This was before *The Lucky Mojo Hoodoo Rootwork Hour* started, so I didn't know anything about Kioni yet. A former Pentecostal preacher who lived near Orlando, he was one of the best rootworkers she knew. Customers she referred to him were often so happy with the work that they called her to tell her so.

"He might talk to you," she said.

I looked on the Web and quickly found his site, but Dr. Kioni's Web presentation was about how to have prosperity. It didn't mention hoodoo, and it seemed that I'd have to go through PayPal to talk to him. I didn't do it. I'd had enough of moneymakers in Salem.

Luckily I had also signed up for Cat's online hoodoo course, which was filled with people avid about magic. For a year I lurked, learning that a hoodoo wagon is a hearse and that if the spirits come in a dream offering food, don't eat it. I learned that to keep a hag from riding you during the night you need to put screens on the window or a sieve near the bed. Hags can't get to your bed until they have counted every hole, by which time it will be daylight. To get rid of a hag forever, find the skin she abandoned before she began to fly and salt it. Cat likes to tell of the hag who returned to find her skin so shrunken she couldn't get back in. "Skinny, skinny, don't you know me?" she wailed.

I learned when burning candles for magic to watch the flame. If it goes out or burns dirty, that's bad. The buzzard is a sacred bird, and a line dance called the buzzard dance has great power. Brushing a buzzard wing over somebody will remove a jinx. The original Dr. Buzzard out of Beaufort, South Carolina, the most famous and powerful of all the hoodoo conjurers, was a white man, according to Cat. Lots of Dr. Buzzards have sprung up since. Legend says that when one of the most powerful African American Dr. Buzzards from St. Helena Island died, his bones were buried in an unmarked grave because so many conjure docs wanted the bones' power that they never would have been allowed to rest easy.

Dr. Kioni was in our class, but he wasn't online much. One day, however, he answered a question from a new rootworker about how to deal with clients. At the end of the message he signed off by writing, "I wish for you all that I wish for myself." A man with a spirit that large might be worth meeting.

So I e-mailed him. He sent me his phone number. I called. We talked. The next day Expedia sent me a message. I could fly straight to Orlando for $135. It seemed like a sign.

Over the years a number of women had volunteered to come to Kioni's suburban Florida home to get to know him better. Unlike the others, whom he hadn't allowed to visit, I kept all my clothes on. He had thrown the photos away, but a lot of women have sent him pictures showing parts of themselves they'd be better off keeping private.

"Some of these women are really bold," his wife, Marilyn, told me. "You wouldn't believe it."

I probably wouldn't.

Dr. Kioni, a tall, well-built man, shaved bald with a goatee, was dressed in an embroidered Mexican shirt and dark pants when he came out to greet me the first day of my visit. He spread his arms wide and said, "Welcome." As well he might. Kioni had done rootwork two years before to bring a storyteller into his life. And there I was, sitting in his driveway with a notebook in one hand and a tape recorder in the other, believing myself to be the captain and sole director of my own destiny. He never doubted that I would arrive.

"I did the work right back there," he said two days later, nodding toward his backyard, where I could see a frost-damaged banana tree and palm trees. "I asked for someone to come here and tell my story."

The only clue that Kioni's white stucco house contains anything mysterious is an eight-sided mirror over the front door. It's easy to overlook. "That's a bagwa," he told me. "It's to deflect energy." Like many magical people, Kioni combines a number of different systems. The bagwa is feng shui.

A row of devil's shoestrings is buried next to the walk leading to his door. That's hoodoo, but no one would know they were there unless Kioni told them. Devil's shoestrings are a powerful root, and Kioni's are meant to keep ill-meaning people away. If anyone particularly unpleasant does get through his door, Kioni might ensure he doesn't return by sprinkling salt along the doorsill after he has left, sweeping it out toward the street, and then placing the broom upside down at the doorway. His magic has worked against a pesky cable television employee and against a young woman whose attire suggested she might be a little too racy for his youngest son. Neither has crossed his threshold since.

"What would happen if someone came here who had ill will toward you?" I asked.

"They wouldn't be able to get in," he said. I wondered if he had watched closely as I approached the door that first time, speculating on whether I would be stopped, and if he would have shut the door against me if I'd stumbled.

One of the first stories he told me was about the evening Mary the Holy Mother of God appeared in the left-hand corner of his bedroom. It was dark but not late. He was in bed but not asleep. The other side of the bed was empty because earlier in the evening Kioni and Marilyn had argued. She was watching a sports program in the den and planned to sleep on the couch, as she sometimes did.

He was lying in their bed feeling sorry for himself and for his wife because of things he had said. He'd let his meanness come out, and it wasn't the first time. Now his back hurt. His head ached. His legs twitched. He felt all the old scars rising, some on his body, many in his mind. They were thirty, forty years old and it didn't matter. The ones on his feet, his ankles, the long gash up his shin, the crescent on his left hip were like puckered snakes slithering against the chocolate of his skin.

In his mind he heard a familiar hiss.

You ain't never going to be nothing. Crippled little bastard. You lucky somebody took you in. Nobody want you. Those words had been said to him too many times to remember. He had tears in his eyes so that when the Blessed Virgin first appeared he had to squint through them to make her out.

"Why do women always leave me?" he was crying when she appeared. "Every woman I've ever loved has left me."

If the Mother of God was in the business of bringing healing and motherly love, as she often seems to be, she'd picked the right bedroom. Kioni's unmarried mother had abandoned him in the hospital when he was three months old and sick with polio. After the first of many operations, a second cousin named Pearlie Mae came for him. Legally blind, she wore dark glasses so that he never was able to look into her eyes. She took him to the boardinghouse she operated. As he grew he learned to mop and wax, to dust and change beds. The boardinghouse was over a bar, and prostitutes often rented the rooms for an hour or two. Kioni, who was called Ken then, would clank up the stairs in his leg braces, bringing them soap, towels, and a basin of water. After they left, he would throw the water out. If he displeased her, Pearlie Mae punished him in ways that he hasn't gotten over yet.

Many operations followed that first one. Kioni can't remember anyone visiting him in the hospital. Nurses and doctors wore masks, afraid of contagion. No one touched him tenderly. At twelve, he refused to have another operation. The only picture he has of himself as a child is from that year. It sits on the television in his den. His cheeks are round and smooth, but a line of mustache makes him look older than twelve. He is scowling.

When Kioni was sixteen, he teamed up with the popular boys at school and began robbing convenience stores. He held the shotgun while the other boys got the money. The gun was empty. At first, they didn't have money for shells; later, when everyone in town was talking about the robberies, they didn't have the nerve to buy them.

His criminal career ended within a few weeks when the other boys panicked and ran for the car one night. He couldn't keep up. They circled back to get him, but not before the shopkeeper saw that he had a limp. Only two black teenage boys in Rockledge, Florida, had a limp. The other boy had an alibi. The city's sole African American policeman visited Kioni not long after that to suggest that he could testify against the other boys and go free or he could go to jail alone. He agreed to testify. Before the trial came up, Pearlie Mae sent him to California. He never believed that she forgave him.

"Why, why do the women I love always leave me?" he was busily imploring when he noticed that a portal seemed to be opening above him. Light came through like a sunbeam through clouds, and in the middle of the light was the face and torso of the Blessed Virgin. Pentecostalism is not a branch of Christianity in which visions of Mary figure prominently, or at all in fact. But Kioni knew who she was. Anybody would.

She was looking at him tenderly. "I've never left you," she said with exactly the tone he yearned to hear from a woman. He'd never realized that the Queen of Heaven was tracking him, but it would have been rude to say that.

She smiled again and said, "Do you remember when you were in the hospital and a woman came during the night? She was dressed in white like the nurses. She took you out of bed and held you in her arms. She sat in a rocking chair and rocked you."

It was a memory that Kioni had forgotten until that moment. And then, yes, he did remember.

"That was me," the apparition said. "I was always there with you."

Kioni then asked her the question that he had never been able to ask his mother, who had died.

"Why did my mother leave me?"

"Your mother loved you. She always loved you, and she loves you still. She's here with me now, and she wants me to tell you that she loves you."

For Kioni, a middle-aged man with five children and a couple of grandchildren, those words fell like cool water on a fresh burn.

"Look into my heart," the Holy Mother said. When he did, the front of her garment opened and he could see her heart, plump and red, just as it is in Sacred Heart paintings. The heart was suffused with a dazzling white light that Kioni looked into. It filled his vision and wrapped around him until he was inside it and finally part of it.

And he felt wonderful—healed and happy and at peace.

I don't know if Mother Mary comes in the night to many people who are alone and in sorrow. I'm willing to bet that if she does, most of them wouldn't tell it. She's never come to me.

But something has. Once.

I was lying in bed with my dog, Pogo, next to me. My husband was working in his study down the hall. I was thinking about how there isn't any God. I wasn't in a particular dither over it. On this night, believing in God seemed preposterous, and so I was turning the ridiculousness of it over in my mind when something came into the room. I couldn't see anything, but I could feel it. It was a presence standing to the left side of my bed about where my shin was. The presence was about my height, maybe a little taller, and as wide as an average person, not so big as to be scary. In my mind I heard the words, *If there's no God, what am I? What is it that just came into this room?*

I didn't answer. Something was there, and I didn't want to disrespect whatever it was, but I couldn't bring myself to answer, so I looked at the spot and said, "Ummph."

About a year later I told a friend about the visitation. She asked, "What was it?"

Her question caught me off guard. It seemed obvious and strange to have to say it. But she had me cornered, so I did.

"It was Jesus," I said. The name felt funny in my mouth, so I emphasized the first syllable the way evangelical preachers do.

JEE-sus. I had considered saying, "God," but that was too much of a reach.

My friend laughed and asked, "So what did you do?"

"I went to sleep."

That's what almost anybody would do, I believe. There's a scientific name for what happened to Kioni and me. It's called a hypnopompic vision, which means a vision that occurs between waking and sleep. Such visions aren't anything real, just a little glip in imagination. Ask the scientists, they'll tell you. They'll advise you to forget about it, just what they would have said to Florence Nightingale, who went to the Crimea and revolutionized nursing after she heard the voice of God calling her to take up his work. They'd have told Walt Whitman to forget about whatever numinous experience it was that changed him from an unheralded reporter to a man so inspired that he became one of America's best-loved poets. They'd have told René Descartes to stop his ears when the Spirit of Truth told him that mathematics is the key to unlocking the secrets of nature. They'd have advised Saul of Tarsus to keep right on pitching Christians to the lions. They'd have told Joan of Arc that she was nuts to think a girl could lead France's armies to victory. They'd have counseled Edison to ditch the idea that his hard work was supported by a universe that could be counted on to feed him one solution after another.

And Kioni, if he'd been listening to the scientists or almost anybody else, would have gone right on to sleep, as I did. Eventually he did go to sleep, but first he let the experience change him. His family noticed in the next few weeks and months that he was gentler. For the first time in their marriage Marilyn didn't feel she had to prove that she wouldn't leave him as his mother had left him. He apologized to his children for times he had lost his temper or failed to come through when they needed him.

lot of people who turn to magic are helpless people, desperate people, and outcasts. Maybe all of us fall into those groups at one time or another. But never mind.

"You have to surrender before you can believe any of this," one of the magical people told me. To my ears that was an echo of evangelical conversion pitches. "You have to surrender your life to Jesus," the evangelicals say. "You have to let go and let God."

One of the hangovers of having been in church so much when I was young is that churchy phrases and Bible verses still float around in my mind, which means that I'm constantly making holy connections out of the strangest things. It's something Kioni and I have in common, but it's worse with him—or better, depending on your perspective—because he knows more of the Bible than I do. Verses come to him more, and he's bolder with his interpretations. If I were talking to him right now, he'd be thinking exactly what I'm thinking: "Raise a child up in the way he should go and when he is old he will not depart from it." It's from Proverbs.

When I was told that to enter magical thinking you have to surrender, I thought that meant that you have to be humble, that you have to let go of ego and rationality. The woman who talked about surrender did mean letting go of the excuses that rationality uses to keep us down, but she didn't mean humble. "It's not a word I use," she said.

In fact, magical people are anything but humble. They don't dwell on sin or fret about their shortcomings. They just decide what it is they want, and they go after it. They think the universe conspires with them. Some, like Kioni, who wears a silver ring with the name Jesus carved in it and says he loves the Christian savior with all his heart, believe they're helping love to rule. Others have baser desires, but I never met anyone in the magical community who felt powerless or hopeless. Some were in quite a fix, and they weren't dealing with it in the way I thought they ought to, but they weren't feeling overly sorry for themselves. No matter what had happened to them, they were sustained by hope.

How did they take so little and turn it into so much? That's a task all of us face at one time or another, and we aren't always up to it. They were deranged, maybe. But maybe that's what it takes to have hope in this world. Were their lives more hopeful than mine?

No doubt.

Take Kioni, for instance. He did a spell to bring a storyteller to his house. And two years later, there I was. That proved his magic to him. The rest of us would be shaking our heads saying, "Wasn't that just the strangest coincidence?" But not Kioni—to him I was a gift from God, a proof of magic and evidence that he wasn't utterly helpless against the princes and principalities of this world.

"Welcome," he had said, his arms wide open, welcoming me and all the good magic he believed I was bringing.

10.

Hoodoo? We Do, in the Graveyard

My magical explorations were taking me into some deep waters, deeper than I'd known existed. I was having to ponder things that I'd never thought much about before, which wasn't altogether comfortable. So when Kioni mentioned that Zora Neale Hurston's grave was in Fort Pierce only seventy miles away in a little segregated cemetery called the Garden of Heavenly Rest, all I heard were the immortal words of the *Animal House* frat boys: *Road trip!!!!*

I said, "Let's go."

Zora was a Barnard-trained anthropologist and novelist who studied African American magical culture during the 1930s. She is also one of hoodoo's biggest names. Unlike other anthropologists of her time, she didn't merely study conjurers, she became one, according to her books. White folks scoff at hoodoo and say it's superstition, but "white folks are very stupid about some things. They can think mightily but cannot feel," she observed. I wasn't born when Zora wrote those words, but she could have been describing me. Anytime I start to feel, I try to stop and think. It's so much safer.

Graveyard work is important in hoodoo. Calling on a spirit while near a grave seems to increase the chances that it will respond. Cemeteries are also used for their symbolism. Anyone who wants to leave a bad habit behind can bury it in the graveyard. Someone who wants to control an enemy might put a baby doll or a mojo hand in a miniature coffin and bury it at the right hand of a grave.

The most common kind of graveyard magic involves taking dirt from graves. The kind of grave the dirt comes from is crucial. Cat said the most common dirt taken from graves is from grandparents or other nurturing relatives because people mostly want the spirits to protect and guide them. But the grave of a murderer or an unrepentant sinner might also be sought for goofer dust, which is an Americanization of the Congo word *kufwa*, which means "to kill." In some spells the method of dying is specified and reinforced by the spell. For instance, an enemy will be led to his death if his shoes are sprinkled with graveyard dust; then a trail of dust is laid from his home and a pinch of dust is laid at every crossroads to the nearest graveyard. An enemy will waste away if his hair and a bit of sulfur powder are mixed with the dirt of someone who "died bad." The mixture is put in a bottle with nine pins, nine needles, and nine nails— three and nine are important numbers in hoodoo—and the bottle is then buried under the enemy's threshold or pathway as the moon is waning. Goofer dust is such bad stuff that after handling it, hoodoo workers often cleanse themselves with a ceremony and special baths.

A soldier's grave might be good for a protection spell but could also be good for a killing spell because a soldier would be familiar with killing and accustomed to following orders. If the conjurer is dealing with a particularly evil spirit, he might be careful about how he comes home so that the spirit charged with killing doesn't follow. One worker recommends crossing water on the way back since spirits may not be able to cross water unless invited. To be doubly sure that spirit doesn't follow, Cat suggests standing in the middle of a bridge while reciting the Lord's Prayer.

Kioni and I didn't have a specific need in mind or anything to bury, but we would definitely take home some dirt from Zora's grave. It could be used for all sorts of work: love spells, court work, breakup efforts. Kioni doesn't do death spells. He won't even do breakup spells unless he's convinced that the cause is justified. Any dirt we took from Zora's grave would most likely be used for positive purposes, which is appropriate because Zora was a positive woman. Her most famous novel, *Their Eyes Were Watching God*, is about a woman who risks all for love. Zora herself had a good number of love affairs. So her dirt might well be used for love spells. For a love spell, dirt is sometimes mixed with Vandal root and then sprinkled on the desired one while the worker asks the spirit to help.

For me, Zora's dirt might be especially potent since she wrote some of the most wonderful work ever done on African American culture. Maybe her spirit would help me write well. Zora's dirt might also have power simply because of her fame. Being a hoodoo celebrity could make it even more potent. Kioni and I wouldn't mind being famous.

Hoodoo doesn't have many nationally known celebrities. Marie Laveau in New Orleans is the best-known hoodoo queen. Laveau, a hairdresser and voodoo priestess, was one of New Orleans' most powerful women in the 1800s. Her grave is still a shrine to thousands of tourists each year. They leave offerings and scratch crosses on the tomb where she is said to be buried. Since New Orleans graves are raised and made of stone, the crumbled stone from the crosses might be used in rootwork instead of dirt.

Kioni and I both hoped we would feel Zora's spirit when we stood over her grave. She might talk to us, or she might come rising up and appear to us. To Kioni anyway. I wouldn't recognize spirit if it punched me. I'd be too busy thinking, *This isn't happening. This isn't happening.*

Believers in spirits generally divide into those who think the dead are uncanny and those who think the dead are friendly, according to Cat. The uncanny camp, which does have its magical adherents, is usually from the Christian, Muslim, or Jewish tradition. To them death could be said to be a kind of defilement. Great saints and holy folk are exempted from the rule and might be called upon. But your run-of-the-mill dead person is to be avoided. Trying to enlist spirit might be considered trifling with demons. Hoodoo follows African tradition in looking kindly on spirits and believing that they look for ways to help the living.

Before leaving Kioni's house, I checked that I had a dime to leave at the grave. Taking dirt without paying would be a bad mistake. We could pay for the dirt with liquor or food or anything we knew the spirit especially liked, but money is always good. Zora had little money during her lifetime. She was never able to make a living off her writing and liked telling the story of the time she was so broke that she took money from a panhandler, saying, "I need it more than you do." Later in her life, when one of her stories was published in the *Saturday Evening Post*, she was working as a maid for a Florida matron, who read the story and was startled to see that the author was her maid. Zora died penniless. Her burial expenses were covered by friends' donations.

Our first mistake was to leave home without getting a tool for digging. "No problem. I'll use my fingers," Kioni said. We also didn't have a container for the dirt.

"We can use my iced tea cup from lunch," I said. It had a lid and was extra large. So we were set.

When we drove into Fort Pierce, Kioni consulted his Internet directions; we seemed to be on the right route. Then we hit a dead end. We turned the other way, and after a mile or so we were lost. We were in an African American neighborhood, which was a good sign that we might be close, but we had forgotten the name of the cemetery, which might be a problem.

Kioni cautioned me about asking just anyone for directions. Ask the wrong kind of person and we'd be likely to get into trouble. We might be directed to a crack house where the helpful citizen's friends were waiting to rob us, he said. We turned down a side street and saw some street workers. They looked safe enough. I stopped next to a tall white man with a big grin. After listening to my question, he shrugged in a bewildered way and replied in Eastern European–accented English that he was not from around there. Across the street we saw an older black man in his yard. I pulled into the driveway next to a black sports car, rolled down my window, and called out to him.

"Hi. We're looking for a graveyard that's around here. Zora Neale Hurston's supposed to be buried in it. Ever heard of it?"

The man looked at me as if I was speaking a language he didn't know. He was shaking his head as he neared the car. Kioni leaned up so the man could get a good look at him and said, "How you doing?"

Then he waited for the man to answer. I could tell that I had violated some law of African American pacing. Kioni was in no hurry. He told the man who he was, who I was, where we were from. He didn't tell him what we were doing, thank goodness, but he did talk about how Zora was a famous writer. He grinned at the old guy. The old guy grinned at him, and then he grinned at me. He looked at Kioni a couple of times, and then he looked at me a couple of times.

Then he nodded and started to talk. "Oh yeah. Oh yeah, I know what you're looking for," he began, pointing first one way and then the other. He was directing us back the way we had come. We were getting more and more confused until a younger man in a utility company uniform got out of the black car and told us where to go. We'd been mistaken about the dead end. We needed to go around a barrier in the road and then go left.

As we retraced our route, Kioni told me, "If you'd been by yourself, they would have never told you where it was." Zora had a name for the overeager friendliness and fuzzy conversation that black people used to misdirect white America.

"The Negro, in spite of his open-faced laughter, his seeming acquiescence, is particularly evasive," she wrote.

> You see, we are a polite people and we do not say to our questioner, "Get out of here!" We smile and tell him or her something that satisfies the white person because, knowing so little about us, he doesn't know what he is missing. The Indian resists curiosity by a stony silence. The Negro offers a feather-bed resistance. That is, we let the probe enter, but it never comes out. It gets smothered under a lot of laughter and pleasantries.

Added to featherbed resistance, there's another problem when white people try to find out about hoodoo. A lot of magical thought is secret, or used to be. When Cat went into conjure shops hoping to talk about hoodoo, she always looked for a particular picture, as a sign that the proprietor might be willing to talk with a white person. It had a yellow background and showed three heads: Martin Luther King, John F. Kennedy, and Robert Kennedy. If she saw that picture, she was usually able to count on a good reception. Cat now has one like it in her own shop.

Being a Jew also helped, she told me. A lot of black people think of Jews as being allied with them, she said, especially in the days before some black Muslims began talking against Jews. In a way, her research and her hoodoo shop were the continuation of a long tradition. When Jewish pharmacists came to the United States in the 1800s, they were often unable to find jobs in white, Christian-dominated parts of town. Many of them opened shops in the black parts of town, and because their clients asked for roots, herbs, and oils used in African American folk medicine, they began to stock them. When the Great Migration north began, some of the pharmacists began mail-order businesses. One built a thriving company, and some of the traditional designs Cat adapts for her products come from his labels.

She advises white people to go out into black neighborhoods, make some friends, be respectful, and listen. "If I can teach my white students *one* thing—just one thing, please, Jesus—it is to go over to the black side of town and make friends and *listen*. All right? You hear me? Make some friends and *learn* something." White people are likely to run into cultural rules they don't know about, but if they watch what's going on, they can figure out what's acceptable and what's not, she said.

As an example, she tells the story of meeting blues great Lightning Hopkins. She was still a teenager. He was playing at a coffeehouse where she worked, and she approached him at the same time that a big-paper journalist did. Lightning had a flask. He took a swig and said to the journalist, who was white, "Will you drink after me?" The journalist took the flask, but before he drank he wiped the lip of the bottle.

"A look of pure hatred passed across Lightning Hopkins's face," Cat said. "I saw it." Lightning took another drink and said to Cat, "Will you drink after me?" She'd never had alcohol, but when he passed it to her she took the bottle. "It was horrible." But she managed a swallow and pretended to drink more.

She saw Hopkins years later backstage at a folk festival. He said, "There's my little girl who drinks after me," and he hugged her.

T he Garden of Heavenly Rest cemetery where Zora is buried sits past a little church at the end of a dead-end street. All the literature notes that it is segregated. Whether that means the black people are buried on one side and the white people on the other, or that there are only black people, I don't know. We didn't see a sign with the cemetery's name or a line showing which ground has black bodies and which has white. There is not much to this graveyard, just a couple of acres.

The cemetery has a dirt road along the side. I pulled in, and we saw a historical marker a little less than midway down and about halfway over. It's a big metal sign with photos and plenty of text, impossible to miss. That had to be it.

In 1973, when the writer Alice Walker decided to find Zora's resting place, the grave was unmarked and the cemetery was covered in weeds waist high. By posing as Zora's niece, Walker was able to get vague directions about the grave being in the center of a circle in the Garden of Heavenly Rest and went there guided by a local woman named Rosalee, who didn't know any more than she did.

Finding the grave seemed so hopeless that Walker began to appeal to the spirit herself. Here's what she wrote in a story called "Looking for Zora":

> "Zora!" I yell, as loud as I can (causing Rosalee to jump). "Are you out here?"
>
> "If she is, I sho hope she don't answer you. If she do, I'm gone."
>
> "Zora!" I call again. "I'm here. Are you?"
>
> "If she is," grumbles Rosalee, "I hope she'll keep it to herself."
>
> "Zora!" Then I start fussing with her. "I hope you don't think I'm going to stand out here all day, with these snakes watching me and these ants having a field day. In fact, I'm going to call you just one or two more times."
>
> On a clump of dried grass, near a small bushy tree, my eye falls on one of the largest bugs I have ever seen. It is on its back, and is as large as three of my fingers. I walk toward it, and yell "Zo-ra!" and my foot sinks into a hole. I look down. I am standing in a sunken rectangle that is about six feet long and about three or four feet wide. I look up to see where the two gates are.
>
> "Well," I say, "this is the center, or approximately anyhow. It's also the only sunken spot we've found. Doesn't this look like a grave to you?"
>
> "For the sake of not going no farther through these bushes," Rosalee growls, "yes, it do."

When Kioni and I arrived, a cold wind was blowing over the open fields. I put on a coat. Kioni had on a sweatshirt, but he shivered a bit as he pulled his forearm cane out of the backseat. We hiked over the ground until we were in front of the sign. It had a few photos of Zora.

Next to it was the headstone Alice Walker bought. It read, ZORA NEALE HURSTON, A GENIUS OF THE SOUTH, 1901–1960, NOVELIST, FOLKLORIST, ANTHROPOLOGIST. "The phrase "a genius of the South" comes from a Jean Toomer poem. I don't know how they chose Zora's birth date, because through her life she gave many, always ones that made her seem younger than she was. Scholars had some trouble tracking the right date down, but they finally did it.

"Hurston was born on January 15, 1891, making her between seven and nineteen years older than she claimed. Neither was she actually born in Eatonville, as she claimed," according to one of them. She did grow up in Eatonville, which was a totally African American town.

A concrete cover was laid over the plot. On it were a doll and a couple of dead flowers. We wouldn't be getting dirt from the top of this grave. Kioni knelt at the side of the concrete.

"Zora, we've come from miles away to visit you and to honor you. We've come to ask your permission to take some dirt from your grave."

There was a long silence. Kioni's head was lowered and his eyes were closed.

"You'd be surprised how many people are interested in having it," he said in a low voice, as though talking to himself, but I knew from the way he said it that he was talking to her spirit. Whether she was talking back, I didn't yet know. "Lots and lots of people want it. People come from all around to honor you.

"Oh, thousands of them," he said, as though someone had asked how many. "A hundred thousand are expected to come to Eatonville this year." Every year a Zora Neale Hurston festival is held there to honor her.

Kioni crouched with his head lowered for a few seconds. Then he laid his hand on the concrete covering. Later he told me that when he touched the grave, he felt virtue flowing into him. The idea of virtue is biblical and magical. Knowing Kioni, I knew that his primary reference was to the story of the woman who was suffering from an issue of blood. She was behind Jesus in the crowd, but she believed that if she so much as touched his garment, she would be healed. So she did. Jesus felt the virtue flow out of him. He turned and asked who had touched him. Seeing the woman, he said, "Your faith has made you whole."

The virtue that resided in Jesus was so real that he could feel it leaving him, Kioni said, but Christ isn't the only person who has such virtue. Everyone has Christ-consciousness virtue in them, Kioni believes, and so does every thing. The natural world is alive with special and specific powers that God has deposited and wants humans to use.

In the case of Zora's grave, Kioni felt the virtue flowing into him from her spirit—not out of him. That convinced him that it was all right for him to take the dirt.

"Okay," Kioni said, now talking to me. "Her feet would be facing east. Her head in the west. So this would be her right side."

Kioni stuck his finger under the grass, peeled it back and rooted around until he had made a little hole. He dropped the dime in before taking any dirt. That's good hoodoo practice. Making the spirit wait for hers might not be a good idea.

"We appreciate this dirt so much that we want to pay you for it," he said. "Lots of people are interested in this dirt. Yes. Lots of them will be excited. We appreciate you letting us take it. We'll take good care of it."

The soil crumbled easily against his fingers so that Kioni quickly filled the large-sized paper cup with dirt.

"Where's the dime?" he said, looking into the hole. "Oh no, I think I've scooped up the dime. It's in the cup." He stirred the dirt around with his finger, but no dime appeared. He poured some dirt into his palm. No dime. Taking the dirt and the dime might be a real bad idea, like trying to fool the spirit. Bad mojo.

"Do you have another one?" he asked, still on his knees.

"I'll get my purse." Clutching my coat against me, I ran across the field. Knowing Kioni must be cold, I didn't want to take longer than I had to. Some teenagers on the corner stood next to a car with its stereo turned up so loud the earth was vibrating. They didn't seem to be paying any attention to us. I grabbed my purse and ran back as I pulled out my wallet. It's red, which Kioni had noted approvingly. Red is a good color for drawing money. I found a dime and handed it to Kioni.

"Good. We'll just put this in there. We wouldn't want to not pay."

Kioni picked up the flowers and doll and put them neatly near the headstone. He turned toward the car and using his crutch on the uneven ground started back to the car at a pretty good pace. I started after him, but before I caught up he swung around and began to come back, muttering, "Yes. Yes. I see. That's right."

He stood as though listening for a moment. Then he looked at me. "This is my path," he said, meaning hoodoo. "I can't get away from it. This is what's right for me. Feeling her here is letting me know that." He'd been moving away from hoodoo toward doing nothing but prosperity spells. Hoodoo is difficult and time-consuming, which he didn't mind, but it also seemed to attract a lot of crazy clients. They took too much out of him, and so he'd been downplaying that type of magic. Now he would stop downplaying it and start practicing it again.

I noticed that the teenage boys were gone, and at the same time I saw big black birds flying in circles high in the sky. "Buzzards," I said. "Buzzards. Can you believe that? That's good, right?"

"I believe those are falcons," Kioni said gently so as not to embarrass me. "There are a lot of them in this area." Two more were at the other edge of the sky.

"That's four," he said. "Seeing them *is* a good sign."

11.

Be Careful What You Say about Zora

Kioni and I drove out of Fort Pierce feeling good. We had enough dirt to share with others in the hoodoo class, and he was certain that he had felt Zora Neale Hurston's presence.

"I could hear her voice," he said. "It sounded like Diana Kroll's, whiskey-husky and sexy. The kind of voice a man likes to hear."

We stopped at a gas station near the freeway. Kioni mentioned that I might want some gas, but thinking only of a restroom break, I didn't take the hint. As Kioni was buying our snacks and drinks, we swiveled a CD rack at the front of the store. It had several old rhythm and blues recordings. "Look at this," he said, grinning. "Oh, here's another one." The CDs were a good sign. Kioni bought two.

As we drove toward Kioni's house in Port St. John, he gave a little shiver. "We used to call these Holy Ghost-a-sisms because they meant that we were being filled with the Holy Ghost," he said. "But that's Zora. She's here with me."

As I drove we talked of hoodoo work. Kioni told me that 99 percent of his clients were female, but two he was working with at that time were gay men. A disproportionate number of gay men are involved in the magical arts.

"Why is that?" I ask. "Why are they coming to you?"

"They're desperate," he said. They're moving toward middle age, he explained, and want what everyone wants, which is someone who will love them faithfully and well. They're often hindered by falling in love with men who aren't gay. Sometimes they want hoodoo to help them turn disinterest into passion. One such client had befriended a straight neighbor in hopes of something more. The straight guy said he wasn't interested and would never be, but he remained friendly. Kioni's client felt he was giving mixed signals. He needed a nudge. Kioni told his client to make up a special powder. At night he was to go to the straight guy's house and sprinkle it from his front door all the way to the client's own bed.

So he did, and the next morning the straight guy came over before the gay guy was even out of bed. As soon as the door opened he gave Kioni's client a hug and turned toward him for a mouth-to-mouth kiss. Startled, the client turned his head.

"He had morning breath," Kioni said, "and he didn't want to kiss him that way." To the client's delight, the neighbor groped him, squeezed him in another hug, and left.

So it worked, Kioni said, and then abruptly, he stopped talking. I glanced over. His brow was wrinkled.

"Oh," he said. "She just rebuked me. That was Zora."

"She did? What did she say?" I asked.

"Why? I don't know why?" he was talking to someone other than me. "Uh-huh. Uh-huh. I do. I understand.

"She just said, 'You shouldn't have done that. It was against his will.'"

That was interesting coming from Zora, who had once boiled a cat alive to get a black cat bone. A black cat bone obtained in that way is supposed to confer invisibility on its owner. Being dead must have softened her nature. That seems to happen. I'd heard of many messages from the dead in my research, and the character of their discourse invariably seemed to have improved since passing over. Stingy, homophobic, mean people come back all apologies. I never heard one of them say, "I was a dirty SOB, and I'm glad of it." Maybe only good people and repenters get an encore.

Kioni had done all the things that he was supposed to do to make sure his work for the gay guy was justified—used his intuition, worked the Tarot cards, done it in the name of Jesus while saying, "Let it come to pass if it be justified." He would not use magic to turn someone gay, but if the straight guy was already veering in that direction, the magic would work with the inclination, he said.

I didn't know whether it was Zora who disagreed with what Kioni had done or some part of himself that doubted he was doing right, but it told me that Kioni wasn't as susceptible to some of the pitfalls of magic as other magicians have been. His conscience, his higher self, his Holy Guardian Angel, his particle of God, call it what you will, was working. In his new life it was having to work hard, maybe harder, than it ever had before.

For a former Pentecostal preacher to be engaging the aid of Jesus to help gay men find lovers was an amazing thing in itself, an over-the-top example of what's happening to many of us in less dramatic fashion. The old ways, which had kept his morality cryogenically preserved for much of his life, had failed him. Forced to enter a world filled with alarming and bewildering new ideas, he had resisted, been anguished, and then groped for new truths. He began to think in ways that he never dreamed he would, and as he did the old guidelines for what was right and wrong fell away. His old friends and relatives disapproved. So he made new friends. He looked to spirits, divination cards, his own intuition, and his own reason for direction in how he ought to behave. He still read the Bible, but now he read it differently. He prayed to Jesus, but now the savior replied differently, using new messengers. Sometimes Kioni stumbled on this strange new path, but that was nothing new. He'd always stumbled. The point was to get back up. And he always did. Within a year after Zora's message, Kioni stopped doing any kind of love spell work at all. He wouldn't make anyone fall in love, and he wouldn't cause lovers to break up. He never criticized those who continued to do it; he just stopped doing it himself.

About ten miles out from Cocoa, which is near Kioni's home in Port St. John, the car's fuel light came on. There wasn't an exit in sight.

"I can't believe this," I said. "We're going to run out of gas. You said get gas, but I didn't. What's wrong with me? I haven't run out of gas in twenty years."

I was waiting to hear the engine sputter when finally an exit came in sight and right beyond it a gas station. As we coasted in Kioni said, "It was all right. I knew we'd be fine. I checked with the spirits, and they said we had enough to get here."

He could have shared the news earlier, but I was too shamefaced about my own behavior to protest. I got out to pump gas. Would I have believed him if he'd quoted his spirits? No. But at least he would have been on record with his prediction. Would that have convinced me? No. I finished pumping the gas, pulled the nozzle out, and spilled gasoline all over my shoes.

Back in the car with a haze of gas fumes rising from my soggy shoes, I asked again, "What is wrong with me? I've never done that in my life." I couldn't feel the spirits. I couldn't hear them. But something had me discombobulated.

"I hope I'm fit to drive us home," I said. "Think we'll make it?"

"It'll be all right," Kioni said. I hoped he was talking for the spirits, but I didn't ask. If he had some mojo working, I'd just let it work.

When we returned to his house, Kioni pulled out a plastic container like people use for leftovers and filled it with dirt. That evening he wrote to members of Cat's class about our day at the grave and said that anyone in the class who wanted some dirt should send him $3 for postage.

"I wouldn't charge for her dirt," he said.

Once the requests came in, he asked Zora who ought to get it and who shouldn't. According to those who got the dirt, she accomplished great things and seems to be doing so still.

I am careful what I say about Zora because her spirit appears to be much at work. She's already chastised me once for being too flip. I'd mentioned to some people that there's dispute about whether all that Zora wrote was truly as she said it was. There's considerable evidence it wasn't. She even wrote somewhat cryptically about the subject: "I am supposed to have some private business to myself. What I do know, I have no intention of putting but so much in the public ears," she wrote in her autobiography, *Dust Tracks on a Road*. And in another place she wrote, "The white man is always trying to nose into somebody else's business. All right, I'll set something outside the door of my mind for him to play with and handle. He can read my writing but he sho' can't read my mind."

Nevertheless, Zora the spirit didn't care for me questioning her veracity. This message was relayed to me by the thirty-four-year-old white rootworker named Adele, who has some of Zora's dirt displayed in tiny perfume bottles on an altar in her spare bedroom. The altar also has a photo of Zora smoking a cigarette and looking sassy.

Zora wanted her dirt in those perfume bottles and nowhere else would do, according to Adele, who lives with two dogs, six cats, and a pistol grip shotgun in a log house on thirty-four acres at the top of a North Carolina mountain. Her land is protected by NO HUNTING signs and dollies. Dollies would be called voodoo dolls by those who don't know the difference. Most people think dollies are used only for bad work. In hoodoo they aren't. On Adele's land they're used for protection. Of course, protection can mean that bad things befall those who transgress, another case of the line between good and bad smudging in the magical world.

Adele, who refers to herself as "just a little country rootworker," had the dolls out not because she objects to hunting. Hunting is fine with her. "But I hate a sneak," she said. When she suspected a neighbor was tearing down her NO HUNTING signs, she smeared ground-up poison ivy on them. A few more disappeared, and that was all. The dollies are to protect against poachers. One poacher left his truck at the edge of the forest and returned to find it stolen. Another shot a deer that Adele was certain had wasting disease.

"I don't know what he saw when he shot that deer," she said, implying that some magical image had interceded so that the poacher would do himself harm by eating bad meat.

It took Adele hours to force grains of Zora's grave dirt down the tiny necks of the perfume bottles, but the rootworker was so determined to please the spirit that she spent an afternoon doing it. Adele has become quite fond of Zora since her dirt went on the altar and her spirit took over the house. I'm not sure exactly why, since as far as I can tell Zora has been nothing but bossy. She demanded that the living room furniture be rearranged immediately, and when Adele's mother came to visit, Zora refused to allow her to share the spare bedroom, forcing Adele to put her mother in another room.

Realizing that even as a spirit Zora's temper remains quite fiery, I want to be clear that I am not insulting her by pointing out that she bent the facts considerably when it suited her. Lots of accomplished people have done the same. And, as Zora pointed out to Adele, who relayed the message to me, I wouldn't be able to do nearly as well as Zora did if I'd been born a black female in Florida in the late 1800s who was soon motherless, deprived of education, and tossed from one relative to another. I can't dispute that even though I am alive and she's dead, which you might think would give me an edge. It would, of course, if we were not dealing in the magical world where spirits are quite accustomed to pushing live folk around.

*M*agical people who embroider their beginnings don't seem to be rare. It was once common to hear Wiccans claim that they were from covens that handed witchcraft down from generation to generation, back to the burning times, but as scholars began to debunk that possibility other witches began to snigger, and those stories have since died back.

I heard so many stories of Wiccans who had stood up to the priests and nuns as children that I began to secretly sympathize with the adults, beleaguered witless by so many mouthy infants. These stories usually involved publicly matching theories with their teachers and besting them with superior logic or moral sense. They had something in common with the story about the boy Jesus awing the elders in the temple, except the magical people are usually insulting the authorities. Often the story ended with the nuns and priests never calling on these cheeky children again or banishing them from class. Such tales were repeated so often that I could have finished them myself, which caused me to wonder. Were these stories true tales or fables that represented what their spirits wanted to do? Either way, they were classic tales of the rebellion against authority that has been so important in magical lore.

In Zora Neale Hurston's autobiography, she tells a wonderful story about her beginnings. When she was being born, all the neighbors and the midwife were at hog killings. Her mother delivered the baby without help and was lying in bed, too weak to cut the cord, when a white man came visiting with fresh meat and vegetables. He cut the cord, wrapped the baby, and had a fire going by the time the midwife arrived. Zora goes on to tell of him taking her fishing later in her childhood, then giving her a nickname and advice about how to live with honor and courage. One piece of advice was not to be a "nigger," a term that, she writes, was not meant to indicate race but rather an inferior way of being.

It's a perfect mythical birth that foreshadows the importance of white patrons in her later life. The story is too perfect, some have said. Zora almost admits as much in the first line of the book chapter. "This is all hear-say. Maybe, some of the details of my birth as told me might be a little inaccurate, but it is pretty well established that I really did get born."

In journalism such fanciful tales would be called fabrications, and any journalist would then disregard everything else said by that person. True and untrue is one of my profession's most sacred distinctions. We might buy all sorts of excuses about all sorts of things. We might confess to all sorts of errors and mistakes, but making up stories, whether you're a source or a reporter, is a bad, bad thing.

In the world of the spirit, however, it may be different. Once again, the magical people were muddying the line between good and bad. James Hillman defends fanciful autobiographies as being more true than the mere facts, and in his book *The Soul's Code* he cites a number of famous people who concocted biographies that matched their sense of true self better than what had actually happened. Hillman refers to this true self as the daimon, an idea he borrowed from Plato's Myth of Er. This daimon is a calling, a soul companion, a doppelganger, or, in Hillman's words, an acorn of the person we are meant to be.

People with a strong sense of their daimon might invent fables that say, "I am not your fact. I will not let what is strange in me, about me, my mystery, be put in a world of fact. I must invent a world that presents a truer illusion of who I am than the social, environmental 'realities.' Besides, I do not lie or invent: Confabulations occur spontaneously. I cannot be accused of lying, for the stories that come out of me about myself are not quite me speaking." Hillman gives a number of famous examples.

Henry Ford liked to tell people that he had taken his first watch apart at seven and would sneak out of the house at night, steal the neighbors' watches, bring them home, and repair them. When he re-created his family's farm home, he put a little watchmaker's bench and tools in his bedroom. His sister Margaret didn't remember him slipping out of the house at night and said there had been no bench.

Leonard Bernstein claimed that his childhood was one of complete poverty and that the Boston Latin School he attended from seventh to twelfth grade had no music program. In fact, his family owned two houses, with maids and at times a chauffeur-butler, and he was in the school orchestra, sang in the glee club, and was a piano soloist.

Conductor Leopold Stokowski spoke with a Polish accent although he and both his parents were born in England. Only his paternal grandfather was Polish-born. He loved to tell the story of getting his first violin at the age of seven from his grandfather. But his grandfather died three years before he was born, and according to his brother and his biographer, no one ever saw him play a violin.

All three men were constructing what Philip Roth calls a counterlife, a fantasy biography. Hillman says that reading a life backward gives us a clue as to why. They told these stories once they had fulfilled the destiny that their daimon ordained for them. Anyone who does that may feel that they were always "themselves" even in childhood and that their stories should reflect that.

"Something in us doesn't want to lay out the facts for fear that they will be taken to be the truth and the only truth," Hillman writes. Everyone reads his life backward to one degree or another as maturity casts new light on personal history. Mark Twain said that the older he got, the more he remembered things that never happened.

Kioni continued to feel Zora's spirit quite strongly after our trip. She took up residence in his house and went pretty much everywhere with him. Once he hit a patch of dark depression during which he could hardly get himself out of bed. He felt shooting pains all over his body that he suspected came from pins being stuck in a poppet. His energy was so low that he couldn't do work for his customers. He went to the doctor, who gave him a good report, but his symptoms didn't go away. He felt as though he were dying. Candles he was lighting for his personal rootwork were burning dirty, full of soot. He was in despair when he heard Zora say that he ought to bathe with her grave dirt.

"Frankly, I was thinking that I was a little off my rocker; but Cat being a wise Sage, urged me to pay attention to the impression I was getting," he wrote in an e-mail.

"After several days of prayer and meditation, I was given two initiation rituals I was to perform with Zora's grave dirt. The first ritual was to be done under the waning moon. . . . Looking at the items Zora instructed me to assemble, I understood the first part of the ritual was to remove some quasi rootwork/voodoo being directed at me. The first part consisted of a strong herb root bath. After stepping from the bath Zora instructed me to rub myself down with her grave dirt! There I stood naked as the day I was born, wet and covered with dirt from my head to the soles of my feet. By the way, the dirt I used had been consecrated on my altar for several weeks and sprinkled with Florida Water—another of Zora's directives.

"After saving some of the previous bath water, I drained our oversize garden tub and filled it again. This time, I placed several scoops of Zora's grave dirt in a stocking and hung it below the faucet. The floral and citrus scent of the Florida Water wafted through the bathroom, transporting me to another time and place. I began to hear drums beating far off in the distance. Caked with Zora's grave dirt, I stepped into the bath again. The Holy Ghost fell on me and I began to speak in tongues as I alternately quoted Scripture and summoned Zora's presence, essence and power. Then I felt a sensation like knives being pulled out of my body. I could hear popping sounds similar to when one cracks their knuckles or pops their bones as we say here in the South.

"Sitting in the warm water, a dream from many years ago flooded to the surface of my mind. In the dream, I was crossing a wide river at the mouth of a beautiful waterfall; however I was not alone. I could see dozens of Africans helping each other cross the raging river by forming a human chain across it. A strong, dark hand took mine guiding me to the next person in the chain until I was standing dripping wet on the opposite shore. We were running to escape capture by the white slave traders.

"Suddenly I shot up out of the tub like a Poseidon anti-ballistic missile. My arms were raised to the heavens and joys flooded from my soul like the water cascading down a waterfall. The drums were louder, or perhaps it was my heart—I don't know. But I do know I heard these words, which cause me to fill with emotion as I share my story. I heard 'Son of Zulu, welcome home. Son of Zulu, the heavens belong to you.'"

Afterward, Zora instructed him to write down what had happened and to send it to someone trustworthy. When he asked why, she said, "You need to make a record." He sent it to me. A few days later a member of our hoodoo class wrote the following: "As I learn hoodoo, I also learn more about the spiritual practices in South Africa through my aunt who lives with me (she's a Zulu and believes in the ancestors and teaches me things even though she's Anglican). I ask her questions all the time and she tries to answer them."

When Kioni read the word *Zulu*, which had never been mentioned in our class, he felt the hair rise on his body. This was the confirmation. This was the reason that Zora had asked him to write down his experience and to send it to someone. His experience wasn't just his imagination. It was real.

Kioni later wrote in a public e-mail, "So, the rootwork done by that certain nefarious person has been removed. I feel pity for this person because I have never done anything to harm anyone, anywhere at anytime in my life." Then, directing his attention toward the person who had tried to hex him, he wrote, "Jealousy of fellow rootworkers will be your downfall, mark my words. Also, from this day on be warned, I will fight fire with fire. Zora scolded me for not having done so sooner because I suffered needlessly.

"I issue a warning here to all who seek initiation into hoodoo. Make sure you are right in your heart before you begin. If you are committing adultery and fornicating like a dog, you will be in mortal danger. If you cheat people in business, you will be deceived in like manner. If you lie, spread rumors and stir up strife online or offline, expect that energy to come back to you triplefold. However, don't expect Zora or the Ancestors to greet you with open arms nor impart to you their knowledge and wisdom. The spirit world is not to be toyed with. *Hoodoo is not a harmless game!* You have been warned."

12.

Every Time You Hear a Bell, a Muggle Has Turned Magical

The magical and the muggle are separated by a river, wide and deep. I could see across, but I couldn't get across, and for a long time I couldn't figure out how other people did. There would come a moment in each interview when I'd squint, shake my head, and ask, "Why? Why do you believe this?" They would try to tell me, and gradually I came to understand some of it. I found four bridges that connect the worlds of the magical and the mundane.

The first bridge is the way of the child. Many people experience magic in childhood. Until the age of puberty, children see the world in what adults would consider quite magical ways. For instance, they recognize no clear dividing line between animate things and non-animate things, according to Piaget. They may agree outwardly with adults who say that animals can't understand and things cannot feel or act, but buried within them is their "true knowledge" of how the world works. Attuned to the spirits within stones and trees, clouds and wind, animals and toys, children believe that they can find answers to their deepest questions and access hidden forces of great magnitude in the world around them. Some outgrow such ideas; others never let them go. Perhaps the difference lies in the intensity of a child's interaction with magical stories, or maybe it comes from experience.

When Cat Yronwode and her friend did their rainmaking ceremony on that Berkeley rooftop, and the clouds came rolling in over the bay, and the terrible drought was ended, young Cat must have felt incredibly powerful. An older person might have quibbled about the link between Cat's act and the resulting rain, but she was a child who had read books about magic since she was able to read. Those books were as important to her as anything that happened outside them and maybe more real. Her rain dance confirmed the truth of that perception.

As she grew up Cat continued to read, and she remembered almost everything she read. Her husband calls her a polymath, which seems deserved. When she told me about the astrological reading that warned her something bad lay in the future for her first child, I did not doubt her experience. I wondered how she explained it.

"How can planets affect individual humans' lives?" I asked. I knew she would have thought about it and might have an answer that would go on for a long time.

She replied, "I don't know, hon. I don't know. All I know is that they do happen."

As for magic, she said, "You can influence the course things are going to take. I've seen it." In addition, there are connections between people and events that have no apparent cause, she said. "You dream about something, and it comes true. I'm just faced with these things happening. They happen. They keep happening, and they are directed."

For people such as Cat, accepting magic is merely a matter of acknowledging their own experience instead of accepting what others tell them. I suspect one reason more people are quietly opening up to magical and spiritual explanations is that the old verities are not holding. Doctors, scientists, preachers, journalists, and government officials have all told us that they know the truth without a doubt, but they don't, and when we discover that, we are like betrayed children, suspicious of received wisdom ever after. We have all become Doubting Thomases, the disciple who had to touch the nail holes in the risen Christ's palms. We want something we can feel ourselves. There's nothing irrational about the choice. In a world where almost every day brings some new information to contradict facts we would have bet our lives on just yesterday, we fall back on what we've seen with our own eyes, felt in our own hearts. Our new perceptions may be wrong, but at least they are firsthand.

A magician named Daniel told me he picked magic over science in the eleventh grade when talking to his favorite science teacher about a local woman who collected herbs and could heal cuts. He had known the woman for much of his life, and she had taught him about the healing power of plants.

"It was a very eerie thing to see," he said of her ability to heal cuts, "more so to actually feel if she was working on you. If you had a deep cut, she could hold her hands over it and chant a sort of prayer or bunch of syllables and the bleeding would stop, and it would sort of pull itself back together over the course of ten minutes or so. In another five to ten minutes, if she kept going, it would seal and heal to a light scar." The science teacher dismissed Daniel's story as impossible and declared it trickery.

"I realized that modern science doesn't actually study all things. Only those that fit within its current theories," he said. "So I decided to follow magic rather than science, even if it meant washing dishes for the rest of my life to make ends meet."

The second bridge to magic is the way of suffering. Those who take this path, adults usually, come to magic after being so knocked down that they need something miraculous to lift them up. If something does, and it could be just some little piece of grace, some moment or message of solace that they would have ignored before, they grab hold. Rationalists will say their new openness is a pitiful kind of coping, but magical people and religious people have long understood that pain and hardship can be ways to reach another consciousness, to forge a new kind of hope that isn't so reliant on whatever fortune may bring.

When they train followers, mages and gurus of all kinds may try to create breakthroughs by putting their students into situations that will thrust them outside everyday routine and thus wake them up. American Indians use vision quests and ordeals. Zen Buddhists use immobility while meditating. Saints have used poverty, hunger, cold, and pain. Russian mystic George Gurdjieff, who settled in the United States, used work. His students would be put to some physically taxing task such as digging in the garden, and he would keep them at it through misery and pain. If they didn't quit even when they felt they couldn't go on, their habitual, predictable ways of being would break down and their subconscious minds would begin to work.

For a woman I'll call Joanie, life itself provided the impetus. She would not have followed a guru or listened for a moment to the idea that she needed waking up. She was perfectly fine, thank you, and her life was perfectly wonderful. When I talked to her, she never used the word *magic*, she used the word *this*, meaning her new belief system. Joanie would never think of herself among the magical people. She's too normal, middle-class, suburban, and self-directed for that. She takes no classes, does no spells, reads no witch books, and belongs to no magical group. Nevertheless, she is among the most common type of magical person in America today.

If magic hadn't come to Joanie's rescue, her story might have been a sad one indeed. She was married for twenty-seven years to a man she described as her best friend. They met when she was fifteen and he was sixteen. Romance developed slowly, which is, of course, one of the best ways if you're looking for a long-term relationship.

So they married, had a child, established careers, bought a home. There was little in their marriage to quarrel about, and so they didn't. With regard to money, they were especially compatible. They were frugal, never left more than a 15 percent tip, and gave almost nothing to charity. This suited Joanie well since her mother had lived through the Depression and passed on all her fears. When Joanie was a child, her allowance was a nickel, which she saved. Eventually it was raised to a quarter, which she also saved. When she married, those nickels and quarters had grown to $1,200, which she was happy to bring into her marriage as a sort of dowry and testament to who she was. Her husband approved entirely.

When she was a year away from retirement, they worked out all the finances. They would sell their home and buy a condo. With the money left over, they could travel more. They were planning with their usual foresight, agreement, and good sense.

Then one day she noticed that her husband was a bit grumpy. He wasn't a moody man. So when the bad attitude lingered for two weeks, she was somewhat alarmed. One weekend afternoon she invited him to lie down on the bed with her. When he did, she lay beside him, stroking his arm. She mentioned that he seemed out of sorts.

"What's the matter?" she asked.

He didn't answer.

Still stroking his arm, she reassured him. "You know you can tell me anything."

With those words, which any reader will hear with a shudder of presentiment, Joanie opened the door that would change her life forever.

"Joanie," he replied, "I love you, but I'm not in love with you anymore."

Hardly original, but it was sufficient to get his point across.

"Are you sure?" she asked.

He was.

"Is there anything I can do?" she asked.

There wasn't.

"Is there anyone else?"

He said no, but that, of course, was a lie. His girlfriend was a woman about their son's age. They would be married not long after the divorce.

Joanie began crying, took to her bed, and didn't get out for a week. One day she decided to kill herself. She'd read a book by the Hemlock Society: sleeping pills to start the job and a plastic bag over her head to make sure it was finished. When she told her husband of her plan, he said, "Everyone will blame me." Joanie recalled that reaction, some years later, with only a bit of wryness in her voice.

But luckily she told some friends of her plan. They said they would be right over, and she was to do nothing before they got there. They nursed her through the worst of it and began introducing her to the idea that she could deal with life in her "earthly" self or with her "higher" self. That was the beginning, rather modest, but enough.

I met her a year after her divorce. She was living alone and pretty certain that she'd never marry again. One afternoon we took a trip to Chicago. On the way back, she began reading the numbers and letters on license plates. "Oh, there's an 8 and 9 and 2," she would say in a loud, excited voice. And then she would say those numbers meant that angels were in charge of the unity of the earth, or something like that.

Then she might laugh and clap her hands and say, "I see a 2 and a 4 and a 2." And that would be God, and God doubled, and then God again or some such thing.

I kept driving, looking straight ahead as though she were suffering from some religious form of Tourette's syndrome and the polite thing to do was to ignore her. Once, as I slowed for a light, I glanced over. She was beaming.

"I know it doesn't mean anything to you, but it does to me. To me it's the universe giving me messages. Wonderful messages." The numbers took their meaning from ancient magic. The idea is that numbers and certain words have great power because they were given to us by God. Other people believe numbers correspond with other essences and set up currents of force. In many magical systems, spells or chants are enhanced if lucky numbers are used; 3 and 7 and 9 are commonly among those.

On the way back from Chicago, when we stopped for ice cream, she told me that she still missed things about her marriage but she wouldn't go back. Losing it had freed her to become who she was meant to be.

"Who's that?" I asked.

It took her a while to answer, and she didn't use this term until later, but basically she told me that she had become an "earth angel," a conduit for love. She told me a number of things that she now did, from being kind to phone solicitors to telling troubled children about the rule of love. That next day she was scheduled to help a friend whose life had gone out of control because of her bipolar disorder. The friend was being evicted because she had let her apartment become so clogged with newspapers and other junk that her landlords considered it a fire hazard. Joanie had hired movers to come in and help. That impressed me greatly because most people run away from the mentally ill. They frighten and annoy us, and they often won't listen to reason.

But the most impressive change was that Joanie doesn't feel the same way she did about money. She now regularly gives large tips. She is also giving away half her retirement income to a needy family. "I'll do that until I die," she said. "I don't see it ending because I don't see their need ending."

Her transformation started when she read a book called *Soul Passages* by Gary Zukav. Then she read books by Deepak Chopra, books by Wayne Dyer, books about Kabbalah and Buddhism and new physics. She marked passages with different colors and decorated the margins with exclamation points and hearts and stars. The more she read, the more Joanie began to believe that her higher, or true, self is part of a larger force and that nothing that ever happens to anyone is an accident. In fact, everything that happened to her was working toward her good, the divorce included.

"There's not one person who knows me who hasn't benefited from the divorce," she said. "It's made me a better person."

The idea of a higher or true self is common in magic. The English mage Crowley called the higher self "true will." One of his famous dictums was "Do what thou wilt shall be the whole of the law," which sounds pretty scary and often was the way he applied it. But he also said that will must be under love. If he had followed that idea, his own life might have turned out better.

Joanie doesn't think of what she's doing as her will, but she describes it as what she most clearly and passionately wants to do. If she had stayed married, she would have never been allowed to follow this higher self, she said. The universal force that she sometimes calls God supports and communicates with her in all sorts of ways—through numbers, of course, and through what others call coincidences, but which she realizes are not. "There are no coincidences" is one of the magical world's most commonly repeated statements.

Hawks are also part of the magic. When she sees them, she believes she's receiving an affirmation. She believes they've been sent for her to see them. She believes they know it, and she thanks them.

So that you won't think she's entirely without any judgment in these matters, know that she tests these messages in certain ways. Sometimes when she's driving, she asks to be shown certain combinations of numbers. And she is. Then she demands another proof, and it comes. Or maybe it doesn't. But she only counts the times that it does. She's aware that the forces can't be made to perform like a trained bear.

Once she was driving home talking to a friend on her cell phone. He mentioned that two hawks were flying in a field near him. "Oh, you always get to see the hawks," she said. "I never do." When she walked in the door of her house, she looked toward the back deck. A hawk was sitting on the rail.

Joanie, once a super-rational atheist, now lives in an enchanted world.

Kioni was also brought to magic by hardship, but he was never a super-rationalist. How could he have been? A child with such a hard beginning needed more than reason to keep him alive. When he was three years old, he awoke one night, went to the window, and looking out saw that the sky was blood red. He'd never read the New Testament book of Revelation, but it was a scene right out of the Book. He realized later that he'd received the anointing on that night. The vision told him that his future lay in serving God.

He was always a hard worker, which is a good thing for a future magical person to be because without hard work to back it up, a lot of magic won't be effective, I was told time and time again. He shined shoes, worked in a laundry, and in the summer visited relatives in the South, where he picked cotton. He rode his bike about town from one job to another, leg brace flashing in the sun.

He sang at school and in the church choir. His cousin Pearlie Mae was a staunch churchwoman who took him every week. He came to Jesus and began to preach. After his brief life of crime, he strayed from the fold for a while. Then he went to the Pentecostals and became their kind of saved.

During the next years he and his family moved from one troubled church to another. Kioni would be sent in as the hatchet man, he told me. His early hardships gave him an edge that made him good at the job, but after the blood-letting, the churches were ready for him to move on. Kioni and Marilyn's last church was a tiny congregation in Georgia, in a town that didn't seem to have been disturbed by civil rights even forty years after the fact. That was the low point, or so they thought.

So he moved his family back to Florida and turned to evangelism. That went well. A black Pentecostal preaches as long as the spirit moves and that can be a long time. He dances and shouts, he huffs and he puffs, he sings, he moans, he weeps and whimpers. He thumps that Bible and rocks that pulpit. He pulls down heaven and stomps down hell. It takes a mighty spirit to do it, a rushing wind, a man filled so full of the Holy Ghost that it won't let him stand still. Kioni's clothes were often dripping when the service finally ended. Some weekends he came home with a thousand dollars of love offering in his pockets.

One morning after he'd preached a long night, he found that he could hardly rise from his bed. He was exhausted beyond anything he could remember. His legs twitched and trembled. And he began to hurt. It wasn't long before he couldn't hold up to the preaching anymore. No one knew what was happening to him. Post-polio syndrome was just beginning to show itself. People who believed that they had been totally cured were finding that the disease wasn't through with them yet.

First he needed a cane, then a wheelchair. When the revival money ran out, there was no more. They lost their house. Many people who had once been their friends were now nowhere to be found. Worse even, some were saying that this new affliction was a sign that something wasn't right in Kioni's relationship with God. If he got right with the Lord, the Lord would take care of him, they said. He knew their thinking. He'd told others the same thing. Preached it even. Now it was being preached back at him, and it was a bitter message.

Kioni's license in the Assemblies of God came up for renewal. The fee was $90. He called the central office and told the administrator that he didn't have the $90 for a license. He needed the money to feed his children. He was told that the fee would have to be paid. He replied that he could pay the $90, but the church would then have to help him feed his family. He said the president of the local assemblies replied, "We're not in the social services business." And that was that, the end of his time as an Assemblies of God minister. Once again, the family had reached the low point. They thought.

Soon he was so weak that he couldn't rise from bed. Marilyn had to help him get to the bathroom even. One day he was lying in so much pain and despair that he couldn't do any more than call out to the Lord. So he did. He called out asking "Why?" basically the same question that the disciples had asked of Jesus before he healed the man born blind. They asked, "Rabbi, who sinned, this man or his parents, that he was born blind?"

And as he asked the question, Kioni remembered that Jesus answered, "No one has sinned, neither has this man sinned, nor his parents: but that the works of God should be made manifest in him." Right there it may sound as if Kioni was on his way back to the Pentecostal church to be risen in glory before the multitudes, but that wasn't what happened. Instead, he kept lying there, but now he was filled with hope.

He began to gain strength. He took his GED test and passed. He enrolled in Brevard Community College. He took a class on comparative religions. The class was taught by a local marvel named Lin Osborne. Kioni's Pentecostal ire was roused many times by the new ideas the professor was teaching, but Dr. Osborne generally kept students like Kioni from fastening onto anything by simply presenting his information, making links between the world's religions, bringing together the ancient myths with current thought, and then letting everyone make their own conclusions.

Kioni began concluding that African religions might be all right to study, maybe even hoodoo. He began to ask about dim memories from his childhood. Hadn't an aunt been some kind of healer? Wasn't there some talk of hoodoo as a way of reaching out for the power that God offers?

Pearlie Mae reminded him that an aunt had cured Jaybird, his cousin who couldn't walk. Jaybird was not much more than a baby when her mother took her to the aunt. The old woman said to dig a deep hole and lower the child into it, feet first. Then pack the sand around the girl until she was buried up to her neck. Leave her there for twenty-four hours, the hoodoo healer said, and then dig her up. She'd be able to walk. And so she could. She walked with a crooked kind of gait like a bird, which is what earned her the name Jaybird, but she did walk and is walking still.

In the early 1980s, when the Internet was just beginning, Kioni and Cat started exchanging e-mails. He began studying magical texts, became a Rosicrucian, delved into Hermeticism, and a modern hoodoo man was born. His new name came after he prayed that God would reveal his true name. The Bible says that God knows our names before we're born. Kioni had several names in his life. His mother's, his father's, and his cousin's when she adopted him. He wished to know the name God called him. So he asked. And one day when he was sitting on the bank of the Indian River, where he often goes to meditate, a goddess appeared to him in a vision. She told him that his name was Kioni.

"Is that all?" he asked. "What about a first name?"

"Christos Kioni," she replied.

That was a little hard for Kioni, then known as Ken, to deal with. Christos would be son of Christ. Wasn't that aiming a bit high? No, not at all, she told him. We are all sons and daughters of Christ. So he took the new name and launched a new life.

I was beginning to see why separating magic and religion was such a difficult task. The ways people come to believe in magic were sounding quite religious. One way smacked of advice given by Jesus: become like a little child. Another way was the route of suffering and trial, also a religious favorite. The third bridge from the mundane to the magical is even more religious. I call it the way of the rebellious disciple. I've noticed that a certain type of person, often a young man, pursues spiritual questions with unusual tenacity and fervor. They read every book that promises wisdom, quest for every answer that seems promising, debate every believer, and push themselves to great extremes. Many go from one religion to the next before finally finding something that seems to fit. Often they are so well versed in different paths and so iconoclastic that they put together various aspects of different faiths to carve their own unique path. My reasons for calling them rebellious is obvious. I call them disciples, even though they may end up following no one system, because they are so inherently and stubbornly dedicated to spiritual matters.

As an aside, individualism is a particularly Western way of questing, according to scholar Joseph Campbell, who traces it back to the Knights of the Round Table. When the knights were sent out to look for the Holy Grail, they were instructed to go forth making their own paths into the forest. Campbell points to this as a mythological call to independent seeking rather than to following a path set out by others. That call to independence defines the Western way of faith and sets it radically apart from the Eastern faiths, in which gurus are more important in finding the right way.

Sam Webster has the kind of intensity and the background often seen in rebellious disciples. He holds a master's of divinity degree from Starr King School for the Ministry, which is part of the Graduate Theological Union in Berkeley; he was once a Pentecostal, incorporates Buddhism into his practice, and is now a leader in a high magic group called the Open Source Order of the Golden Dawn in the San Francisco Bay Area. Like many other magical people, he has extensive experience in a number of magical systems. His group is set apart from other Golden Dawn groups because it publishes the ceremonies and secrets of the Golden Dawn system of magic. For them the term "open source" is the same manifesto of free information that it is in the computer world. Putting Golden Dawn teachings on the Web was a controversial move that has inspired some amount of enmity, even though anyone who wants to know Golden Dawn magic can buy copies of its secrets at second-hand bookstores.

Sam's group wants to normalize high magical practice, which they believe could benefit everyone. It would make people happier, more sure of their purpose in life, and more in tune with reality. Golden Dawn's high magic would put them in touch with the Cosmos, the Absolute, the Divine, call it what you will, and engage them in consciously completing the Creation. Sam calls this the Work, short for the Great Work, which Jews call *tikkun olam*, or the healing of the world. Sam and his group of magical mystics believe people have specific work to do while on earth. Conversing with their Holy Guardian Angel, which is the goal of Golden Dawn teachings, helps them to know what they are to do and how to do it.

The Open Source Order descends from a magical group formed in England in 1880. It relied on Masonic and Rosicrucian teachings as well as a mysterious enciphered manuscript that supposedly contained ancient wisdom. Called the Hermetic Order of the Golden Dawn, the group counted among its members Irish poet W. B. Yeats, the infamous Aleister Crowley, and Irish revolutionary Maud Gonne. The Golden Dawn magical order, like Wicca and Hermeticism, was founded on what appear to be fabrications, or at least misunderstandings.

A Mason named W. Wynn Westcott claimed that he translated the enciphered manuscript, which led him to correspond with a German woman named Anna Sprengel, who was supposedly a member of an ancient Rosicrucian order. Rosicrucians, another magical group with a shadowy past, were a secret magical group that used Hermetic teachings. Sprengel empowered Westcott to establish a similar group. No one but Westcott was ever in touch with Anna Sprengel, and in later years many people came to doubt that she existed. The origin of the enciphered manuscript is also in doubt.

Westcott may have written it himself. The Golden Dawn rose to about eighty members and collapsed in the early part of the twentieth century. Crowley went on to form his own system, which still exists and is now known as the OTO, short for Ordo Templi Orientis.

The Open Source Order of the Golden Dawn includes women, as did the original Golden Dawn, but unlike the original, it does not rely on Christian teachings. Instead, it is distinctly pagan. Sam's reasons for becoming pagan go back to his days as a Pentecostal, when he was a "sock puppet" for Yahweh, as he puts it. Among the gifts of the spirit that Sam possessed was giving prophecies, which are thought to be the direct words of God funneled through a human. As Sam describes it, God would pull part of him out of his body and insert Himself so that he was in God and God was in him. God would enter through the back of his head, take over his mouth, and then say whatever he wanted to the church people. Sam, filled with love, bliss, and total adoration, would remember nothing of what had been said, but he did remember snatches of being in what might be called a realm of the gods. He could sense the presence of the other gods and goddesses, and over time he came to think that they were better than the one he was serving. They all had dark sides, but only Yahweh delighted in setting his followers one against another, Sam said.

"He's quite violent. He enjoys the war amongst his children. He has set three nations against one another, and he has enjoyed that for several thousand years. I do not respect that, and no other kinds of deities have done that," Sam said. So he decided that he would worship other gods. Giving them his energy and devotion would make them stronger and Yahweh less strong.

"It's the only way to vote," he said.

The Open Source Order of the Golden Dawn has about thirty members. Among them are an anthropologist, physicians, secretaries, a bookstore owner, technicians, and computer programmers. As one member pointed out, their membership is as mainstream as a Masonic lodge in some ways. One spring afternoon they allowed me to attend an initiation ceremony for the first level of magical training. Inviting me was so controversial within the group that some people didn't attend the event. Those who did were apprehensive about being mocked but nevertheless eager to talk about what they were doing.

It would have been easy to make fun of them. The rites and ceremonies they follow include wearing robes of various colors, using symbols of the Kabbalah, employing special handshakes and signs, and memorizing ritualized speeches. They worked hard at it. A row of robed members sat to the side. Each member was assigned to bring the power of a certain god into the ceremony by concentrating on that god power constantly. Each initiate was led into the room wearing a long black robe with a hood over his head and a rope at his waist. The Open Sourcers, some of whom have theatrical backgrounds, likened the initiation to a play being performed for an audience of one: The audience was each initiate, who was "pinged," they said.

By that they meant that the ceremony was supposed to thump the newcomers into awareness of who they are and of the information being beamed at them by the cosmos, the gods, the spirits, the whatever it is. Their first task was to learn how to listen; symbols and rituals are an ancient language for such communication.

"That's how you write to the universe, and that's how it writes back to you," said Sam. "It responds. There's an echo." The echo may come later in experiences, dreams, visions, realizations, synchronicities, omens. The Open Sourcers believe that every phenomenon a person experiences is part of that communication, but they also realize that anyone who took every experience as an omen would go crazy. So people must learn how to listen and how to filter at the same time.

Sam said the Golden Dawn process attempts to do what shamanic training does, but in a less traumatic way. "They totally shatter you, and then try to piece you back together again, and hopefully they will pick up most of the pieces. Okay. This [Golden Dawn magical system] is a method that evolved after someone looked at that and said, you know, we are losing pieces here. So they invented a little more orderly process. We do each of the pieces one at a time, and we assemble it into something a little more effective."

"You're trying to induce non-normal states of mind, but doing so in such a way that you don't hurt yourself," said Joseph Maxx, another Open Sourcer. As for the ordeal, life will provide that. "You don't need to ask for ordeals. They're going to happen anyway. You are going to get hit."

Magical people often talk about magic as being fueled by energy. Sam and Joseph prefer to say that magic is about information. In Golden Dawn practice, "you are manipulating the information matrix of the universe," said Joseph. "The whole universe is information. DNA is information. The atomic structure is information."

"All of the world is the mind of God," said Sam, who works in computers. "That's one of the Hermetic statements. So it's all data. It's all the thought of God."

The fourth bridge over which people cross the divide between reason and occult wonder is the way of the mind. In this way, people embrace magic because of their experience, but then the reverse occurs. They experience magic because they've embraced it, writes Tanya M. Luhrmann. The second part is something like the socialization that happens within any profession. People adopt a group's methods, its language, and finally its vision of the world, which means they pay attention to certain things and ignore others.

There's nothing odd about that process or unusual. It happens to lawyers. Their schooling teaches them to pay attention to fulfilling the law. They talk of justice, but their true allegiance is to law, not justice. Journalists learn to value freedom of information. Their allegiance is to the public's right to know. People's privacy is secondary. Doctors learn to value life. When they keep humans alive at any cost, they are simply following the socialization of their group. At some point each profession behaves in a way that differs dramatically from common wisdom. It happens in religion too. Once again, magic is the same.

Magic is fostered by shared beliefs that are set out, developed over time, and reinforced by experience. Perhaps the most common idea is the idea that I've used as a definition of magic itself: that there is an energy or force in the universe that can be tapped by certain actions, words, and intentions. People who believe in magic believe that objects and events respond to human intention and that when that intention is backed up by certain words or actions, the response is even stronger. Magical groups and magical literature say, "Do this spell or ritual and watch what happens." If subsequent events seem related to the spell or ritual, they say, "See, it worked." If events don't relate to the spell, they may say, "Try a new spell," or, "Try doing it during the full moon and watch what happens."

Perhaps the most important shift is not that the student affects reality—that may or may not happen—but that the student begins to notice in a new way. His relationship with experience has shifted. Now he is looking for meaning and pattern and connections. Life starts to have a flow, and he begins to be a participant in the direction of that flow. The groups and the books reinforce this experience by talking about it, putting it in stories, making jokes about it, and even critiquing it. All this gives magical experience weight and reality. Over time the many shared assumptions and experiences begin to be described in jargon or code words that have deep meaning within the group.

Another stage of magical development may come when magic teachers instruct their students to meditate, as they often do. They sometimes provide guided meditations that have students imagine themselves traveling into magical realms. Teachers might also encourage students to remember their dreams and interpret them. Magical practitioners often set up altars where they perform rites and pray. All these practices foster a turning inward. As the student begins paying more attention to his interior world, his thoughts and visions seem more and more real. The world of meditation and dreams is, of course, often filled with surreal, magical images that have great meaning if they are taken seriously. Joseph Campbell believed that Tibetan Buddhism and other Asian religions have such extensive pantheons of gods because in their extensive meditation the monks encounter inflections of experience that are personified as deities. It's an intriguing idea that dovetails with Carl Jung's thoughts. One scholar of religion, J. Gordon Melton, gave Jung credit for rescuing magical thought. He said Jung's ideas about archetypes and the universal unconscious gave credibility, theory, and fuel to neo-pagans who embrace ancient gods and goddesses. Some pagans agree and think of their deities as parts of themselves projected into human and animal forms.

None of the four bridges to magic would work for me. I had no good magic memories from childhood, no terrible events propelling me, no call to rebellion, and no inclination to join a magical group and be socialized. The only way to magic for me was to stop talking about it and start experiencing it.

13.

Follow the
Weird-Looking People

I was often surprised at how modest magical stories were. People asked for more prosperity in the new year. They wanted a shut-mouth spell to silence a gossip. They wanted to get somewhere on time during rush hour. They needed a job. One man wanted a prostitute to sleep with him. I assume he didn't want to pay. He made a bargain with a succubus, which is a spirit woman who comes to men in the night, and not long afterward the prostitute got drunk and slept with him. He was well pleased with his magic, but a drunk prostitute isn't exactly like asking for a Mennonite virgin.

When I asked for examples of magic they'd done, their stories were sometimes amazing but rarely matters of great braggadocio. Joseph Maxx was once doing a spell to banish bad work done on a friend. His friend was holding a piece of paper in her palm as ceremonial words were said over it. The paper began to crinkle as though being affected by great heat. I'm not saying that wouldn't have spooked me out, but still again it's not on par with making frogs fall from the sky.

Zardoa the Silver Elf told about doing magic to bless all the babies in the world. Women all around him began to get pregnant, which was not his intention. Zardoa wasn't claiming immaculate conceptions, and he wasn't saying he fathered any of those babes except his wife's. His story was merely an example of magical surprises, easily passed off as coincidence. Silver Flame told of seeing a black spirit cat run across the floor while she and a friend were having coffee. They both saw it and believed it meant something protective was around their children, but the cat didn't prophesy. It didn't jump on their laps and disappear in a puff of smoke. It merely ran through the room.

Shawn the Witch's highest compliment was to call someone really magical, and he didn't say it often. One of his candidates was a pagan named Michael Pendragon, who runs a Salem shop called The Oracle Chamber. Pendragon claimed that he could dream about a certain convenience store, and if he bought a lottery ticket there the next day he would win. Shawn backed him up, but Pendragon never claimed to win huge sums, and the dreams didn't happen every week. In Pendragon's opinion, the most powerful magicians might be people who don't consciously practice magic. People who amass great wealth, celebrities, and great generals are all able to cause change in accordance with their will, which was Crowley's definition of magic. They may never know their will is activating magical principles, Pendragon said.

I immediately thought of Arnold Schwarzenegger. How much more magical could a story be than his? The columnist George Will wrote of him, "Arnold's confidence approaches mysticism. Extending an arm, his palm toward his face and his fingers curved as though holding an invisible orb, he says ingenuously, 'If I can see it, I can achieve it. And I have the ability to see it.'"

Shawn also praised a witch named Jen. She smiled at his description and replied, "I don't always feel magical." For her, being magical was more a feeling about her own ease and buoyancy in the world than the success of any particular spell. Her example of successful magic dealt with a time when her daughter wanted to transfer to another class. Jen asked the principal for the transfer and sent an e-mail to her magical friends asking for help. Shawn had replied at once: "Consider it done." And so it was. Jen saw magical workings. I didn't. I thought the letter to the principal had done it.

I'd pledged to put my skepticism aside, but I couldn't. Many times I wanted to ask, "How do you know that what happened wasn't a coincidence or the result of the ordinary effort you put into it?" Finally I realized that other people's experiences were never going to be enough. Just as I was coming to that conclusion, Kioni volunteered to do some rootwork for me, whatever I wanted.

"How about a root to help a friend lose weight?" I asked.

No, he said. Hoodoo doesn't do weight magic. "Just push back from the table. That's the only way," he said. "And besides, you do hoodoo for yourself. Not for other people." If they want work, they get it for themselves.

"Okay then. We ought to do something specific. So I'll know if the hoodoo works or not."

"No," he said. "You can't test hoodoo. You have to have faith. It won't work for you if you test it. How's your sex life?"

"Fine."

"Fine? That means not great."

"Fine," I said, drawing out the *i* in the middle.

We were driving toward his house. For half a block the car was silent. Then I spoke.

"Okay, okay. Could a spell make it great?"

Maybe it could, he said.

"What would we need? I didn't, uh, bring anything." I was too shy for the plain speak of hoodoo. Hoodoo sex spells often require semen or vaginal fluid or menstrual blood. I hadn't brought anything like that along and would feel pretty strange if Kioni sent me to the bathroom with a Q-tip.

Pubic hairs could also be used for sex magic. One of the best conjure stories I heard was Cat's hoodoo interpretation of the most famous pubic hair in America. When Anita Hill testified that her boss Clarence Thomas had gotten up from the table where they were working, gone to his desk, picked up a Coke, and returned asking, "Who has put a pubic hair on my Coke?" white people might have thought he was making some strange sexual play. But black people who know hoodoo would have known that he was suggesting a woman had hoodooed his Coke by putting the hair on it, according to Cat.

Kioni didn't mention anything about fluids or hair. For such spells, he might use a blue penis candle and a red vulva candle, plus herbs, roots, and magnetic sand. He would watch how each candle burned, and he might gradually pull the two together, using a dark blue thread, until they were burning together. Sex spells can increase male or female "nature," which is the word conjurers use for libido. They can also make it so that the partners won't be able to perform with anyone else. In one spell, the woman masturbates with the penis candle and does a ritual afterward that includes putting nine needles in the candle. Whenever she wants to have sex with her beloved, she pulls out the needles. Afterward, she puts the needles back in the candle, and he, poor man, goes as limp as a hanky.

Kioni offered to have some candles overnighted from Lucky Mojo. I shook my head. I'd never had relations with a candle, and if I did, I could never keep quiet about it. Somebody in my family would get the story out of me, swear secrecy, then whisper it around, and nobody would ever forget. They'd pass it through the generations. Children would giggle about Auntie Christine and the candles long before they knew the joke. Thirty-five years from now I'd be an old woman tottering and doddering into Christmas dinner, and they'd be off in the kitchen whispering, "Hide the tapers." Wink, wink. Snigger, snigger. "Y'all be sure to count those candles before she leaves." Har, har, har.

Or worse, I'd do the spell and get my wish, and it would be like the fairy tale about the fisherman's wife who made such foolish wishes. My nice husband would become some raging sex animal and run off with another woman, or he wouldn't run off with another woman and I'd become one of those wives who make up excuses for why they can't come to bed just yet. He'd want me to wear black Merry Widows and fishnet stockings and walk around the bedroom in high heels even though we live in Wisconsin and my thighs get goose bumps.

"How about a spell for the success of your book?" Kioni said.

"I'd like that," I said, thankful we'd moved to another topic.

"And we could do a general blessing."

"I never turn down a blessing."

He asked me to bring a purple hanky. "Where would someone get a purple hanky?" I asked. Maybe it was a black folks thing, like big hats for church ladies. Just go to any Wal-Mart, he said, which

was a tip-off. This wasn't a black thing. Wal-Mart doesn't sell hankies. Women use tissues and throw them away. They have for forty
years. It's amazing what guys haven't noticed.

When I pointed that out, he told me to buy some purple material and some yellow material. Fabric stores are almost as rare as
hankies. I couldn't find one, but the night before we were to do the
work I drove deep into the neighboring city of Cocoa looking for
any kind of store that might have cloth.

When I spotted a Bealls far back from the street in a strip shop-
ping center, I turned in. Outside the store were racks of T-shirts.
The first one I touched was purple. Beside it was a yellow one. I
pulled the tags to see their price, $2.87 a piece. It was a sign, right?

The next morning I took them out of the sack all proud. We
hated cutting new shirts, but we would. Hoodoo requires sacrifice.

Then he asked again, "What do you want?"

And I said, "Look, maybe we shouldn't do this."

"Why?"

"I'm sorry. You said it won't work if someone doesn't believe. If
someone expresses any doubt, you send them away, tell them not to
waste their money."

I hadn't offered to pay, and he hadn't asked, but payment was
important. People pay Kioni hundreds of dollars for work. I'd seen a
$500 money order on his desk. I ought to pay. That's how hoodoo
works. People pay for what they get. You pay for the hoodoo hand.
You pay for the skill and time and power of the conjure. When you
evoke the saints even, you pay. What you don't pay for, you don't
get. I could pay, but if I gave the money knowing all the while that I
considered it wasted, what kind of magic would that be?

I didn't believe. I wanted to, but I couldn't.

"Well, sometimes someone else can believe for you," Kioni said
carefully. "I could do that for you in this case."

That might do it. But I'd seen Kioni work. I'd seen him shout and sweat, incant and cry. He constructed magical symbols. He mixed roots and herbs and oils. He displayed photos and told them what was expected of them. He opened his Bible and read the Psalms. He etched names into the candles, dressed them ritually with the right oils. He lighted the candles and watched how they burned. He did it with all his big, open, warm heart. If I didn't pay and didn't believe and wouldn't give hoodoo credit, I'd be just spitting on his effort.

"It's whatever you want to do," he said. He grinned and put his palms face up. "I'll do it if you want." In an echo of the Dapper Gent at the vampire ball, Kioni was telling me that I had to choose.

"No," I said. "No. Why don't we just go get some lunch and you can show me where you used to live?" So that's what we did. We also drove along the Indian River looking at the rich people's mansions, talking about which kind Kioni would have someday.

Jesus said that in his father's house are many mansions. He said he went to prepare a place. Magic says, "As above, so below." Put them together, which Kioni does, and there's a mansion in his future. He believed it without a doubt, and, for a little while, as we drove along and I listened to him, I believed it too. It was a great afternoon.

But I left Florida disappointed in myself. If I was going to get below the surface of magic, I would have to be more intrepid. I obviously wasn't ready to commit. If I could *feel* something, maybe I'd move a little closer.

For feeling, I looked to the vampires, because they specialize in that most important concept of magical thought: energy. As I've already noted, the idea of an energy or vital force available in the universe for human use is a central idea of magic. It got a boost in the 1700s from a man named Franz Anton Mesmer, who believed that a kind of psychic ether pervades all space. This ether is moved by the heavenly bodies just as sea tides are. Ill health comes when a person's etheric tides are blocked in some way. Mesmer believed he could use energy that he called animal magnetism to cure people of illness, and he seemed to have success. Mesmerism, as his method came to be known, is so close to hypnosis that the terms are still sometimes used interchangeably. Mary Baker Eddy also thought an atmospheric vital force was the secret of good health. Today thousands of people practice forms of energetic healing. Some are based on Asian medicine, some channel divine energy, and others remove energy blockages and tangles.

One primary difference between what the psychic, or psi, vamps are doing and what other energy workers and religious folk do is that the vampires don't draw energy out of the ozone or from gods or goddesses or from natural objects—they pass it back and forth among themselves and other humans, not as a healing force but as life energy. They believe they need the energy of other people to survive. The idea of feeding off other people seemed a rather wacky notion to me. Why would people who thought such things about themselves admit it, much less adopt a name for it and tell everyone? Another magical mystery.

When I heard that a vampire family called the House of Kheperu was having an open weekend of workshops, I signed up. The house's founder is a long-legged thirty-two-year-old named Michelle Belanger. She is a woman who definitely has strong energy. She wears her hair man-short, henna-colored with a blond forelock. The way she moves about a room reminded me of the rangy ease of cowboys. One year when I was at a Wyoming guest ranch, I asked a group of cowboys to stand before a weathered old barn so I could take their picture. They were reluctant to do it, but once in position, they effortlessly fell into the world's most understated macho poses. Then I took a photo of their wives, who were beautiful women with great force of their own, but their photos seemed so pallid and lifeless in comparison that I despaired. Michelle would have posed with the guys.

Early on during the House of Kheperu weekend, we formed circles to trade energy. About forty people were there, most in their twenties or early thirties and most in black, with a bit of leather and a few chains. Some had shaved heads, some sported fluorescent hair, but mostly the hair was black. I saw a few things that you don't see every day, at least I don't. One evening a very pretty thin girl with long red hair asked a bald guy if she could lick his head: "I just love to lick bald heads." He noted that his head was shaved and might not feel too good, but she insisted she would love it. She started at the back of his head but couldn't reach the top. So he knelt down, and she licked from the base of his neck over the top of his head and finished looking very satisfied.

Before we formed the circle for exchanging energy, the vamps cleared the space by walking through it pushing energy out. Neopagans and Wiccans clear sacred space by performing banishing rituals and calling the watchtowers in all four directions. Watchtowers are something like guardians of the world and are manned by gods and angels, as I understand it. Some magical people clear space by simply standing in the middle of the room and telling everything to get out. Others envision a sort of sphere in the center of their mind.

As we stood in our circles holding hands the plan was to send our energy left to right. A pretty little woman with glossy black hair apologized for hitting people with her wings. Her wings had a forty-foot span, she said. They were invisible, of course. I didn't feel them, but someone else in the circle said, "So that's what that was."

At one point she and Joe, another vampire, stood facing each other with their palms held shoulder high, in patty-cake position, but not touching. They were making ozone, they said. Nobody could make ozone like they could, I was told. Some people could smell it. I couldn't. Others smelled pine and lilacs. I couldn't. I never felt a thing either, but others also noted that our circle had been kind of a bust.

A guy I'll call Will seemed to be the problem. He was described by his girlfriend, the glossy-haired woman with wings, as a dead zone. Will generally stood with his arms dangling at his sides, a lank flop of hair hanging over his forehead, pale and serious but seemingly not offended by talk of his deficits. During the circle he was next to me, his hand trembling in mine. The girlfriend said Will had no hands energetically and a big block at the knees that balled up the energy.

After the circle, the vampire leader, Michelle, worked on him. She ran her hands over his body without touching it and then opened his shirt between buttons, put her mouth on his chest, sucked the energy, and then blew it out. But it didn't seem to work. The only way he had ever been able to ground was through his ass, he said, which sounded intriguing but meant only that he had to sit on the ground. A couple of us migrated out to the parking lot where he could sit on the pavement.

He sat and was worked on for some time by Joe, who finally gave up.

"Have you ever seen anything like it?" his girlfriend said, shaking her head in wonder.

Another vamp who described himself as having no energetic legs ("I have to sort of hotwire myself to get energy moving") told the girlfriend that she would have to construct an energetic body for Will, but it would take a lot of work. It might take all day, he said.

"To tell you the truth, I'd just off your legs," he told Will.

It was clear that they felt something real was happening. I had promised myself I'd stop rationalizing, but I couldn't. In past times, people interpreted the world through religious lenses. Now we psychologize. I put the two together with the help of Joseph Campbell. He believed that the sense of original sin comes from humans' knowing that in order for them to live other things must die. Being meat-eaters is so traumatic that cultures make sacrifices to animals, ask their permission, bless them as they are killed, or, in our case, package meat in such a way that makes it completely separate from the idea of a living being and give it names that distance it even further from the reality of what it is. Campbell believed that vegetarians have the same guilt because they too must kill living things.

Were the vampires responding to that old guilt but giving it a different name? They had adopted one of the bloodiest archetypes available, one that sucks blood and gives the "kiss of death" in order to live, but then they modified vampirism so that it was about energy, a renewable resource that doesn't require the death of others. Or maybe there really is energy and they need it to survive, just like they say.

"Vampire" is a clumsy term for what her family actually is, Michelle believes. Some psi vamps have abandoned the term altogether and simply call themselves by the name of their house, or they change the spelling to "vampyre." Michelle and a New York City vamp called Father Todd Sebastian have helped lead the vampire community away from exchanging blood. They've written a code of ethics for the community that forbids taking energy from others without their knowledge.

They believe that exchanging energy can be good for everyone. People often feel sexual energy rising when they are fed upon. One woman had an orgasm that she proclaimed to be the best she'd ever had. Her name was Jody, and she came to Michelle because she was lethargic and her libido was down. Michelle hardly touched her, but afterward Jody's libido returned to a satisfying degree.

Michelle's story of being a vampire began when she was still a child and would induce neighborhood children to play a game of chase in which she was the vampire and they were her prey. In her late teens she had a past life memory of herself as a ten-year-old in an Egyptian temple. She was stamping her foot in protest over the cosmic rule that said that reincarnated beings would not remember their past lives. If people couldn't remember what they'd learned, then they would have to start over each time, she told the adults, who weren't sympathetic. "That's just how it is," they told her.

But the little girl who became Michelle many lifetimes later wasn't satisfied. There is a connection between the universal life force and each individual, Michelle came to believe. It comes out of the belly area. The universal life force feeds energy through that connection, but along with that energy comes amnesia about past lives. If that connection were cut, a person would be free to roam back through other lives and pick the wisdom found there, Michelle reasoned.

So sometime in her late teens she went into a trance state and cut the connection. That severed her from the energy that is available to normal human beings. It made her a vampire who cannot survive without the energy of others. But in return she gained access to wisdom. Her vampire family's title, the House of Kheperu, would translate as House of Transformation, she said. She described her house as following a pre-Egyptian wisdom tradition.

At one point, hoping to get a PhD in English and become a professor, she resisted the idea that she was a vampire and stopped exchanging energy. She began to sicken and almost died. Her heart was damaged by the experience to the point that she required surgery, she said. Later, when she wore a low-cut shirt, I was able to see clear scars on her chest.

One afternoon we went to a local park said to be the site of extraordinarily excellent energy, with lots of ley lines, which are energetic lines in the earth. We were there to learn dowsing, which is still so popular that classes are held on it all over the country. There's even an association of dowsers, I was told.

When I arrived, the vamps were gathered in a little knot of about eight people at a picnic table. In pitched tents around the parking lot were troops of Boy Scouts. The scouts were in uniform. The vamps were too. They were mostly wearing black with tattoos. One girl in a bustier showed a vast amount of bruised breast. Another wore a black shirt with white lettering: "I'd rather be masturbating." There were a few chains and some leather. Conversation was about what they planned to wear to the ball that night. One mentioned four-buckle leather boots called stompers. They exchanged information about fangs. A good set costs about a hundred dollars, and not many in the group had that kind of money.

Eyeing the bare-kneed Boy Scouts, one raven-haired vamp said happily, "No one told me lunch was being provided."

The vampires were showing each other various knives and other weapons when one of the Boy Scouts began blowing a trumpet. One of the vamps stood still to listen.

"'Ode to Joy,'" she said, as if citing memories from another life.

Another grimaced and said, "Maybe you could blow him up with your mind."

As a half-dozen cars swung into the parking lot, one of the vamps sang out a fanfare, "Dum, da, da, dum," and said, "Now we can attack."

A dozen black-clad vamps piled out. A vampire-leprechaun named Dreaming Squirrel, wearing his faded red DON'T TRY TO OUTWEIRD ME T-shirt with a Terry Walsh autograph scrawled across the chest, was carrying a large lance with feathers down the length of it. A vampire named Sorrowsheart, who was to teach us dowsing, wore a long leather coat and high lace-up boots. Married with a small son, Sorrowsheart holds down two jobs, one of them at night. Vamps prefer night jobs. A number of the Kheperians work as hotel desk clerks. He looked sleepy. He was carrying an armful of coat hangers and some wire cutters.

He instructed the group to cut their hangers and bend them so that they had two pieces of wire bent into an "L" shape. They would hold the short end and let the long ends float free, he explained. The direction the wires pointed would show where ley lines were. It took a while for everyone to get the wires fixed, but eventually it was done.

"Are we ready?" he shouted out.

"Hell, yes. Tallyho," someone shouted back.

As we stomped past the scouts' tents into the forest, a middle-aged man sitting in a lawn chair smiled and shook his head. A younger man, short-haired in a clean-cut way, glowered as the vamps marched by.

Sorrowsheart called out, "Follow the weird-looking people." Then reconsidered. "No. Follow the normal-looking people. If you follow the weird-looking people, you'll end up with the Boy Scouts."

By the end of the weekend I'd experienced nothing. It was all just talk. So on the last afternoon of the open house I asked Michelle if she would feed off me. It was a risk to ask. I knew she might refuse for all sorts of reasons.

She wouldn't take energy from anyone who was physically ill; even touching someone sick might affect her. She also wouldn't take energy if she didn't have a good feeling about the person. In her work as a hotel desk clerk, she often set up energy shields between herself and guests so that she didn't absorb too many negative energies. Once a man came in who seemed so evil to her that she thought he must be up to no good. All the while he was there she expected something bad to happen, but nothing did.

She had me sit in a straight-backed chair as she stood behind me. I could tell that she was waving her hands about my body in the way of energetic healers. She held them over my head, then ran them along the contours of my back, not touching. When she placed her hands on my shoulders, they felt like long blocks of ice. I could feel the chill through two layers of clothing. She moved her hands slightly forward so that they rested on my upper chest.

She asked that I take off my cloth jacket. Energy would flow more easily with less cloth between our skins. Skin to skin was best. My hands rested on my knees, palms up. Taking one hand at a time, she cradled it with her left hand and stroked the palm with her fingers. My hands began to feel cold. Hers were feeling warmer.

When she moved behind me again, I could feel the heat from her body, radiating like a portable space heater. I was feeling more and more chilly. At one point she stood to my right side, kneeling with my hand held in hers again. The left side of my body tingled briefly. If I felt pressure around my heart, we would stop immediately, she said. I didn't.

Standing behind me once more, she asked if she could put her mouth on the back of my neck. I tilted my head forward as she put her mouth over the vertebra. After a few seconds she turned her head to the side and exhaled with a whooshing sound. The exhalation released the parts of my energy that her body didn't need to take in, she said.

"Your energy is delicate," she said. "It's almost papery. When I exhaled, it felt as if I was breathing out a powder." Later she said the powder was gone. My energy was clearer, still delicate.

"Your energy flows. There don't seem to be any blockages. It's very balanced and calm. That's probably a reflection of your personality." Calm and balanced? Maybe compared to vampires. She was being gentle with me, she said, because if she was too aggressive even the touch of her fingers might leave marks on my skin. That would have been something to see, but it didn't happen.

By the end of the exchange, my forehead felt hot and damp. The rest of me was chilly, and my hands were icy. My face was hot because she had drawn the energy through the top of my head, Michelle said. Her hands, once so cold, were now warming mine. I could feel the heat coming from her when she was a foot away. My change in temperature might have come about because I took off my jacket, but I hadn't felt that the room was cool before. Her change in temperature was a common by-product of her feeds, she said. Her hands were often so cold before a feeding that the nails were blue. "I die a little," she said.

I wasn't entirely convinced that our shift in temperature was magical, but I did experience it. It isn't easy to believe your own perceptions, much less to make something of them. It's easier to wait for the scientists or the preachers or your own anxieties to tell you what you can believe, but if you want to be magical, you have to choose your own feelings over what authorities tell you. I had learned that much.

My first magical experience had been the lessoning of my travel fear when I purchased the mojo bag and burned the candle as I said the Psalms over it. It hadn't been much, a slight shifting toward being more hopeful and courageous. The second experience had been the eerie dream of being paralyzed by the jailer's injections and then reading that a similar paralysis is typical of voodoo possession. Because of my old ideas about Jesus, I'd taken a terrible dream as a good sign. If you want good magic, you have to claim the good even if you feel like a fool for doing it. I had also learned that good is a stronger force than most of us think. Just as evil can claim people, so can good. Put together with the change in temperature when Michelle fed on me, I'd experienced three events that could be called magical. Were they self-fulfilling prophecies? Wild interpretations. Maybe.

I didn't count these things as big magic, and maybe not as magic at all, but they had been experiences deep within myself. I often tell myself that I don't feel what I feel. I say that I'm not angry when I am, that my feelings aren't hurt when they are, that I'm not jealous when I am. Anytime I experience anything not on my list of acceptable behaviors, I deny that I feel it. What would it be like to simply believe that if I felt something that made it true? I wouldn't have to put together a committee to back me up or do an experiment to prove it. I wouldn't have to justify it. I would just have to stand on my own perceptions. Could I do that? Probably not. How many people can?

I'd had a little taste of magic. I wanted more. Silver Flame, the fairy I'd visited in California, said the outcome of magical workings is a "sacred retort" in response to the intention and actions of humans. I loved that idea. Could I evoke such communication? Maybe, but only if no one was watching. Either I didn't trust people enough for the magic to work, as in the Wiccan rituals, or I liked them too much and felt exploitive, as with Kioni—which is what brought me to the chaos magicians. Privacy and simplicity are among the virtues of their system. They also are completely independent and iconoclastic.

Chaos magicians, who have thrown out many rules that other magicians follow, also don't ask for belief. Open Sourcer Joseph Maxx, who is a noted chaos magician, advised, "If you don't believe it, do it anyway." Fake it until you make it. I could do that.

Some people are afraid of chaos magicians because of their name, because of their interest in the dark side, and because they sometimes strut around in leather and brag about doing nasty things. But I liked that they didn't care much for secrecy, which always irks me and causes me to suspect there's nothing to tell. I also liked that they didn't require a lot of ceremonies and rituals to get started.

My first magical experiment was to construct what's called a sigil. It's a symbol that becomes magical when you charge it by putting energy into it. Some people call sigils doorways to other realms. The idea that a symbol or picture can contain some energy beyond its actual self is an ancient, respected one. It's somewhat like the idea behind Christian icons, which are "mediums of holy presence," writes Peter Schjeldahl in the *New Yorker*. "Think of icons as visual cell-phone calls from the beyond: you don't look at them; you receive them, and you respond."

The difference, of course, is that the power of sigils comes not from God but from the person who creates them, and they are created for a specific magical purpose, not for worship. The magic book recommended that I do two sigils, one for important magic and one for something trivial, such as seeing a woman with a little white dog.

My husband was about to leave for a conference in Saudi Arabia. The U.S. State Department had recently issued a warning about the danger of traveling to that country, and the embassy had sent home all non-essential personnel and families. My important magic was to bring my husband home safely. I was also using Cat's mojo for that. My trivial magic would be to see a woman in a red hat. It was summer, and not many women were wearing red hats.

I made the sigils, as directed, by writing what I wanted, crossing out the vowels and repeated letters, and then forming a symbol using the letters that were left. When I finished making the symbol, the original letters were completely unintelligible. The sigil is empowered when it is focused on at a critical moment and thus imprinted on the creator's mind. A critical moment would have to do with energy. For instance, you might charge your mind with the image of the sigil just as you are having an orgasm or just as you've exercised to exhaustion. Your intention and energy fuel it. I jogged on my treadmill until I was out of breath and couldn't run any more. Then I fell on the bed and imagined the sigils.

Once I'd charged them, I put them away and stopped thinking about them, which is what the book directed me to do. In many magical systems it is important to do the magic and let it go. Often when hoodoo work is done at a crossroads, for instance, the conjurer walks away and does not look back. It is important not to fret the magic, but to let it happen. Joseph says that you want to shift your attention by laughing or distracting yourself so that your consciousness shuts around the sigil and nothing else comes into that opening.

The book had warned that the magical event might not be exactly as expected. The next day I didn't think about the woman in the red hat until early afternoon. A friend and I were returning from lunch. She stopped for gas. The pump wasn't working, so she moved the car up to another one. As I sat waiting I remembered the sigil and realized that I hadn't seen a woman in a red hat. My friend got back into the car. As we pulled out I glanced at the pumps on the side of the building. An African American woman wearing a dark red scarf with blue flowers was standing next to a car. She was laughing. I couldn't see what she was laughing at or hear anything being said because the windows were up. Her scarf was rolled and tied so that it made a kind of Aunt Jemima head covering, a do-rag.

I laughed. I'd expected a different kind of hat and a different shade of red, but I was looking for a red hat just as one appeared as if by magic. Later the Silver Elves said they believed that my consciousness was drawn to the magic at the moment it appeared, which was a good indication that the sigil worked. But I couldn't decide if a scarf counted. I asked my friend.

"No," she said. "A scarf is not a hat."

Probably not, or maybe a scarf made into a hat by a black woman seen by another woman doing magic and studying hoodoo was better magic than I'd asked for, personalized just for me. If I wanted to deny it, I could. If I wanted to affirm it, I could. Perfect. All about perception, faith, and hope.

A shudder of delight mixed with fear went through me. It would be wonderful to believe in something powerful and personal and good, especially if that something could be activated by my actions. All I had to do was choose. Make the correct choice, and this could be true life-changing enchantment. That scared me.

If I could have claimed it and then laughed it away, I might have, but the more I thought about it, the more bizarre it seemed. For my sigil to have caused the woman in the red hat to appear would have required a long chain of events. She would have to have decided to wear that hat, go to the gas station, and stand outside her car at exactly that time on that day. All the while she would have believed herself completely in control, never knowing that my wish had brought her there. My friend who picked the restaurant would have had to pick one in the same part of town as the gas station. She had to offer to drive and fail to fill her tank with gas. She needed to buy the gas after lunch, not before, at that gas station and pull out at exactly that moment. Maybe the pump had to break at just the right time. Maybe she even had to go to the broken pump first so that the timing was perfect. She too would have been utterly controlled by my magic without either of us knowing it. And for the final step, I had to be looking at that side of the gas station and not the street.

It would mean that our thoughts and actions, our lives, are connected in a vast web that trembles every time anything—a thought, an emotion, an action—brushes it. Or was it all foreordained even before I did the sigil? Was the whole chain of events, including my wish, inevitable? The more I thought about the woman in the red hat, the more dizzying it was. If I accepted that I'd done real magic, I'd be committing myself to a universe utterly unlike the one I've always thought I lived in. I couldn't do it.

My husband did return safely from Saudi Arabia. So my big wish was granted. But did it prove anything? No. Not to me. Not that I was complaining.

*C*haos mages also provide simple starting exercises to prepare the mind for magic. Perhaps that was what I needed, preparation. Joseph said he sometimes tells people to start by merely noticing everything they see of a certain color, red or blue maybe. The point is to start people noticing what's around them. The magical exercise I chose to do first was to walk through my neighborhood looking at everything as though it were occurring only for me, which some mages say is literally true. That was easy enough and wouldn't require much effort.

I was wearing a red jacket as I walked my dogs. One is a terrier mix and the other a black Labrador. I passed a woman wearing a red jacket walking a black dog that looked like a Labrador mix. She was going one way. I was going another.

I said to myself, *She's on this street dressed like me, walking a dog that looks like mine. I have two dogs. She has one. I have a mixed breed and a Labrador. She has a mixed Labrador.* She was skinnier and younger than I was. I asked myself, *What does this mean?* Maybe it meant that I could get skinnier and younger. No, probably not.

I saw three black birds flying high in the sky. I said to myself, *Three black birds. Just for me. Three is a magical number. The Trinity. The number of Wiccan archetypes: maiden, mother, and crone. The number of days before Jesus rose. Three black birds. What does it mean?*

I saw a tree that had been split by a windstorm. A limb had fallen across a walkway leading to the front door of a house. I said, *A broken tree blocking a doorway. Just for me. The entrance is blocked by the fall of a great symbol of life. What does it mean? What does it mean? It means I'm becoming an egotistical nut case.*

Imagining myself as the cause of so many events was exhausting and made me feel silly. So I stopped doing it and turned home. But having honed this new perception, I found it difficult to stop. For the rest of the walk I noticed trees I'd never looked at, animals I wouldn't have usually seen, shapes and colors and configurations that I'd never been aware of. I didn't ask what they meant. As I neared my house a half-dozen yellow finches burst out of the bushes in a light-flecked flurry so beautiful I gasped. I did not ask what they meant. Witnessing it was meaning and magic enough.

Perhaps that seems a cop-out. Open Sourcer Sam Webster might not think so. He might call it high magic. "I'm interested in trying to stay as present to my experience as possible so I hear the world when it's echoing to me," he said. That's especially important because in the magical view the world is not an opponent but rather a support, he said. "The world is what gives rise to me. God or the cosmos has always been there with me, or in biblical terms, I have dwelt in the presence of the Most High every day of my life. I have never known otherwise."

I had been changed just the littlest bit by that walk, just as I'd been changed by the uncommonly beautiful light of the candles I'd lighted before going to Salem. It wasn't much, but I remembered that Joseph said changing oneself is the best magic.

"It's the most effective by far," he said and then gave an example. "If you want to get money, don't invoke magic money falling from the sky. Invoke your employability to make more money. This works much better."

My magical walk had also discombobulated me in a way that none of the other magic had. Merely playing with the idea that I might be the center of the universe, the recipient of constant messages from divinity, made me feel a bit crazy, as though it wouldn't be hard to tip me over. I'd only done it for about an hour, but I knew that if I kept thinking that way, it would change my brain. If I told myself those things as I walked every day, at the end of a month I would not think in the same way I had before. If I did it for six months, I might not recognize myself. I was so certain of that walk's power that the thought frightened me. I couldn't prove that it would change me so radically, but I knew it would.

Six months later I read a study in *Mind*, the new *Scientific American* magazine, that gave substance to my ideas about the malleability of the human mind. Researchers seated a test subject with one hand on a table before him. They also placed a rubber hand on the table. Between the real hand and the rubber hand, they placed a partition so that the test subject could not see his own hand but could see the rubber hand. The researcher then randomly stroked and patted the test subject's hand at the same time that the rubber hand was stroked and patted. After 20 to 30 seconds, the test subject began to "feel" the touch on the rubber hand. Other researchers discovered that they could produce the same effect without the rubber hand. Merely stroking and tapping the table while stroking and tapping the hidden real hand would cause test subjects to feel that they had been touched when the table was touched. Even more strangely, in other experiments, test subjects reacted with alarm when the table was struck a blow, as though they themselves had been struck.

The brain works by percentages, authors Vilayanur S. Ramachandran and Diane Rogers-Ramachandran wrote in explanation. "As you feel your unseen hand being tapped and stroked and see the table or dummy hand being touched the same way, your brain in effect asks itself, 'What is the likelihood that these two sets of random sequences [on the hidden hand and on the visible table or dummy] could be identical simply by chance? Nil. Therefore, the other person must be touching *me*.'"

The brain makes its decision automatically based only on sensory input. Higher consciousness that might involve logic is never consulted. "Even a lifetime of experience that a table is not part of your body is abandoned in light of the perceptual decision that it is. Your 'knowing' that it cannot be so does not negate the illusion," the authors wrote. The researchers then went on to link this deep 'knowing' with people who cling to superstitions even when their logic tells them that such things cannot be true.

I took the studies as verification that I'd been right to be afraid of the walk's power. It wouldn't be difficult to program my brain so that it saw events in a completely different way. If I told myself every day that all events have special meaning for me, soon they would. Conversely, if I lived in a society that told me events are all random and utterly separate from me, I would see them that way.

Either way, I would be stroking my brain, giving it example after example of truth, until it took over and began feeding the examples back to me.

The brain is a powerful and deceptive instrument. Science has demonstrated that again and again, and so has experience. But it is all we've got. If we trust it too much, we're in trouble. If we trust it too little, are we in worse trouble? Will we then trust someone else's brain? Or a computer? Humans are good at making meaning, which is not to say they are good at finding the truth, wrote Richard A. Friedman in the *New York Times*. So what to make of this? I'm not sure. But here's an idea that seems radical and a little frightening to me: if we're not good at truth and we are good at meaning, maybe those of us who are merely trying to live our lives as best we can would do better to give truth a bit of a rest and pursue meaning.

Take Kioni, for instance. He saw a figure in the corner of his bedroom and took it to be the Virgin Mary with a message he longed to hear. Was she there? I don't know, but he was healed whether she was or not. A young man in my dream declared me innocent. I took him for Jesus and was emboldened. A voice spoke to Siva the Satanist. He took it to be Kali, and it began to refer him back to his own best judgment. Twelve-year-old Cat did a rain dance, it rained, and a lonely young girl thought herself powerful. I remembered asking Cat, about astrology, "How can such things happen?" And I remembered her answer: "I don't know, hon. I don't know." And then she had said, "All I know is that they do happen."

14.

Werewolves Just
Want to Have Fun

I flew to Kitchener, Canada, to attend the spring gathering of Otherkin, hoping to connect with the elves, who are perhaps the magical world's most dedicated embodiments of gentleness and light. In Tolkien's work, they are immortals of great beauty and nobility. In Gael Baudino's *Strands of Starlight*, they are called the Fair Ones and live by the rule of love. They worship the Goddess and receive strength and direction from the stars. They refuse to cut trees and are so in tune with animals that they ask permission of their horses before riding them.

Those are fictional Otherkin, of course. The living Otherkin are a loosely affiliated group of mostly young people who believe themselves to be magical and spiritual creatures: elves, werewolves, dragons, fairies, angels, hobbits. I was fascinated from the first time I read about them in a *Village Voice* story by Nick Mamatas, which pointed out that Otherkin believe they age slower than others and heal faster. They feel alien and frequently have an aversion to iron and other new-fangled instruments of progress. Mamatas wrote,

A number of Otherkin claim that they are especially empathetic toward others, and toward the ebb and flow of the natural world.

Of course, once upon a time another species was widely believed to have this kind of connectedness: human beings. Before industrialization and urbanization, people depended on their feelings and intuition rather than on shrinks and Oprah. People lived in tune with nature, thanks to a largely agricultural existence, until the Enlightenment and its attendants—calculus, petroleum, and animal vivisection—turned the universe into clockwork, work into wage slavery, and the family into a demographic market segment. Elves are now what people once were, before we all got office jobs, health insurance, and credit card debt, before life became like running across a flaming rope bridge. Thanks to modern society, we're all Frankenstein's monster. None of us fit.

The Otherkin are making a Romantic appeal for a better world and a better life.

My first impression when walking into the hospitality room of their convention was, yes, these people are different. I felt a little like Han Solo walking into the bar. Tattooed people with dark figures writhing up and down their arms. Pale thin-faced kids with iridescent hair, blue, pink, purple, and green, overlaying rough-textured tresses of the deepest black, frizzing down their backs, falling in heavy wings around their faces or spiking around their heads. Pierced, studded, and clad in lumpy clothes, mostly jeans and black T-shirts. I was by far the oldest person in the room, more than twice as old as many. If anyone was a freak in this group, it was me.

And yet in the most unobtrusive and sensitive ways, they paid mind to me. One caught my eye, held up his cup, raised his eyebrows, and murmured, "Can I get you some coffee?" Others sidled up to me with a soft "Hi" and then looked away, like friendly deer, too polite to nibble at my pockets but ready to befriend me. These were outcasts, geeks, misfits—their words, not mine. I would have never called them that, but they almost always made that point about themselves within seconds of meeting me.

They are often dismissed as fan boys who live in their mothers' basements. "Fan boys" is a term for people whose lives as Trekkies or whose love of stories from comic books or whose devotion to roles they play in computer fantasy games are more real to them than anything else. Junior high and high school were hell for many of them. You could tell that instantly, and they could give you details that would shrink your soul. Their status hadn't changed much. Appearance, interests, manner, everything marked them. Look at them and you instantly thought of the kids who sat in the back of the room sleeping during class, sullen or worse, some of them openly terrified when called on, chosen last for team sports, uninvited to the popular kids' parties. If they went to the prom, they went in ripped black or camouflage pants or in something flamboyantly inappropriate, like elf ears or vampire teeth. They were the freaks, the druggies, the kids bullies loved to target. If they'd been meaner, they might have had a chance, but mean was the last thing they were. Too sweet was more like it, too sensitive and too smart not to know all the dreadful nuance of their place.

Since so many are computer geeks, they often express themselves in computer-ese. Some mention being science majors. When one girl lectured the group on new science, it was obvious that the group knew enough to argue. But they didn't. Afterward, I heard her saying to another Otherkin, "I know that string theory isn't proven, but. . . ."

They knew that thinking themselves elves or werewolves, dwarfs or dragons, left them open to being called crazy. They questioned themselves on that point quite a bit. Some had been diagnosed with

various types of mental illness: depression, bipolar disorder, disasso-
ciation, multiple personalities, suicidal tendencies. They had reason to
be wary of outsiders. Many had been attacked by Internet-savvy haters
who flooded their chat rooms with so much threatening talk that
they'd sometimes had to shut down and open new rooms. There were
only about sixty of them in attendance, but three guys were assigned to
be security, not so much to police their behavior as to protect them
should some meanie try to crash their convention.

Never once did they set me apart. Nobody tried to show me
how cool he was by letting me know that I wasn't. One afternoon a
workshop given by a handsome werewolf featured everyone breaking a board karate-style, a lesson on how to use energy. I was afraid
to try. The Wolf, who had well-cut, light-colored hair and looked
more like the young businessman he was than a werewolf, invited
me to try several times before I would.

Everyone broke the board in one try, but not me. I whammed
my hand twice against the board. Nothing happened to the wood,
not even a splinter.

"Try again," he said softly, positioning my hand differently.

"You can do it," the crowd yelled each time I failed. "Try again."
When the board finally broke, I'd hit it so hard that my whole body
followed through and I fell against the floor. Anybody might have
laughed. They cheered. They knew the multiple ways in which people can be made to feel apart. They had forsworn them all. I'd never
seen anything like it.

The man called Dreaming Squirrel was there, and said he was
elf and leprechaun. I'd heard that his three-year-old daughter had
one pointed ear and one normal ear. When I asked, her mother
pulled back the little girl's brown curls. Sure enough, one ear was
pointed and the other wasn't. When the child was born, her mother
told me, her ears were the first body parts she checked.

Dreaming Squirrel jumped around a bit, talking excitedly about various topics and then exclaiming, "Excuse me. I had to say that." The first night he was carrying a cudgel made of green cloth and foam shaped like broccoli. Twice I heard him tell the story of how he would go to gentlemen's clubs, and when the dancers complained of pains or tension, he would reach out and touch them magically.

"They would go, 'Ooooh, how did you do that?'" he said, which demonstrated how amazed and grateful they were for his magical healing.

"So I guess that makes you the Jesus of the Gentlemen's Clubs," said the Wolf, demonstrating his wolfish edge. Dreaming Squirrel blinked and said nothing, demonstrating a limit to his aspirations.

Of course, being an Otherkin doesn't solve all one's problems. Spark, a young woman with shining red hair that fell softly about her shoulders, creamy glowing skin, and a silver nose ring, told me she was a vampire. She wore fashionable black-rimmed glasses, a pentacle pendant, and long flowing skirts. She had a handsome boyfriend, with a fringe of a beard outlining his chin, who sat silently beside her. She described herself as having been a shy, depressed, easily frightened, low-energy child who cried easily. She had grown up to be a woman with many health problems that caused her to feel frequent pain and lassitude. I asked if discovering her magical self had helped with the ailments. She said they had actually gotten worse. At the Come as You Really Are Ball, she sat in the back, far from the dance floor.

"I'd like to dance," she said, "but I'm afraid to. I'm that kind of person who wants to but doesn't."

A guy named Gleef told me that he was some kind of prehistoric lizard. Another guy called himself Kibble. When I asked why, he said that he serves the Wolf god. "I'm kibble for him," he said.

Another woman calls herself The Crisses because she harbors so many different personalities inside her—dozens already and adding all the time. Many are magical beings, some are not, she said.

Otherkin call each type of magical being a race, and you often hear them ask, "What race are you?" Discovery of one's race is called the "awakening." Awakening is often a terrifying process, they told me, during which the person doubts his or her sanity. Each race has personality traits. Angels are among the most popular otherworldly creatures to be, but I didn't meet any at the convention. They aren't universally appreciated among the Otherkin. They tend toward rigid, anal-retentive personalities, I was told. Their posture reflects their personalities so often that Otherkin like to say, "We know where they keep their flaming swords."

Appearance doesn't necessarily correspond with identity. One elf whose lean body, high forehead, blond coloring, and sharp features would have made him central casting's first choice, said some Otherkin have the ability to change how they look to conform to their true selves. He didn't look elven at all when he first discovered his race, he said, but over time he has been able to magically change his body to look more like his true self.

Sexual preference, even sexual identity, is variable in Otherkin circles. Roger, who was pointed out to me as an East Asian dragon, is a he with long blue and black hair and noticeable breasts. The dragons at this convention were of the Eastern kind, which was fortunate, because Western dragons are often portrayed as stupid, rash, and greedy, like the one in Tolkien's *The Hobbit*. Eastern dragons are much wiser and powerful in better ways.

These dragons were all women of average to below-average height and impressive width. I'd watched them make their way through gatherings carefully maneuvering in space set up for humans of less girth. They were light on their feet and careful it seemed to make sure others weren't pushed around by their physical presence. If considered human, the dragon family might be thought of as humans suffering from bad genes or poor eating habits or laziness or gluttony or any of the other insults that are thrown at people whose weight is above average. But as dragons, their shape is not a drawback or even an oddity. A dragon ought to have some heft. It is their size, in fact, that helps make them so magnificent.

That evening during the Come as You Really Are Ball the Wolf spotted me sitting on the sidelines. I'd arrived late. My costume was a pen and notebook, jeans and a sweater, just me being my exciting self. He'd come as a party boy with handcuffs hanging from his belt. I saw him on the dance floor, gyrating wildly, shirtless. Shirtless suited him. When he saw me, he came over, took my hand, pulled me from my chair, and said, "I've been watching for you. Come upstairs where there's a real party."

If my husband had been there, he might have pointed out that when a half-naked man with handcuffs on his belt invites you to the real party, the right response is "No thank you, please." But my husband wasn't there.

As we walked down the long hall toward his room I asked, "Are you from around here?" He laughed and said, "That's the oldest pickup line in the world. Can't you do better?"

Before he poured me a triple shot of tequila, he jangled the handcuffs hanging off his belt and said, "I'd like to get a pair of these on you." Typical Otherkin, so considerate, always trying to make a person feel part of the group.

We went into his bedroom, where people were sitting on the bed and against the wall. I was quiet as I sat on the edge of the bed, taking small sips of the tequila.

Along with enough liquor to fill a refrigerator, the Wolf had brought a whip to the gathering. He invited a long-haired woman to scourge him, which she did with an admirable amount of flourish. Obviously here was a woman with some experience in handling a whip.

"Is that the best you can do?" he taunted her, and she applied herself with even more vigor. I hardly looked around. Bondage games are big in some magical circles, but they don't interest me. Performance sex of any kind makes me feel that the polite thing to do is look away. I know that's not what they're hoping for, but it's the best I can do.

After a while the Wolf lounged on the bed. I stayed on the edge while he and Michelle Belanger, the vampire leader of the House of Kheperu, explained to me about sex and energy.

Otherkin don't merely have sex, they exchange energy, Michelle said. It's the energy that makes sex with them more exciting than it would normally be. They touch the hidden energetic body of their partners, which is something everyone longs for. It's intimate and intense in a way that mundanes don't understand, Michelle said. As a result, they often believe themselves to be in love with vampires and Otherkin after having had nothing more than sexual energy exchange.

I wondered whether whipping and handcuffing played any part in touching the energetic body and whether I knew anybody who would think that meant love. One group of magical people, called Beasties, is known for dressing up like animals to have sex. Another group is involved in what they call sacred prostitution, modeled on ancient ideas of goddess worship, I suppose. Compared to them, the Otherkin might be considered fairly tame.

"That beautiful creature gave me one of the most exciting times of my life using just her fingernails," said the Wolf, referring to Michelle.

Telling me to push up the sleeve of my sweater, she demonstrated the exchange of energy by having me hold out my arm with my palm flat, facing the floor. Then she put her hands on either side of my hand about two inches from it.

"Feel the energy," she said. She began to stroke my arm with her fingernails, which were translucent white and filed to sharp points. Like animal claws or vampire fingers, which is what they were, I guess.

This time I didn't feel anything. She told me to relax and sense.

"I feel some heat," I said, which was a lie. I didn't feel a thing, but I'm sensitive to peer pressure, even when people aren't my peers. When I was little, my mother never taunted me by asking, "If everyone else was jumping off a cliff, would you?" She knew I would.

I left the party at 3:00 A.M. It went until seven. By the time I saw the Otherkin at eleven, they were looking quite human in a bilious way. Hungover and sleep-deprived, many sported newly created hickies on their necks and who can say where else.

"Looks like you exchanged a little energy last night," I said to the Wolf.

"I gave as good as I got," he said, straight-faced. Fighting words. As though he had been in a battle. Perhaps he had.

Later, when I went to Michelle's website, I saw that she was selling note cards with photographs of herself clad in black leather, glowering into the camera as she punished a bound young woman referred to as Kitty. It looked so stagy that I wondered, *What is she telling us in this piece of playacting? That she is powerful and dangerous and always in control?*

Well. Okay. That I understood.

But is binding and whipping people magical, and if it isn't, why pair it with sex? I'd learned enough now to understand why sex and magic so often go together. It's not merely that sexual energy is powerful enough to derange even the steadiest among us, although it is. And it's not just that orgasm is such an overwhelming experience that the French are right on when they call it the little death, although they are. And it isn't even that what turns us on and what turns us off is so mysterious and wondrous, or even that good sex makes us feel more alive than any other thing. What makes sex magical isn't merely orgasm. It's the selfsame thing that makes magic magical—the connection with something beyond ourselves. If it's the right kind of sex, it makes us more than we were before, happier, healthier, more powerful. Connecting with someone else in a real and intimate way is not the only way to have sex, as most of us know quite well, but it might be the only magical way.

Granted, being bound and whipped is a lot less scary than intimacy with another human, especially one who's lying nose-to-nose naked with you, and some people say that sadomasochism helps overcome that scarier fear. Maybe it does. Or maybe it's just another wrong turn in the road to real magic.

When we ran into each other at the elevator, the Wolf talked me into going for breakfast. I'd already had breakfast, but he suggested I have coffee while he ate. I was about to invite some others to go with us when he moved between the other Otherkin and me. His back was to them, but he slid between us like a wolf cutting off the rest of the pack. They took the message and turned away wordlessly. When we got to the diner, he said, "I don't like to eat alone," and ordered us both chocolate milk shakes and then plates of eggs with potatoes. He avoids meat. First I met a vegetarian vampire, then a meat-avoiding werewolf. Wonders never cease.

He told me he had been a sickly child who became aware of his true nature while studying with native people in the north woods of Canada. He did not claim to grow fur or fangs, but he did hint that a wolf's capacities for enduring pain and fighting fiercely were in his genes. His father had a wolfish element in him, he said. As a child, he admired it, sometimes feared it, and now believed he had inherited it in a way that was more than human. He often called upon his wolf nature when boxing, he said. As he felt himself losing a bout, he would summon the wolf and fight so tenaciously that he felt no pain and he usually won.

When I asked for a magical story, he told me that he had once come upon a bear in the forest. As they stood facing one another, the Wolf had called on his animal nature, hoping to intimidate the bear. After looking at him for a few seconds, the bear turned and walked away.

I asked for another magical story, and the Wolf talked of a business decision he once had to make. He was unsure which way to go. So he sat in meditation invoking the Goddess.

"Why the Goddess?" I asked.

"I'm a big tough guy," he said. "I don't need a male god who can protect me. I do need comfort and warmth, the kind that I wanted as a child and didn't get." For that, only a goddess will do. We were silent a minute.

"It's not as though I think there's a big vagina in the sky," he said.

"Good," I murmured. "That could be distracting."

During his call upon the Goddess and his meditation, he believed himself able to see paths before him. He could see how each one would turn out. None took him where he wanted to go. And then he received a message. He was to go to a man whom he knew only slightly. This man would know how to move forward.

The Wolf did what the vision told him, and that man is now his business partner.

This was the last day of the workshop, and after the closing ritual I was busy interviewing people. The Wolf kept coming to me as I talked. He would stand at my side, and without a word he would smooth my hair back, stroke the curve of my ear, and then move his fingers down my neck. I would continue talking. No one mentioned what he was doing, and I didn't have a clue. Without a word, he would leave.

He returned several times, and then finally he found the touch he was looking for. What had been merely contact was now a caress. It was exactly the same motion and yet nothing like what he'd done before. I stood quite still like a dog being scratched under the chin.

"I believe that's it," I said when he stopped. "I think you've found it." He backed away again, without a word.

Later, as I stood alone finishing some notes, he came close to me. I kept my head down, and his low voice was in my ear. "You didn't feel the energy when Michelle did it. I wanted you to feel it before you left."

"How did you do it?" I asked in the same low tone, my head down, my eyes on the notebook.

"I put emotion into it," he said. His words were so soft I could hardly hear them.

Then he was gone. If I had known what he was about, I could have told him what he needed the first time he touched me. Magical people had been teaching me that for more than a year. You must connect. Call it emotion, call it commitment, call it surrender. Whatever you call it, you can't have magic without it.

15.

Voodoo Takes the Big Banana Down

Perhaps the werewolf's touch was a turning point that the energies of the universe responded to, maybe the gods looked down and were pleased, or maybe it didn't make one bit of difference. I had one more visit to make in my magical research. My Jesus dream and its connection to voodoo made me determined to experience at least one voodoo ceremony. I particularly liked New Orleans' Sallie Ann Glassman, a voodoo priestess, or manbo, whom I'd talked to a number of times. I liked her for exactly the reason that some other voodoo practitioners didn't like her. Among her followers, animal sacrifice is not done. Instead, they generate the energy that spirits want by meditation that brings up prana, or life force, energies.

Her teacher in Haiti does conduct animal sacrifices, and Sallie Ann has been to some of them. But Haiti is a far different place than New Orleans, she says. Sallie Ann believes that religions adapt to new circumstances. She believes voodoo deities will come to devotees just as forcefully when enticed by less bloody offerings.

Sallie Ann invited me to come to New Orleans. For more than a year I couldn't seem to get there. I'd almost given up when she sent an e-mail saying that her teacher, the Haitian oungan Edgar Jean-Louis, was coming to visit for a week. Anyone who wanted a head washing, which is a sort of blessing, could pay $50 and get one. It seemed like an opportunity too good to miss.

The front of her house is plain and fits into the neighborhood well. Shutters give it the closed, blank look of many city houses in New Orleans. Lots of people were on the street during the early evening, and most were black. In the front room and the middle room that led to the kitchen, much of the floor was filled with two mattresses without bed frames. The beds were made up, and nothing about the rooms was untidy, but they made the place feel a little like a crash pad. A Bart Simpson doll sat on a shelf among more Haitian-looking figures. The walls were covered with bold colorful paintings that seemed Haitian. Two featured a woman who looked like Sallie Ann. In one she was looking into a mirror while spirits swirled around her.

Edgar was a tall thin man of eighty-three with the look of hollowed-out, longtime hunger that is often seen in developing countries but rarely seen in the United States, except among AIDs patients or drug addicts. He was dressed in a white T-shirt and blue pants with stripes. His bones were so close to the skin that when he hugged me he felt loose and gangly in my arms. His hands hanging at the end of long sinewy arms were big and knobby. His smile was sweet under a well-trimmed mustache. His hair was grizzled and short enough that it was easy to see the shape of his head. On the back of his head was a big knot. After the ceremony he smoked, holding what looked to be a hand-rolled cigarette between his thumb and forefinger, like a Frenchman or a stoner with a joint.

There was an altar in the kitchen with plates of food set on it. Off the kitchen was the peristil, or temple room, with a black-and-white-checked floor and black walls. The apartment had high ceilings, which gave the room a grand feeling. Haitian drums sat at the edges of the room. People were expected to take their shoes off when they went into the peristil. I didn't at first because no one told me, but no one corrected me or seemed to notice. Edgar didn't take his shoes off either, and of course, no one corrected him.

I wore black trousers and a white shirt. Sallie Ann was dressed in a white skirt and a lovely white sleeveless blouse that had a feminine touch of eyelet fabric in the front. She was thin, a tiny woman, and looked to be quite tanned, although that could just have been the color of her skin. She had reddish hair and a wide smile. She was soft-spoken and seemed almost retiring. She was not ordering people around or seeming to be in charge at all. She tended to Edgar assiduously, watching him and interpreting what he said in a low sweet voice. He spoke no English. Sallie Ann speaks French and taught herself enough Creole to understand him.

When she saw my black pants, she said, "If you want a head washing, he'll want you to be in white." I knew who "he" was. There were only three other men there: one devotee with a white satin head covering, a film student making a documentary, and an anthropologist from the University of New Orleans. For a while it seemed as though there were more people studying the group than people in the group. The women were all dressed in white, and they wore long white cloths tied about their heads with the knot in the back. Sallie Ann opened a closet at the back of the peristil filled with white clothes. She chose a skirt with gathered tiers of filmy material.

I went into one of the two bathrooms off the kitchen to put it on. Later a woman volunteered to tie a long piece of cloth around my head. She was shorter than I am. So I knelt while she did it.

The peristil's altar was dedicated to many spirits and had many images on it. In front of them were plates of food: a white cake, Turkish figs, vanilla cookies, bananas, watermelon, grapes, and cups of what looked to be coffee. There was also Florida Water. A replica of a human skull with the butt of a cigar hanging out of the mouth and the image of a very black woman with a long red tongue were also in the room. Edgar's skin was almost as black as the statue's, a shade of black that you see most often in Africans, of such a deep, rich shade that it seemed to swallow the light around it. He was the only black man there.

Edgar began placing things in front of the altar, walking back and forth with a cigarette hanging off his lips. The head-washing liquid was contained in a metal basin on the floor in front of the altar. I was unhappy to note that the liquid looked something like vomit. It was grayish brown in color. A sludge seemed to have settled to the bottom, leaving a thick film of clear liquid on top. Something protruded from the middle of the concoction. It might have been an egg.

Before the ceremony started, Edgar moved about the room as he counted a stack of bills Sallie had collected from us. Using cornmeal, he made a symbol on the floor to bring forth the lwa, or spirit, we would be seeking. Then he sprinkled cornmeal into the basin. I could hear the rough friction of his fingers, like sandpaper. He put an egg on the plate of cornmeal, rolled it around a bit, opened a bottle of Florida Water, and splashed a good bit of it into the basin. The hot room, which already smelled of candles, filled with a pungent smell like aftershave.

Then he rose and began to shake a rattle as we stood watching from the edges of the room. Someone passed a short-legged, cane-bottom chair over the crowd. Edgar put it in front of the basin and sat. As people came forward, he made the sign of the cross on their heads, on their foreheads, and then on their lips. Each person took off the scarf, knelt before the basin, and put her head over it so that her hair could be splashed with the liquid. Some people ducked their faces into the basin. Others seemed to be kissing the floor. A few were crying. Afterward, the scarves were re-tied about our heads. One tall woman with a snake tattooed across her shoulders wore the beads that she had been given during her initiation in Haiti. Edgar took off her beads, piled them on top of her head, put the egg over them, and then bound her head in the white cloth. The egg would provide a conduit for the spirit to enter through her head, I was told. Afterward, he hugged her.

Edgar then went through the room, shaking hands. He would take one hand, shake it, and then jerk it toward the ground. Then he took the other one and did the same.

I had no idea what any of this meant. Before we dispersed, however, he spoke to us as Sallie Ann translated. She spoke softly and with great humility. But the praise he gave her made her proud, and she didn't try to hide that. He said that she had never lied to him. He said that she had brought many people to be initiated and that they were his children now. He said it didn't matter if you were in Haiti or the United States, you could still serve the lwa. This head washing would open up the way for the lwa to be with us. It might be the first step for us to become initiated ourselves. We would be changed, he promised. Sallie Ann told us to remember our dreams that night because they could be important messages from the lwa.

We were told that boys were not to sleep with girls or girls with boys that night. There was to be no sex, in other words, and we were to keep our kerchiefs on. In the morning we might wash our hair.

My head smelled awful that night, and the friend who was with me mentioned how happy she was to be across the room in another bed. "I didn't let them wash my head because I was afraid of what it might do to my color," she said.

"Color?" I wailed. "My color? I didn't think about that." She meant those highlights we'd paid so much to have streaking through our hair. I hadn't worried about the lwa doing anything to my soul, but if my hair was green in the morning I'd be out a fortune getting it right. Still, I kept the scarf on. To back out would mean that I'd never know whether the blessing could have changed me. I didn't dream at all that night. I washed my hair the next morning, and my color was fine.

My friend wanted an authentic voodoo flag. To get one we walked over to Sallie Ann's shop, the Island of Salvation Botanica, which is outside the French Quarter. Sallie Ann had first become acquainted with voodoo when importing flags, and she had a great selection, well priced. I didn't intend to buy one, until I saw them. I knew the one I wanted immediately, but I didn't say anything as my friend chose hers. We were both ready to buy when my friend said, "I think I'd like to have two. I could put them on my wall and they would match." She looked around the shop and picked one. But Sallie Ann shook her head. Those two don't go together, she said. The spirits aren't compatible. "It would be better to pick another one."

My friend looked at mine. "I wish you would pick another one so I could have that one," she said. "Yours would look so good with mine."

It was true. Mine was a perfect match, right size, right colors, right shape, and the spirits worked well together. I looked at all the other flags. There were so many I could have. I ought to give it to her. The old curse of the big banana was hanging over me, saying, *Don't be selfish. You'll regret it.*

If you keep that flag, the sequins would fall off and the edges would unravel. I could hear the voice as loud as ever, but I shook my head.

You'll lose it. You'll get it home and not even like it. Put friendship first. What kind of person are you? Is this the kind of person you want to be?

But this time I didn't give in. Something had changed. I could hear the voices, but they weren't quite as sure of themselves. We spent an hour looking, debating. Again and again my friend urged me to take another flag. Again and again I almost did. I'd be on the verge of giving it up, and then I wouldn't. It was completely unlike me. Who was this person so stubbornly holding on to what she wanted? What would Sallie Ann think of me?

Then Sallie Ann said, "Every bead in these flags is sewn on with a prayer." I looked at my flag. A ripple of light flashed across the sequins.

"No," I said. "I want this one."

Was that me saying so loudly, *I want this one,* as though I were a two-year-old child? Yes, it was me. I bought it. And all weekend my friend, like some force sent from heaven to help me cement my new resolve, kept giving me one chance after another to trade my flag for the one she had eventually bought. But I never did. And the sequins didn't fall off; I didn't lose it; I didn't get it home and realize that I hadn't really liked it. My friend didn't get mad. She never reproached me. She just said, "Okay." Nothing bad happened. Nothing at all.

The curse of the big banana was broken. Maybe Papa Edgar was right about the head washing having changed us. I hadn't felt any different afterwards, but I was.

Was this good magic? How could it be? The curse of the big banana had tempered my selfishness. Without it, I would think of myself first instead of putting myself last. That's bad, right? Not what Jesus would do. Even so, it felt like good magic to me. It felt like liberation and strength, as though I had been freed from always stepping to the back of the line, helplessly, wordlessly, inevitably. I could advocate for myself now instead of standing like a mute child hoping someone else would take up for me. The next time someone stepped in front of me in line, I would do more than shrug and wince. I'd say something. Nothing rude probably, but something. The next time someone said, "Do you want that last cookie?" I wouldn't have to look away nobly and say, "No. You take it." I might not be able to eat the whole thing, but I could take half of it. I felt like a doormat that had finally gotten up and walked away.

It didn't mean that I would never be generous again, but when I was generous I could be that way with a free heart and not because I was afraid. I had a choice. This was good magic for me, even if it wasn't that great for everyone else. Well, that's how magic is, I guess. That's always how it has been, focused on one person at a time. I'd seen that again and again.

I put the flag in my study and made a sort of altar around it so that I would never forget. In front of it I put my Buddha from Hong Kong, a crucifix bought in the French Quarter, a Madonna and child icon from Romania, photos of my family, and a Josefina Aquilar statue of a *dama de la noche* smoking a cigarette. The voodoo flag is near the door, and every time I go in or out of the room the sequins wink at me, like a blessing.

I half expected that I would return to my former self at some point and regret my decision, reproach myself for greed and repent, but I never did. I e-mailed Sallie Ann to say that I was surprised I'd wanted that flag so much, and I wondered if it was the lwa who made me cling so tenaciously to that particular one.

"It was the lwa," she wrote back. "I'm sure it was."

16.

Do This in Remembrance

My magical experiences were too little to convince me and at the same time too much to dismiss. Together they made a pretty good list: the mojo bag that reassured me about travel; the Jesus dream in which I was paralyzed and the voodoo book with its ceremony of paralysis; the cold that had fallen on me when Michelle the vampire fed off me; the change in the werewolf's touch when he put emotion into it; and the voodoo head washing that brought about the end of the big banana curse. What did it all amount to? I didn't know.

When Christmas arrived, I was in London with my husband, who was attending a conference. One of my oldest friends and her eleven-year-old daughter joined us for the holiday. None of us attends church, but Westminster Abbey was only a short walk from the apartment we rented, and so Christmas morning we went there for a service.

Throughout the singing and the reading and the sermonizing, I felt puzzled and out of sync, as I often do in church. I remembered my days of fervent, unquestioning belief, but the emptiness I felt made those earlier times seem odd, like the imaginings of a child. At the end, when it came time to take communion, I went forward. My friends and my husband stayed in their seats. I suspected that the eleven-year-old was staring at me with disappointment and perhaps disdain. A tenderhearted, passionate girl of great idealism, she was in a terrible struggle with life's inability to live up to what it promises. She was furious with Christianity for harboring so many hypocrites. Perhaps having learned that good is good and bad is bad and never the twain should meet, she was caught in disillusionment, as I have been so many times. It had taken a lifetime and a trip deep into the magical community to deliver me from that error. I hoped she would find an easier, quicker path.

I was aware that my young friend might think me a hypocrite for taking communion, but, despite the coldness of my heart, I had some dimly understood aversion to sitting while others stepped up for that ancient sacrament, and so I took the blood and body of Christ with its promise of forgiveness and new life. To anyone who doesn't share that heritage, it's a strange thing to do, every bit as strange as any magic I'd seen. What happened next will seem like pure imagination to anyone who has never felt it, but anyone who has felt it will know precisely what I mean.

After solemnly taking the wafer and the wine, I returned to a seat in that arching cavern surrounded by stone statues and tombs and other living humans who like me are only on this earth for one bright, burning moment and then will be gone. We were all completely alone in the universe with not even an echo to keep us company, and in the next instant I was connected. To what? I don't know. It came into my consciousness like a shaft of light, only it wasn't light; like warmth, only it wasn't warmth; like understanding, only it had no content. The vampires might have called it energy. Siva the Satanist might have called it Kali. Kioni and I would call it God.

Taking communion had been an act of magic for me, a technology of the sacred. I had believed just enough to step forward for the ritual, and that was enough. First, the voodoo head washing had changed a deep-seated part of me. Then Christian communion had connected me to something that was bigger than myself. Nothing happened until I took some action. Action and results—the two go together. You can call it religion, you can call it spirituality, you can call it magic. Maybe what you call it doesn't matter. What matters is that you don't settle for being cut off, that you take the power, that you demand the completeness of human experience. To taste fully of all that we perceive, to expand our hopefulness beyond the heavens is our birthright. We aren't here only for confusion and disillusionment. We aren't born merely for death. We are here also for transcendence, to savor the numinous, to wander through the shifting corridors of meaning, and to follow them wherever they take us. If we go too far, we can stop. We can backtrack, we can recant, we can be inconsistent, illogical. What we must not do—no matter what the scientists tell us—is allow ourselves to be cut off from our own experience of life as it presents itself to us. If we do, we will have lost the very ground beneath our feet.

I am not saying that we must believe that a spell can turn a frog into a prince or that bewitched dolls will blink and move their heads. Many of the magical things I witnessed and even those I believed to have happened might have been coincidences or the result of suggestion. Those two factors could be enough to explain everything. But I believe it was no accident that Jesus showed up in my dream during the days when I was most avidly pursuing magic, and it was no accident that I interpreted his appearance as encouragement to go further. It was also no accident that Bible verses came to me again and again during my investigation. Those touchstones of my earliest faith led me forward when nothing else could have.

One verse that hadn't occurred to me would have helped me understand what I was seeing at the very beginning, on that night early in my travels when I attended Mistress Tracy's Vampire and Victims Ball. It was something Jesus said. "The kingdom of heaven is at hand."

Some people thought he meant that the world was soon to end, but I don't think he meant that. I think he meant that the truth of life's wonders is constantly revealing itself all around us. The sacred text that waits patiently for us to read it is life itself. The rituals, the magical workings, the symbols and incantations of magic, the writings of religion, maybe even the ponderings of personal just-make-it-up spirituality are the technology that opens channels for what might be called life energy, or God, or virtue, or—I like best of all how the elf Silver Flame put it—the sacred retort. Whether those things exist outside the human imagination or merely inside it doesn't matter as much to me as it does to some people. If the Jesus who showed up in my dream lives only within my heart, he's still there. What matters to me is that we can allow ourselves to participate in the richness available to us.

All we have to do is choose.

After the Westminster service, I went up for a closer look at the grand monument to Sir Isaac Newton that stands at the front of the chapel. A few steps to the side, I stood on the stone engraved with Charles Darwin's name. These two men did more to aid human progress and more to destroy the traditional beliefs of religious life than anyone on earth. Both are buried at Westminster. Still filled with that wondrous feeling of connectedness, I stood right on top of Darwin's name.

SOURCES

1. THE WAITRESS WEARS A PENTACLE

Luhrmann, *Persuasions of the Witch's Craft.*

2. EAT ONLY CHICKEN THE DAY OF THE GAME

Cohen, "A Surge in Popularity in Jewish Mysticism"; Piccalo, "On E-Bay, New Meaning for 'Spirited' Bidding"; Faires, "The Curse of the Play"; Bettelheim, *The Uses of Enchantment;* James, *Varieties of Religious Experience;* Schneider, *Culture and Enchantment;* Bailey and Bledsoe, *God, Dr. Buzzard, and the Bolito Man;* Shorto, *Saints and Madmen;* Galbreath, "Explaining Modern Occultism."

3. AMERICA THE MAGICAL, I SING OF THEE

Finke and Stark, *The Churching of America;* Crèvecoeur, *Letters from an American Farmer;* Ellis, *Lucifer Ascending;* Boyer and Nissenbaum, *Salem Possessed;* Butler, *Awash in a Sea of Faith;* Ellis, *Raising the Devil;* Melton, *Magic, Witchcraft, and Paganism in America;* Hoffman, "Modern Alchemists"; Stavish, "History of Alchemy in North America"; Godbeer, *Devil's Dominion;* Fuller, *Religious Revolutionaries;* Galbreath, *Explaining Modern Occultism;* Kyle, "The Occult Roars Back"; Hill, "Imaginary Friends Perfectly Normal"; Dunnewind, "Just Imagine That"; *New York Times,* April 13, 2004, D3; Fuller, *Spiritual but Not Religious;* Luhrmann, *Persuasions of the Witch's Craft;* Burton and Grandy, *Magic, Mystery, and Science;* van de Broek and Hanegraaff, *Gnosis and Hermeticism;* Kieckhefer, *Magic in the Middle Ages.*

4. LOOKING FOR LIVING DOLLS, WHACK JOBS, AND THE LUCKY MOJO CURIO COMPANY

Catherine Yronwode's collection of slave narratives at southern-spirits.com; Sutin, *Do What Thou Wilt*; Yronwode, *Hoodoo Herb and Root Magic*; Hemenway, *Zora Neale Hurston*; Dewey and Jones, *King of the Cold Readers*; Saville and Dewey, *Red Hot Cold Reading*; Duriez and Foster, *Christianity Today*.

Lyrics to hoodoo and blues songs are reprinted from luckymojo.com, which carries an extensive copyright disclaimer. "Due to certain social, economic, and political paradigms in place at the time of their composition," Yronwode explains, "many early blues songs were improperly copyrighted or not copyrighted at all." She adds that unethical practices on the part of some music publishers and arrangers have further muddied the copyright status of these songs. "It is my sincere belief," she notes, "that the song transcribed on this [web] page bears the implied moral copyright of its composer, whoever that may be. If you believe that you control the copyright by virtue of authorship or legal legerdemain, you may contact me in a civil and polite manner and I will attempt in good faith to satisfy your needs in the matter of obtaining formal permission to quote the lyrics in this scholarly publication."

5. NEWTON'S ALCHEMY, HEGEL'S *GRIMOIRE*, AND WHAT CIVILIZATION OWES TO MAGIC

Adler, *Drawing Down the Moon*; Wilson, *The Occult*; Luhrmann, *Persuasions of the Witch's Craft*; Sutin, *Do What Thou Wilt*; French, *John Dee*; Burton and Grandy, *Magic, Mystery, and Science*; Armstrong, *The Battle for God*; Gleick, *Isaac Newton*; Gleick, "Isaac Newton's Gravity"; Magee, *Hegel and the Hermetic Tradition*.

7. *MALEFICIA DU JOUR:* SERVED HOT, COLD, AND CASH BEFORE DELIVERY

Haskins, *Voodoo and Hoodoo*; Pinckney, *Blue Roots*; Teish, *Jambalaya*; Twyman, *Book of Lies*; Borg, *Meeting Jesus Again for the First Time*.

9. WHAT TO DO WHEN THE MOTHER OF GOD COMES CALLING

Pinckney, *Blue Roots*; Burton and Grandy, *Magic, Mystery, and Science*.

For information on Catherine Yronwode's hoodoo class lessons and *The Lucky Mojo Hoodoo Rootwork Hour;* go to luckymojo.com and discussions.

10. HOODOO? WE DO, IN THE GRAVEYARD

Hemenway, *Zora Neale Hurston;* Catherine Yronwode's hoodoo class, lesson 27.

11. BE CAREFUL WHAT YOU SAY ABOUT ZORA

Kaplan, *Zora Neale Hurston: A Life in Letters;* Hillman, *The Soul's Code.*

12. EVERY TIME YOU HEAR A BELL, A MUGGLE HAS TURNED MAGICAL

Luhrmann, *Persuasions of the Witch's Craft;* Toms, *An Open Life;* Melton, *Magic, Witchcraft, and Paganism in America;* Schjeldahl, "Striking Gold."

BIBLIOGRAPHY

Adler, Margot. *Drawing Down the Moon* (New York: Penguin Compass, 1986).

Armstrong, Karen. *The Battle for God* (New York: Alfred A. Knopf, 2000).

Bailey, Cornelia Walker, and Christena Bledsoe. *God, Dr. Buzzard, and the Bolito Man: A Saltwater Geechee Talks About Life on Sapelo Island* (New York: Doubleday, 2000).

Barnard, G. William, and Jeffrey J. Kripal, eds. *Crossing Boundaries: Essays on the Ethical Status of Mysticism* (New York: Seven Bridges Press, 2002).

Barzun, Jacques. *From Dawn to Decadence: 500 Years of Western Civilization* (New York: HarperCollins, 2000).

Baudino, Gael. *Strands of Starlight* (New York: Roc, 1994).

Belanger, Michelle. *The Psychic Vampire Codex: A Manual of Magick and Energy Work* (Boston: Weiser Books, 2004).

Berg, Wendy, and Mike Harris. *Polarity Magic: The Secret History of Western Religion* (St. Paul, MN: Llewellyn, 2003).

Bettelheim, Bruno. *The Uses of Enchantment* (New York: Alfred A. Knopf, 1976).

Black, S. Jason, and Christopher S. Hyatt. *Urban Voodoo: A Beginner's Guide to Afro-Caribbean Magic* (Tempe, AZ: New Falcon, 1995).

Bodin, Ron. *Voodoo: Past and Present* (Lafayette, LA: University of Southwestern Louisiana Press, 1990).

Borg, Marcus J. *Meeting Jesus Again for the First Time* (San Francisco: HarperSanFrancisco, 1984).

Boyd, Valerie. *Wrapped in Rainbows: The Life of Zora Neale Hurston* (New York: Scribner, 2003).

Boyer, Paul S., and Stephen Nissenbaum. *Salem Possessed: The Social Origins of Witchcraft* (Cambridge, MA: Harvard University Press, 1974).

Bradley, Marion Zimmer. *The Mists of Avalon* (New York: Ballantine, 1982).

Breslaw, Elaine G., ed. *Witches of the Atlantic World: A Historical Reader and Primary Sourcebook* (New York: New York University Press, 2000).

Brown, Karen McCarthy. *Mama Lola: A Vodou Priestess in Brooklyn* (Berkeley: University of California Press, 1991).

Bruce, Eve, MD. *Shaman, MD* (Rochester, VT: Destiny Books, 2002).

Burton, Dan, and David Grandy. *Magic, Mystery, and Science: The Occult in Western Civilization* (Bloomington: Indiana University Press, 2004).

Butler, Jon. *Awash in a Sea of Faith: Christianizing the American People* (Cambridge, MA: Harvard University Press, 1990).

Cabot, Laurie. *The Witch in Every Woman* (New York: Delta, 1997).

Campbell, Joseph. *The Power of Myth* (New York: Anchor Books, 1991).

Carnes, Mark C. *Secret Ritual and Manhood in Victorian America* (New Haven, CT: Yale University Press, 1989).

Carroll, Peter J. *Liber Null and Psychonaut: An Introduction to Chaos Magic* (Boston: Weiser Books, 1987).

Case, Shirley Jackson. *The Origins of Christian Supernaturalism* (Chicago: University of Chicago Press, 1946).

———. *Experience with the Supernatural in Early Christian Times* (New York: Benjamin Blom, 1971).

Chatwin, Bruce. *The Songlines* (New York: Penguin, 1987).

Clark, Stuart. *Thinking with Demons: The Idea of Witchcraft in Early Modern Europe* (Oxford: Oxford University Press, 1997).

Cohen, Debra Nussbaum. "A Surge in Popularity in Jewish Mysticism," *New York Times*, December 13, 2003.

Crèvecoeur, J. Hector St. John. *Letters from an American Farmer* (New York: Fox, Duffield, 1904).

Crossan, John Dominic. *Jesus: A Revolutionary Biography* (San Francisco: HarperSanFrancisco, 1994).

Cuhulain, Kerr. *Wiccan Warrior: Walking a Spiritual Path in a Sometimes Hostile World* (St. Paul, MN: Llewellyn, 2000).

Cunningham, David Michael. *Creating Magickal Entities* (Perrysburg, OH: Egregore Publishing, 2003).

Cunningham, Scott. *The Truth About Witchcraft Today* (St. Paul, MN: Llewellyn, 2001).

———. *Wicca: A Guide for the Solitary Practitioner* (St. Paul, MN: Llewellyn 2003).

Dewey, Herb, and Bascom Jones. *King of the Cold Readers: How to Tell Fortunes for Fun and Profit,* 2nd ed. (1989; Marc Sky, 1996).

Dowdy, Thomas E., and Patrick H. McNamara. *Religion: North American Style,* 3rd ed. (New Brunswick, NJ: Rutgers University Press, 1997).

Dunnewind, Stephanie. "Just Imagine That," *Atlanta Journal-Constitution,* December 26, 2004.

Duriez, Colin. "Tollers & Jack," *Christianity Today,* August 25, 2003.

Ellis, Bill. *Lucifer Ascending: The Occult in Folklore and Popular Culture* (Lexington: University Press of Kentucky, 2004).

———. *Raising the Devil: Satanism, New Religions, and the Media* (Lexington: University Press of Kentucky, 2002).

Faires, Robert. "The Curse of the Play," *Austin Chronicle,* October 13, 2000.

Farrar, Janet, and Stewart Farrar. *The Witches' Goddess: The Feminine Principle of Divinity* (Blaine, WA: Phoenix, 1987).

Farrar, Stewart. *What Witches Do* (Blaine, WA: Phoenix, 1971).

Finke, Roger, and Rodney Stark. *The Churching of America, 1776–1990: Winners and Losers in Our Religious Economy* (New Brunswick, NJ: Rutgers University Press, 1992).

Flowers, Arthur. *Mojo Rising: Confessions of a 21st-Century Conjureman* (New York: Wanganesgresse Press, 2001).

Foster, Michael. "An Unexpected Party," *Christianity Today,* August 25, 2003.

Frazer, Sir James George. *The Illustrated Golden Bough* (New York: Doubleday, 1978).

French, Peter J. *John Dee: The World of an Elizabethan Magus* (London: Routledge & Kegan Paul, 1972).

Fuller, Robert C. *Spiritual but Not Religious: Understanding Unchurched America* (Oxford: Oxford University Press, 2001).

———. *Religious Revolutionaries: The Rebels Who Reshaped American Religions* (New York: Palgrave Macmillan, 2004).

Galbreath, Robert. "Explaining Modern Occultism," in *The Occult in America: New Historical Perspectives,* edited by Howard Kerr and Charles L. Crow (Urbana: University of Illinois Press, 1983).

Gamache, Henri. *The Master Book of Candle Burning* (Old Bethpage, NY: Original Publishing, 1998).

Garfield, Joseph R. *Performing Action: Artistry in Human Behavior and Social Research* (New Brunswick, NJ: Transaction Publishers, 2000).

Glassman, Sallie Ann. *Voodou Visions: An Encounter with Divine Mystery* (New York: Villard, 2000).

Gleick, James. *Isaac Newton* (New York: Pantheon Books, 2003).

———. "Isaac Newton's Gravity," *Slate*, October 21, 2004.

Godbeer, Richard. *The Devil's Dominion: Magic and Religion in Early New England* (Ann Arbor: University of Michigan Dissertation Information Service, 1990).

Greer, John Michael. *Inside a Magical Lodge: Group Ritual in the Western Tradition* (St. Paul, MN: Llewellyn, 1998).

Hanegraaff, Wouter J. *New Age Religion and Western Culture: Esotericism in the Mirror of Secular Thought* (Leiden, the Netherlands: E. J. Brill, 1996).

Harner, Michael. *The Way of the Shaman* (San Francisco: HarperSanFrancisco, 1990).

Haskins, Jim. *Voodoo and Hoodoo: The Tradition and Craft as Revealed by Actual Practitioners* (Plainview, NY: Original Publications, 1978).

Hemenway, Robert E. *Zora Neale Hurston: A Literary Biography* (Urbana: University of Illinois Press, 1977).

Hill, Frances. *A Delusion of Satan: The Full Story of the Salem Witch Trials* (New York: Doubleday, 1995).

Hill, Richard L. "Imaginary Friends Perfectly Normal," *Milwaukee Journal Sentinel*, January 30, 2005.

Hillman, James. *The Soul's Code* (New York: Random House, 1996).

Hine, Phil. *Condensed Chaos: An Introduction to Chaos Magic* (Tempe, AZ: New Falcon Publications, 1995).

Hoffman, Jascha. "Modern Alchemists," *Boston Globe*, July 27, 2003.

Hopman, Ellen Evert, and Lawrence Bond. *Being a Pagan* (Rochester, VT: Destiny, 1996).

James, William. *The Varieties of Religious Experience* (New York: Modern Library/ Random House, 1994).

Kalder, Raven, and Tannin Schwartzstein. *The Urban Primitive: Paganism in the Concrete Jungle* (St. Paul, MN: Llewellyn, 2002).

Kaplan, Carla. *Zora Neale Hurston: A Life in Letters* (New York: Anchor Books, 2002).

Kerr, Howard, and Charles L. Crow, eds. *The Occult in America: New Historical Perspectives* (Urbana: University of Illinois Press, 1983).

Kieckhefer, Richard. *Magic in the Middle Ages* (Cambridge: Cambridge University Press, 1990).

Kyle, Richard. "The Occult Roars Back: Its Modern Resurgence," *Directions* 29, no. 2 (Fall 2000): 91–99.

Le Guin, Ursula. *The Dispossessed* (London: SF Masterworks, 1974).

Long, Carolyn Morrow. *Spiritual Merchants: Religion, Magic, and Commerce* (Knoxville: University of Tennessee Press, 2001).

Luhrmann, Tanya M. *Persuasions of the Witch's Craft: Ritual Magic in Contemporary England* (Cambridge, MA: Harvard University Press, 1989).

Masters, Robert. *Swimming Where Madmen Drown: Travelers' Tales from Inner Space* (Makawoa, Maui, HI: Inner Ocean, 2002).

Metzger, Richard, ed. *Book of Lies: The Disinformation Guide to Magick and the Occult* (New York: Disinformation Co., 2003).

Mac Liammóir, Micheál, and Eavan Boland. *W. B. Yeats and His World* (New York: Viking Press, 1971).

Magee, Glenn Alexander. *Hegel and the Hermetic Tradition* (Ithaca, NY: Cornell University Press, 2001).

Mason, Michael Atwood. *Living Santeria: Rituals and Experiences in an Afro-Cuban Religion* (Washington, DC: Smithsonian Institution Press, 2002).

McLelland, Lilith. *Out of the Shadows: Myths and Truths of Modern Wicca* (New York: Citadel, 2002).

Melton, Gordon. *Magic, Witchcraft, and Paganism in America* (New York: Garland, 1982).

Mishlove, Jeffrey. *The Roots of Consciousness: Psychic Liberation Through History, Science, and Experience* (New York: Random House, 1975).

Narby, Jeremy. *The Cosmic Serpent: DNA and the Origins of Knowledge* (New York: Jeremy P. Tarcher/Putnam, 1998).

Neihardt, John G. *Black Elk Speaks: Being the Life Story of a Holy Man of the Oglala Sioux* (Lincoln: University of Nebraska Press, 1932).

Norton, Mary Beth. *In the Devil's Snare: The Salem Witchcraft Crisis of 1692* (New York: Alfred A. Knopf, 2002).

Ochs, Carol. *Women and Spirituality*, 2nd ed. (Landham, MD: Rowman & Littlefield, 1997).

Piccalo, Gina. "On E-Bay, New Meaning for 'Spirited' Bidding," *Los Angeles Times*, January 8, 2005.

Pinckney, Roger. *Blue Roots: African-American Folk Magic of the Gullah People* (St. Paul, MN: Llewellyn, 2000).

Polson, Willow. *The Veil's Edge: Exploring the Boundaries of Magic* (New York: Citadel, 2003).

Pratchett, Terry. *Witches Abroad* (New York: HarperTorch, 1991).

Puttick, Elizabeth. *Women in New Religions* (New York: St. Martin's Press, 1997).

Rice, Anne. *Interview with a Vampire* (New York: Ballantine, 1976).

———. *The Vampire Lestat* (New York: Ballantine, 1995).

Rigaud, Milo. *Secrets of Voodoo* (San Francisco: City Lights, 1969).

Robbins, Thomas, and Dick Anthony. *In Gods We Trust: New Patterns of Religious Pluralism in America* (New Brunswick, NJ: Transaction Books, 1981).

Saville, Thomas K., and Herb Dewey. *Red Hot Cold Reading: The Professional Pseudo Psychic* (privately printed, n.d., photocopied typescript).

Schjeldahl, Peter. "Striking Gold: The Final Installment of the Met's Byzantium Shows," *New Yorker*, May 17, 2004.

Schneider, Mark A. *Culture and Enchantment* (Chicago: University of Chicago Press, 1993).

Sedgwick, Mark. *Against the Modern World* (New York: Oxford University Press, 2004).

Seligmann, Kurt. *The History of Magic and the Occult* (1948; New York: Harmony Books, 1975).

Silver Elves. *The Magical Elven Love Letters* (Sebastopol, CA: Silver Elves Publications, 2001).

Shorto, Russell. *Saints and Madmen: Psychiatry Opens Its Doors to Religion* (New York: Henry Holt and Co., 1999).

Smith, Huston. *Forgotten Truth: The Primordial Tradition* (New York: Harper Colophon Books, 1976).

———. *Why Religion Matters: The Fate of the Human Spirit in an Age of Disbelief* (San Francisco: HarperSanFrancisco, 2001).

Starkey, Marion L. *The Devil in Massachusetts: A Modern Enquiry into the Salem Witch Trials* (New York: Doubleday, 1949).

Stavish, Mark. "History of Alchemy in North America," *Alchemy Journal* (May–June 2002).

Stewart, R. J. *Power Within the Land* (Lake Toxaway, NC: Mercury Publishing, 1992).

Summers, Montague. *The History of Witchcraft and Demonology* (Edison, NJ: Castle Books, 1992).

Sutin, Lawrence. *Do What Thou Wilt: A Life of Aleister Crowley* (New York: St. Martin's Press, 2000).

Teish, Luisah. *Jambalaya: The Natural Woman's Book of Personal Charms and Practical Rituals* (New York: HarperCollins, 1985).

Tickle, Phyllis A. *God-Talk in America* (New York: Crossroads Publishing, 1997).

Tolkien, J. R. R. *The Hobbit* (New York: Ballantine, 1937).

——. *The Return of the King* (New York: Ballantine, 1965).

Toms, Michael. *An Open Life* (New York: HarperCollins, 1990).

Twyman, Tracy. Interview with Peter Levenda, in *Book of Lies: The Disinformation Guide to Magick and the Occult,* edited by Richard Metzger (New York: Disinformation Co., 2003).

Vale, V., and John Sulak. *Modern Pagans: An Investigation of Contemporary Pagan Practices* (San Francisco: RE/Search Publications, 2001).

Van den Broek, Roelof, and Wouter J. Hanegraaff. *Gnosis and Hermeticism: From Antiquity to Modern Times* (Albany: State University of New York Press, 1998).

Walker, Alice. *In Search of Our Mothers' Gardens* (San Diego: Harcourt Brace, 1983).

Walker, Cornelia, and Christena Bledsoe. *God, Dr. Buzzard, and the Bolito Man: A Saltwater Geechee Talks About Life on Sapelo Island* (New York: Doubleday, 2000).

Webb, James. *The Occult Establishment* (La Salle, IL: Open Court, 1974).

Weisman, Richard. *Witchcraft, Magic, and Religion in Seventeenth-Century Massachusetts* (Amherst: University of Massachusetts Press, 1984).

Whitaker, Kay Cordell. *The Reluctant Shaman: A Woman's First Encounters with the Unseen Spirits of the Earth* (San Francisco: HarperSanFrancisco, 1991).

White, Michael. *Isaac Newton: The Last Sorcerer* (Reading, MA: Helix Books, 1997).

Whitehead, Nicholas. *Patterns in Magical Christianity* (Albuquerque: Sun Chalice Books, 1996).

Whitman, Walt. *The Portable Walt Whitman* (New York: Viking Press, 1974).

Wilson, Colin. *The Occult: A History* (New York: Random House, 1971).

Yronwode, Catherine. *Hoodoo Herb and Root Magic: A Materia Magica of African-American Conjure* (Forestville, CA: Lucky Mojo Curio Co., 2002).

Zalewski, Pat, and Chris Zalewski. *Z-5 Secret Teachings of the Golden Dawn* (St. Paul, MN: Llewellyn, 1992).

Zell-Ravenheart, Oberon. *Grimoire for the Apprentice Wizard* (Franklin Lakes, NJ: New Page Books, 2004).

ACKNOWLEDGMENTS

I am grateful to all the magical people, named and unnamed, who helped me by sharing their experiences and knowledge with me. Thanks particularly to Frank Takei for his good humor and clear explanations of philosophical matters. To Sharon Grigsby, who read some of the early chapters, and all my friends who listened to many strange stories with great patience, many thanks. To my family, who support me no matter how far-out the topics I write about are, I am always grateful. My wonderful agent, Jandy Nelson, was an unfailing support. Endless thanks to all the people at HarperSanFrancisco, who are talented, hardworking, and always a delight to deal with, especially Gideon Weil, my editor, who worked the best kinds of magic on the manuscript and on my aspirations for it. He made even the most impossible parts of the writing seem imminently doable.